The Fast Close Toolkit

Founded in 1807, John Wiley & Sons is the oldest independent publishing company in the United States. With offices in North America, Europe, Asia, and Australia, Wiley is globally committed to developing and marketing print and electronic products and services for our customers' professional and personal knowledge and understanding.

The Wiley Corporate F&A series provides information, tools, and insights to corporate professionals responsible for issues affecting the profitability of their company, from accounting and finance to internal controls and performance management.

The Fast Close Toolkit

CHRISTINE H. DOXEY

WILEY

Library of Congress Cataloging-in-Publication Data

Names: Doxey, Christine H., 1955- editor.
Title: The fast close toolkit / edited by Christine H. Doxey.
Description: Hoboken, New Jersey : Wiley, [2020] | Series: Wiley corporate
    F&A | Includes index.
Identifiers: LCCN 2019024543 (print) | LCCN 2019024544 (ebook) | ISBN
    9781119554493 (hardback) | ISBN 9781119554523 (adobe pdf) | ISBN
    9781119554448 (epub)
Subjects: LCSH: Closing (Accounting) | Financial statements.
Classification: LCC HF5681.C45 F37 2020 (print) | LCC HF5681.C45 (ebook)
    | DDC 657—dc23
LC record available at https://lccn.loc.gov/2019024543
LC ebook record available at https://lccn.loc.gov/2019024544

Cover Design: Wiley
Cover Image: © fanjianhua/Getty Images

Printed in the United States of America

V10015419_110719

Contents

Preface

REGARDLESS OF COMPANY SIZE or complexity, all successful fiscal close processes require continuous communication, comprehensive documentation, and a flexible, responsive organization that is focused on people, processes, transactions, reconciliation, and reporting. The degree to which each building block is implemented will vary based on company size, type of industry, availability of resources, and management commitment.

However, omitting one or two of these building blocks may result in some type of failure during a month-end close. The building blocks for the fiscal close are explored in Chapter 3, "The Components of the Fiscal Close." When executing these building blocks, executing the fiscal close correctly helps achieve the following benefits.

- A reduced cycle time for the fiscal closing process
- A more transparent, better documented process with better insight into the close process
- Finance and accounting executives being more confident in the close
- Well-managed and less-stressed employees
- More time for analytics and the calculation of metrics

The fiscal close process is one of the most fundamental indicators of the efficiency of your fiscal infrastructure, and is the critical foundation that must be in place before your finance and accounting team can even begin to optimize its role as a true consultative business partner and trusted advisor, assisting in achieving strategic goals and creating shareholder value.

Over the last decade, the financial reporting landscape has seen significant change. Finance executives face mounting pressure to increase the accuracy of financial reporting while decreasing turnaround time. Costs are being highly scrutinized as the longest recession in U.S. history continues. Regulatory agencies have introduced a host of new standards and accounting rules changing materiality thresholds and requiring detailed schedules and new disclosures for public filings. To complicate matters, many finance organizations are being asked to do more with less as headcounts are reduced in response to economic pressures.

The current legislation has strict requirements for the timing of preparation and the quality of financial statements. It is especially important for chief financial officers (CFOs) of large companies who receive fiscal information from multiple entities, from different systems, and in incompatible data formats.

Since the adoption of the IFRS throughout the EU and the demand for greater transparency as far as external reporting is concerned following the collapse of corporate giants such as Enron and WorldCom, there is a great need for reliable fiscal information on a real-time basis.

Today's finance organizations face multiple priorities that include the oversight of fiscal transactions, management of enterprise performance, attestation of financial reporting, and timely close and consolidation of fiscal data. As they grapple with these issues, CFOs are always seeking ways to increase the efficiency and timeliness of their fiscal close and compliance processes. However, merely improving the speed of the fiscal close process is not enough.

There is a competing demand for improved fiscal governance and increased transparency and reliability of data. The pace of regulatory change also continues to increase as a result of the current economic challenges as well as ongoing regulatory initiatives such as the mandate of eXtensible Business Reporting Language (XBRL) as the reporting standard format and the likely move to International Financial Reporting Standards (IFRS).

Finance organizations need to proactively manage the challenges of data quality and prepare for new regulatory requirements to avoid creating a "perfect storm" for their fiscal close and consolidation processes. As regulations and requirements become tighter around responsibility accounting, more and more companies are continually reevaluating their closing processes to meet up with their statutory requirements, but also to integrate multiple financial reporting systems requiring a "Fast Close Toolkit."

HOW THIS TOOLKIT IS ORGANIZED

This toolkit provides the guidance, best practices, tools, templates, and policies to enable a faster fiscal close. The Guide to Toolkit Organization table provides the applicable chapter number for each section.

For easy reference, each best practice, policy, checklist, process narrative, and standard of internal control is numbered throughout this toolkit. Tables for these important references are provided in the following tables:

- Table of Best Practices
- Table of Policies
- Tables of Checklists
- Tables of Process Narratives
- Table of Standards of Internal Control

GUIDE TO TOOLKIT ORGANIZATION

Chapter Number	Chapter Title
	Introduction
	Executive Summary
1	Why the Continued Focus on the Fiscal Closing Process?
2	Key Pain Points and Bottlenecks
3	The Components of the Fiscal Close
4	Governing the Fiscal Close Process
5	The Transaction Accumulation, Reconciliation, and Sub-Ledger Close
6	Introduction to the Standards of Internal Control
7	Roles and Responsibilities During the Fiscal Close
8	The General Ledger and Trial Balance
9	The Common Chart of Accounts
10	Cost Centers
11	The Journal Entry Process
12	Spreadsheet Controls
13	Checklists for Transaction Accumulation, Reconciliation, and Sub-Ledger Close
14	Sample Policies for Transaction Accumulation, Reconciliation, and Sub-Ledger Close
15	Process Narratives for the Transaction Accumulation, Reconciliation, and Sub-Ledger Close
16	Standards of Internal Control for the Transaction Accumulation, Reconciliation, and Sub-Ledger Close Process
17	Corporate Close and Consolidation
18	The Number of Consolidation Points
19	The Number of Closing Cycles
20	Post-Closing Entries
21	Communication and Accountability

TABLE OF BEST PRACTICES

TABLE OF POLICIES

Policy Number	Best Practice
1	Account Reconciliation Policy
2	Accounts Payable Accruals
3	Spreadsheet Controls
4	Financial Close and Consolidation Process
5	Basic Policies on Financial Reporting

TABLE OF CHECKLISTS

Checklist Number	Best Practice
1	Transaction Accumulation and Fiscal Close Checklist
2	Fiscal Year-End Sample Schedule
3	Accounts Payable Roles and Responsibilities Year-End Checklist
4	Reconciliation Template
5	Corporate Close and Consolidation
6	Executive-Level Closing Checklist
7	Twenty Critical Areas to Review at Year-End
8	The Year-End Financial Statement Checklist
9	The Year-End Transaction Checklist
10	The Year-End Payroll Process Checklist
11	Quarter-End Fiscal Close (10Q)
12	Year-End Fiscal Close (10K)
13	Performing Financial Statement Analysis
14	Trend Analysis

TABLE OF PROCESS NARRATIVES

Process NarrativeNumber	Best Practice
1	Journal Entry (JE) Process
2	Management Approval of Journal Entries
3	Other Current and Long-Term Assets
4	Other Current and Long-Term Liabilities
5	Balance Sheet Consolidation
6	Assets Held for Sale Due to Discontinued Operations
7	Disclosure Checklist
8	Fluctuation Analysis
9	Cash Flow Reconciliation
10	Reporting Debt

TABLE OF STANDARDS OF INTERNAL CONTROL

Standards of Internal Control Number	Best Practice
1	Journal Entry (JE) Process
2	Management Approval of Journal Entries
3	Other Current and Long-Term Assets
4	Other Current and Long-Term Liabilities
5	Balance Sheet Consolidation
6	Assets Held for Sale Due to Discontinued Operations
7	Disclosure Checklist
8	Fluctuation Analysis
9	Cash Flow Statement Reconciliation
10	Reporting Debt

Introduction

ACCORDING TO THE *Journal of Accountancy*, fiscal close systems, processes, people, and their interconnectivity can be complex, but successful improvements to the process can be achieved by introducing some simple building blocks and basics as provided throughout this toolkit.

No matter what the company size, industry, or complexity of systems and process, all successful fiscal close processes require a solid governance and infrastructure, checklists and documentation, standards of internal controls, and continuous communication throughout every phase of the process to ensure accurate and timely fiscal results and reporting.

There are many factors that place the spotlight on the fiscal close process, which is usually led by a team of individuals in the corporate finance and accounting department managed by the corporate controller. The complexity of the process is driven by the nature of the company (private, public, nonprofit, or government subcontractor) and the type of industry or industries the company has responsibility for. Well-defined fiscal closing processes for monthly and quarterly close are foundational to establishing the discipline needed to obtain accurate and timely results throughout the fiscal year.

The fiscal year (FY) is usually the primary accounting year for a company, organization, or government. The fiscal year serves as the organizing basis for economic measurement and financial reporting. The fiscal year also serves as a basis for budgeting and planning. The budget, forecast, and planning process will be discussed later in this toolkit.

Sometimes the organizational structure of the company, the fiscal systems and tools, and the management style can impact the fiscal close. As an additional consideration, a company that has recently been through a merger or acquisition (M&A) activity will have a whole new set of "closing challenges."

This toolkit will focus on the general best practices for the fiscal close that will enable a "fast close." With the closing process, I've found that it's critical to do the basics well. In comparing the monthly, quarterly, and annual processes, I've determined that there may be differences in closing schedules, the number of journal entries processed, the types of reporting, the level of scrutiny for external and internal reporting, and the preparation of external communiques for public companies but the need to "close the books" sooner and more efficiently is a universal goal. The ultimate deliverables for the fiscal close process include the following two requirements.

1. **Achieving timely, accurate, and consistent data.** It's all about the data! Controllers and corporate finance and accounting departments often find themselves in the eye of today's market whirlwinds with both internal and external reporting requirements to fulfill. Timely, accurate, and consistent data is always of critical importance.

   Operational and strategic decisions are dependent on this rapid, precise, and reliable data. This data drives the planning and budget processes of an organization. The digital age has created a class of investors and shareholders who expect immediate access to the data created by current business activities for rapid decision making, to meet regulatory requirements and to complete reporting and review results with metrics and analytics.

2. **Adhering to statutory, regulatory, control, and compliance requirements.** Statutory, regulatory, control, and compliance requirements add another layer of complexity. Global organizations are required to support reporting with multiple accounting standards, and new legislation requires new systems. Global organizations need to be concerned with the accuracy and regulatory requirements for intercompany accounting processes. Here are two examples and definitions of regulatory requirements that impact the fiscal close. We'll focus on the Sarbanes Oxley Act of 2002 (SOX) and the Foreign Corrupt Practices Act (FCPA). Additional regulatory requirements are provided in the Fast Close Compliance Toolkit located in the addendum of this book.

   The Sarbanes Oxley Act of 2002 (SOX) was designed to enhance the reliability of financial reporting and to improve audit quality. SOX strengthened corporate governance, shifting responsibility for the external auditor relationship away from corporate management to independent audit committees. It instituted whistleblower programs, CEO and CFO certification requirements, and stricter criminal penalties for wrongdoing, including lying to the auditor. These measures and others were geared toward improving the reliability of corporate financial reporting.

The Foreign Corrupt Practices Act (FCPA) adds a new level of anti-bribery controls to the closing process for global organizations. Under the FCPA's Anti-Bribery Provision, it's unlawful to make a corrupt payment to a foreign official (official, political party, political official, or candidate for political office) for the purpose of obtaining business, retaining business, or directing business to any person. This includes ordering, authorizing, or assisting others to violate or conspire to violate these provisions. This applies not only to a successful corrupt payment—the offer or promise of such payment can also cause violation. Under the Accounting Provision, corporations must make and keep books and records that accurately and fairly reflect the transactions of the corporation. Corporations must devise and maintain an adequate system of internal accounting controls.

IMPROVING THE FISCAL CLOSE

Many chief fiscal officers (CFOs) and controllers face ongoing challenges with the fiscal closing process. In some cases the process is still very manual and spreadsheets are used throughout the process. Many companies can't seem to get a handle on the fiscal closing process and find that a checklist with well-defined roles and responsibilities is needed for every component of this critical and highly visible business process. In some cases, automation is not always the "silver bullet" but gaining a true understanding of the full fiscal closing cycle along with the processes that impact the cycle is a recommended direction.

Several years ago, I managed the fiscal consolidated process at Digital Equipment Corporation (DEC), which is now merged with Hewlett Packard. We faced two very unique challenges that I had the opportunity to address.

1. We had 32 individual general ledgers that were sent to corporate finance every month. Each ledger needed to be individually reconciled before we consolidated the results. Our CFO decided to implement financial management centers which combined multiple ledgers by region. This greatly reduced the time spent collecting data from several locations. The financial management centers were also responsible for reconciling the results in a "mini-corporate consolidation" process, which ensured that clean data was transmitted to corporate finance. Of course, we had some glitches along the away, but the process change in our fiscal architecture

took out two days from the fiscal close. This was before the concept of shared service organizations was even fashionable.

2. During the mid-1980s DEC was using a tool called Software International General Ledger (SIGL). We found that our finance team was not using the correct programs to run the corporate work papers, which was a critical step in producing our financial reporting. There were hundreds of incorrect reports that were never purged. My team developed a set of standard reports for the monthly, quarterly, and annual close. All we needed to do was change the reporting period. This process change removed another day from the fiscal close.

I mention these two examples because best practices cannot replace empowerment and a culture of continuous improvement. Lastly, technology and automation are great tools to support the fiscal close, but it's important to ensure that your staff understands how to use them. I suggest the ultimate best practice combines people with automation, and when establishing a goal for the completion of the fiscal closing process, ensures there is enough time to analyze results, metrics, and potential risk. Let's take a look at some best practices.

 ## BEST PRACTICE 1: CONSIDER THE USE OF A SINGLE ERP SYSTEM

Gartner's current definition of ERP in the postmodern era is:

> Postmodern ERP is a technology strategy that automates and links administrative and operational business capabilities (such as finance, HR, purchasing, manufacturing and distribution) with appropriate levels of integration that balance the benefits of vendor-delivered integration against business flexibility and agility.[i]

The original ERP systems were developed for product-centric companies, which typically have the broadest ERP functional footprint. Product-centric companies traditionally are manufacturing companies and distribution companies.

---

[i] Gartner, "IT Glossary." Accessed May 6, 2019. https://www.gartner.com/it-glossary/single-instance-erp.

A single- instance ERP reduces the number of consolidation points and allows the integration of financial transactions across a company. There is no need for uploads to a "system of record" to properly record a transaction.

A single-instance strategy is compelling in that it helps lower cost in the many organizations that struggle with redundant data, high training costs, and lack of insight across disparate systems and processes. A single-instance strategy is related to the desire of a business unit for more autonomy; others are of a more technical nature. There are three factors to consider when evaluating a single instance deployment:

1. Global organizations with legal entities operating in different countries need to comply with local statutory reporting and legal requirements. Trying to comply with these different requirements in one single code base can add system complexity, both in configuration and management as well as user experience.
2. Whenever many users access the same single instance it is critical that access to data and business processes is restricted in a way that can be easily monitored and managed.
3. Although there might be a high degree of commonality across entities, there still needs to be support for industry-specific requirements and specific processes and policies.

BEST PRACTICE 2: EMPLOY CLOUD-BASED COMPUTING

Cloud-based computing (also called *software as a service*, or *SaaS*) allows users access to software applications that run on shared computing resources (for example, processing power, memory, and disk storage) via the Internet. These computing resources are maintained in remote data centers dedicated to hosting various applications on multiple platforms.

Cloud ERP is software as a service that allows users to access Enterprise Resource Planning (ERP) software over the Internet. Cloud ERP generally has much lower upfront costs, because computing resources are leased by the month rather than purchased outright and maintained on premises. Cloud ERP also gives companies access to their business-critical applications at any time from any location and is an excellent enabler of a faster close process and supports business continuity and contingency requirements.

CHAPTER ONE

Why the Continued Focus on the Fiscal Closing Process?

NTRODUCTION: THE FISCAL CLOSING process is one of the most fundamental indicators of the efficiency of your fiscal infrastructure, and is the critical foundation that must be in place before your finance and accounting team can even begin to optimize its role as a true consultative business partner and trusted advisor, assisting in achieving strategic goals and creating shareholder value. Getting accurate and timely fiscal information is critical in today's global market because:

1. Financial statements are the ultimate scorecard for a company. A company's financial statements reflect the company's business results and trends—its products, services, and macro-fundamental events.
2. The critical information obtained from fiscal information is used to perform analysis. The absolute numbers in financial statements are of little value for shareholder and investment analysis. These numbers from financial statements must be transformed into meaningful relationships to judge a company's fiscal performance and determine its fiscal health at the current time. The resulting ratios and indicators must be viewed over extended periods to spot trends and predict performance.

If your finance organization is bogged down in a never-ending closing process, they have little time to focus on enhanced reporting or analytics.

Visibility to accurate fiscal information and underlying operating metrics are critical to your management team in any economic environment, but particularly in times of uncertainty, where rapid and knowledgeable responses to changing business and market dynamics are imperative.

There are many factors that place the spotlight on the fiscal close process, which is usually led by a team of individuals in the corporate finance and accounting department managed by the corporate controller. The complexity of the process is driven by the nature of the company (private, public, nonprofit [tax-exempt or mission based], or government) and the type of industry or industries the company has responsibility for. Sometimes the organizational structure of the company, the fiscal systems and tools, and the management style can impact the fiscal close process cycle time and the resources needed.

Key Point: The signs that the fiscal close needs attention include:

- The close is completed later than four days after the period end.
- No formal management review of the fiscals is done after every close.
- The driving force behind completing the financial reports is an external reason—bank covenant reporting, tax payments, government reporting, etc.—rather than a sincere belief it is a key management tool.
- The current fiscals are not integral to the company's forecasting system.
- The accounting and finance team is focused on past shortcomings, not getting the most out of the company's future potential.
- Executives are not pushing to get the fiscals as soon as possible each month.
- Every fiscal close event results in chaos, delays, and unexpected results.

The fiscal closing cycle is also referred to as the Record to Report (R2R) process. Record to Report (R2R) forms an important aspect of the finance and accounting process. It provides the necessary insights on the strategic, operational, and fiscal facets, which gives an in-depth idea of an organization's performance. It involves complex processes of gathering, converting, and supplying information to stakeholders who want to know if their expectations have been met.

Regulatory bodies and analysts expect organizations to review their account books in less than a week and release their earnings statements within a month. Industry-specific regulations and the ever-increasing financial reporting has put a huge burden on an organization's reporting process.[i]

Key Point: When fewer days are devoted to month-end close activities, more time can be spent providing performing analytics and addressing finance and accounting process improvements.

AN OVERVIEW OF THE FISCAL CLOSE

The accounting process can differ slightly from one business to another based on variances in the chart of accounts, revenue and expense recognition, and cost center breakdown. Despite these differences, the overall monthly closing process is the same. Following the same standard procedures to close the books each month will help ensure consistent and accurate reporting. Here are some basic processes that will add discipline to the fiscal close. These processes will also help to expedite closing processes.

1. Establish a Closing Date

Establish a closing date by which all expenses and revenue must be posted. Communicate the closing date to everyone who has access to modify the ledger. Close the books for the month as of the date communicated, prohibiting any further changes to the ledger for the period.

2. Trial Balance Report

Start the closing cycle with a trial balance report. Review the balances to identify any anomalies from what is expected. Review the transaction details for any accounts you are uncertain of and note any adjustments that need to be made.

3. Adjusting Entries

Create the adjusting entries to recognize prepaid expenses, accrue outstanding invoices, relieve accruals that have been paid, and recognize depreciation and

---

[i] Senthil Kumaran, Operations Manager—Finance and Accounting, "6 Best Practices for Record-to-Report Process," Invensis Technologies. Last modified February 12, 2016. Accessed February 8, 2019. https://www.invensis.net/blog/finance-and-accounting/6-best-practices-record-report-process/.

other amortizations. Post adjusting entries to correct the current balance of any ledger account that reflects expense postings in error.

4. Adjusted Trial Balance

Generate an adjusted trial balance report to review the final balances in the ledger. Verify that the trial balance matches on the debit and credit side. Verify that the balances are accurate, checking the account activity if needed. Trial balances will vary from the initial report due to the adjusting entries. This helps you identify any entries that posted incorrectly.

5. Reporting

Create reporting to show the final expense activity for the period and year-to-date. Include documentation of the balance sheet, income statement, and depreciation schedules. Save copies of the entire journal entries posted along with the documentation supporting their necessity for audit purposes.

 CYCLE TIME TO MONTHLY CLOSE

The following background on the "cycle time to monthly close" comes from APQC's General Accounting Open Standards Benchmarking survey. For this open-ended question, the metric is defined as the cycle time in calendar days between running the trial balance to completing the consolidated financial statements. Cycle time is the total time from the start of the process to process completion, including time spent actually performing the process as well as time spent waiting to move forward.

Of the 2,300 organizations that answered this survey question, the bottom 25% said they need 10 or more calendar days to perform the monthly close process. The top performers, or the top 25%, can wrap up a monthly close in just 4.8 days or less—about half the time of the bottom 25%. At the median are the organizations that need 6.4 calendar days to close out a month's books.[ii]

[ii] Perry D. Wiggins, "Metric of the Month: Cycle Time for Monthly Close," CFO.com. Last modified March 5, 2018. Accessed February 11, 2019. http://www.cfo.com/fiscal-reporting-2/2018/03/metric-month-cycle-time-monthly-close/.

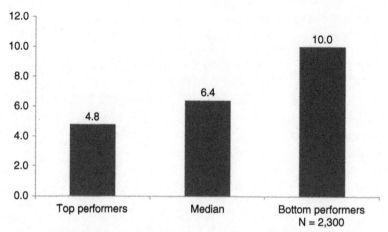

Cycle Time in Days to Complete the Monthly Consolidated
Financial Statements

For multisite companies with separate reporting entities, finance has to ensure the chart of accounts' naming and numbering conventions are as closely matched as possible. Organizations that strictly adhere to common fiscal definitions need fewer days to complete their monthly consolidated financial statements.

Common data definitions set the business rules for every aspect of the fiscal close and can prevent transactional errors and will help set the foundation for accurate metrics and support consistency through all phases of the fiscal closing process.

CHAPTER TWO

Key Pain Points and Bottlenecks

NTRODUCTION: ALTHOUGH THERE ARE different reporting requirements and levels of complexity for each fiscal close process, the closing is very similar regardless of industry or company size. Here are some of the common challenges that continue to place the fiscal close in the corporate spotlight. Understanding these key pain points and bottlenecks will help identify the areas of focus when implementing process improvements to achieve a faster close.

Common Financial Close Process Challenges

- The fiscal close process exceeds a desired benchmark and never seems to end.
- All participants in the fiscal close are in "fire-drill" throughout the process.
- All other finance activity (such as analysis, ROI calculations, and project support) shuts down during the close.
- Reports are late, difficult to understand, and overly complex, data is suspect, and last-minute revisions are needed.
- There are differences between internal and external financial reports with conflicting internal report requirements.
- Multiple systems and data warehouses are used during the close process.
- There is no clear ownership of the data.

Common Financial Close Process Challenges

- Reports are usually created in spreadsheets and document control is a challenge. Spreadsheets are further used to support multiple manipulations of the same data over and over to meet various reporting requirements. Financial documents (including spreadsheets) are created and stored on individual computers within and outside of finance, which can result in:
  - Too many surprises
  - Lack of timely reporting
  - Period-end cutoff errors
  - Lack of supporting documentation
  - Lack of consistent processes
  - Excessive post-close adjustments
- The fiscal hierarchy is too complex.
- There is no time and a limited capacity or ability to report operational metrics or key performance indicators (KPIs). An absence of staffing and training plans creates a resource gap during each closing cycle.
- There are too many cost centers, and many are inactive and can be consolidated.
- There are disparate and disconnected business process and fiscal systems.
- Multiple, nonstandard, or overly complex charts of accounts are used. These are the basic "bones" of the accounting system.
- There are too many adjusting entries during the fiscal close.
- There is no time to worry about fiscal close internal controls or perform any risk analysis.
- Multiple general ledgers and disparate transactional systems with inconsistent data structures must be mapped to achieve a consistent reporting format.
- There is a lack of visibility into the status and execution of the closing process and the related tasks and evidence gathering performed by finance, with the knowledge of these processes in the heads of just a few employees.
- Limited reporting capabilities that have propagated spreadsheet-based reports that house critical fiscal results have become the company's "corporate records."
- There is a lack of focus on the process "basics" such as closing process checklists, reporting templates, standard operating procedures, and business continuity plans.
- There are concerns with systems limitations, intercompany issues, and nonstandard procedures during the fiscal close.
- Systems and software:
- There are multiple systems for payroll, accounts payable, accounts receivable, general ledger, and consolidation.
- Little or no adherence to closing checklists, which creates a delay in submitting data and documents.
- Incorrect classification of expenses causes errors and increases the risk of fiscal statement miss-statements.
- The field accounting staff is not following established procedures.
- Lack of support for internal controls by management.

CHAPTER THREE

The Components
of the Fiscal Close

NTRODUCTION: THE FISCAL CLOSE process starts with: (1) Transaction Accumulation, (2) Reconciliation, and Sub-Ledger Close process component, and is pictured in the diagram below. It focuses on recording and reporting accounting transactions during a specific and defined period—monthly, quarterly and annually.

All activities that comprise the fiscal close are driven by cutoff dates that ensure fiscal results are accurately reported as part of the Close and Consolidation process.

The Corporate Close and Consolidation component is considered part of the fiscal close and consolidation process and includes the close of business units and the completion of the adjusted trial balance, and the first pass of consolidated financial statements. The "final mile" of the process is (3) the Analysis and Reporting cycle.

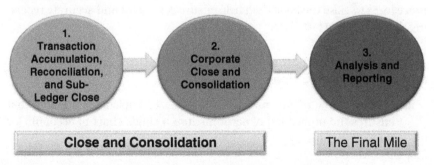

Components of the Fiscal Close or Record to Report (R2R) Process

CUTOFF DATES

Cutoff dates are a critical component of the fiscal close since they drive all the accounting activities that will be included in a specific fiscal period to ensure that the information in the financial reports for the company is accurately stated.

Here's a definition of a cutoff date.

In accounting, the cutoff date is the point in time that delineates when additional business transactions are to be recorded in the following reporting period. For example, January 31 is the cutoff date for all transactions that will be recorded in the month of January. All transactions occurring after this date will be recorded in February or later months.[i]

The fiscal year (FY or financial year) is usually the primary accounting year for a company, organization, or government. The fiscal year serves as the organizing basis for economic measurement and metrics, and establishes the deadline for the fiscal close process and the preparation of financial statements. The fiscal year is usually one year in length, composed of four fiscal quarters. The fiscal year may or may not always correspond to the calendar year or to a company's tax year.

BEST PRACTICE 3: IMPLEMENT CUTOFF DATES

Establish a cutoff date by which all expenses and revenue must be posted. Communicate the closing date to everyone who has access to modify the ledger. Close the books for the month as of the date communicated, prohibiting any further changes to the ledger for the period.

The fiscal close process can differ slightly from one business to another based on the industry and the size of the company. Despite these differences, the foundation for the closing process is very similar, and following a set of standard procedures to close the books will help ensure consistent and accurate reporting that supports a fast close.

1. Transaction Accumulation, Reconciliation, and Sub-Ledger Close

    a. **Single chart of accounts:** The goal is to implement a policy that ensures the unification of accounts into a single chart of accounts for the entire company.

---

[i] Accounting Coach, "Cut-off Dates." Last modified August 8, 2018. Accessed February 7, 2019. https://www.accountingtools.com/articles/2017/5/14/cutoff-date.

b. **Trial balance report:** Start the closing cycle with a trial balance report. Review the balances to identify any anomalies from what is expected. Review the transaction details for any accounts you are uncertain of and note any adjustments that need to be made by considering the following processes.

1. **Streamlined data flow:** Streamlining the data flow and dissemination in such a way that ownership resides at the point of entry and information is considered to be a readily available corporate resource

2. **Sub-ledger and general ledger integration:** Integration of sub-ledgers with the general ledger through the use of cross-validation rules and error (control) fields and/or reports

c. **Adjusting entries:** Create the adjusting entries to recognize prepaid expenses, accrue outstanding invoices, relieve accruals that have been paid, and recognize depreciation and other amortizations. Post adjusting entries to correct the current balance of any ledger account that reflects expense postings in error.

d. **Adjusted trial balance:** Generate an adjusted trial balance report to review the final balances in the ledger. Verify that the trial balance matches on the debit and credit side. Verify that the balances are accurate, checking the account activity if needed. Trial balances will vary from the initial report due to the adjusting entries.

2. Corporate Close and Consolidation

Create reporting to show the final expense activity for the period and year-to-date. Include documentation of the balance sheet, income statement, and depreciation schedules. Save copies of the entire journal entries posted along with the documentation supporting their necessity for audit purposes.

a. **Flexible consolidation options:** Consolidation may be realized at several levels and for different entities. Any consolidation technique can be realized (full or proportional consolidation, and equity method).

b. **Control of reporting process:** Flexible capabilities of tracking and alignment of data at any stage, reviews of input data and final reports, use of registers for making manual adjustments, and audit trail of reporting data.

3. Analysis and Reporting

a. **Limit the use of spreadsheets.**

b. **Reduced closing time:** Minimize of the overall close and consolidation time frame, and meeting management reporting deadlines.

c. **Centralized application architecture:** All the information is stored in a centralized database, which is accessible from any place in the world. All users can see real-time information after it has been input in the system. At the same time the system provides an opportunity to work offline with subsequent simple synchronization of modified data.

d. **Data security and contingency plans:** Secure data access is ensured by the distribution of user privileges according to their roles and by configuring the rights of access to different analytical dimensions (directories) or particular reports, folders, and other objects.

e. **Accurate results:** Consolidated financial statements that provide accurate financial reporting.

f. **Integration of statutory and management information:** Statutory and management information via the implementation of specialized software packages are integrated.

g. **Compliance:** Transformation of financial statements in compliance with IFRS (GAAP).

h. **Analytical capabilities:** Reporting items, companies, currencies, periods, versions, geographical regions, and products.

i. **Environment of communication:** Reporting process becomes more comprehensible with the capability of inputting instructions and comments, as well as sending notifications either automatically generated by the system or customized by the user.

CHAPTER FOUR

Governing the Fiscal Close Process

NTRODUCTION: ACCORDING TO THE American Productivity & Quality Center (APQC), good governance goes beyond standard data definitions The focus should be on creating systems for accountability that improve data quality and consistency and reduce the risk of regulatory repercussions. No matter where data comes from, vendor invoices, emails, the addition of new customer accounts, or other sources, should align with your organization's technology and finance processes. Good data governance includes procedures for data accountability, confidence in data reliability, and the reduction of unnecessary tasks that decrease efficiency.

In general, the fiscal close process should have a defined governance process to ensure that roles and responsibilities are defined and that there is consistency in the process. A well-governed process can help reduce "fire drills" during the process and establishes the structure for scrutiny, accuracy, and continuous improvement.

Effective finance organizations address these issues by establishing a ledger close governance framework. Central components of a fiscal close governance process include the following best practices.

BEST PRACTICE 4: IMPLEMENT A FISCAL CLOSE GOVERNANCE PROCESS

<u>Introduction:</u> A well-defined governance process for the fiscal close also reduces the risk of fiscal statement fraud, error, and management overrides resulting in fiscal restatements. Many of the tools contained in this toolkit can help you build the foundation for the governance process for your fiscal close. I recommend the following 12 best practices.

1. Implement a Financial Close Architecture
2. Standardize Templates and Processes
3. Implement a Financial (GAAP) Hierarchy
4. Implement a Controlled Journal Entry Process
5. Automate Variance Analysis
6. Follow a Best-in-Class Documentation Philosophy
7. Automate Manual Tasks
8. Provide Training
9. Implement a Communication Strategy
10. Collaborate Across Organizations
11. Involve Other Functional Areas
12. Implement Metrics

1. Implement a Financial Close Architecture

The concept a fiscal close architecture is comprised of several components which help make the close successful. These components are included below:

- The ability to superimpose a complete suite of governance; risk management and compliance applications on a miscellany of operational systems with the minimum of disruption
- The ability to seamlessly connect period close, fiscal close, external filings, and controls in a single overarching environment
- The ability to merge quantitative information in the form of fiscal results with qualitative information about workflow status, tasks, issues, and controls to create a complete picture of financial reporting readiness
- The ability to implement standard processes on a global or enterprise-wide basis to smooth out the differences in time zones and connect disparate reporting entities and to give complete end-to-end visibility of the financial reporting and controls environment

- The provision of specialist functionality that allows tracking and reporting of tasks, issues, and controls throughout the fiscal close process
- Tight integration with consolidation applications and a variety of other data sources so that fiscal outcomes are inextricably linked with underlying controls (through reporting and dashboards) to prove that reported fiscal results are dependable

2. Standardize Templates and Processes

Standardized closing templates guide your closing in completing the tasks that are accurate and consistent across your organization. Templates should include timelines and clear definitions of the tasks to be completed by the specific individual, and should build in time for a review and approval process.

3. Implement a Financial (GAAP) Hierarchy

Generally Accepted Accounting Principles (GAAP) is the single most important body of accounting standards in the United States as it defines how financial statements are produced. These guidelines provide the framework that allows investors to understand what the statements say. GAAP is composed of a variety of resources, some of which contradict each other. As a result, a hierarchy of authority was established that clearly defines which standard to use in case of conflict. It is important to note that GAAP is not the only set of standards that a business must use to meet all of its disclosure requirements.

 COMPOSITION OF GAAP

GAAP standards are drafted by three separate organizations. The first is the Accounting Principles Board. The APB was one of the earliest organizations that established accounting guidelines. The APB issued 31 opinions and four statements prior to its dissolution in 1973. The APB was followed by the Financial Accounting Standards Board. The FASB is a private organization of accounting professionals and its main focus is to provide better accounting standards. It issues several different types of reports on accounting standards which have varying authoritative value. The final organization is the American Institute of Certified Public Accountants. The AICPA is in charge of establishing the industry's ethical standards and induction qualifications. It also provides guidance on reporting standards.

GAAP HIERARCHY

The hierarchy is composed of four groups of resources. The most authoritative references are the FASB Standards and Interpretations, APB Opinions, and AICPA Accounting Research Opinions. If the answer for an accounting issue cannot be found in one of those sources, the next step of authority is composed of the FASB Technical Bulletins, AICPA Industry Audit and Accounting Guides, and AICPA Statements of Positions. If this level of authority lacks the necessary information, the next step is to look at the FASB Emerging Issues Task Force position papers or in the AICPA Practice Bulletins. If the answer still cannot be found, the lowest form of authority is composed of AICPA Accounting Interpretations, FASB Implementation Guides, and using "widely recognized and prevalent industry practices."

 ## OTHER DISCLOSURE STANDARDS

While a business must utilize GAAP to prepare its financial statements, other sources of disclosures require other standards. U.S.-based businesses must file their taxes in accordance with the federal tax code. The reporting measurement standards between GAAP and the U.S. tax code differ in several key respects, such as in calculating depreciation, revenue recognition, and inventory measurement. Also, federal regulations may come into play. Sarbanes Oxley (SOX) came as a federal response to accounting scandals of the early part of the century. The focus of SOX primarily is on ensuring strong internal controls are in place over corporate assets and an increased oversight on financial reporting.

4. Implement a Controlled Journal Entry Process

A Journal Entry process can provide a controlled, templated approach to centralizing manual journals. Companies can create, review, and approve journals, then electronically certify and store them with all supporting documentation. Journals can be posted to the general (or sub-) ledger systems either on demand or in a batch on a schedule. Moreover, pre-posting validation means journals are not rejected from the general ledger due to entry errors.

5. Automate Variance Analysis

An automated variance analysis approach replaces the spreadsheet flux analysis that is manually completed by many companies as part of their risk identification and mitigation process. The business owner identifies which accounts need monitoring, and when new balances are imported, variance analysis templates are automatically created for the accounts that deviate from defined parameters.

6. Follow a Best-in-Class Documentation Philosophy

Not only do the standardized templates assist your staff in preparing clear and concise explanations for elements in the account balance, but supporting documents should also be electronically attached so they never get lost or changed. This integrity of control is critical to a best-in-class documentation process.

7. Automate Manual Tasks

Many manual tasks can be automated during the fiscal close. These include auditor Provided By Client (PBC) lists, operational checklists, exception handling and research, tax filings, compliance controls, recurring journal entries, and high-volume reconciliations.

Example of Automation: High-volume reconciliations can be some of the most time-consuming and painful components of the fiscal close process. The need to tick-and-tie millions of individual transactions can occupy hundreds of hours each month. An automated transaction matching module can streamline and automate detail-heavy reconciliations, such as bank reconciliations, credit card matching, intercompany reconciliations, and invoice-to-PO matching. Additional examples of automation and recommendations for process improvements will be explored throughout this toolkit.

8. Provide Frequent Training

All participants in the closing process should be aware of the impact that they have upon your company's fiscal results. Your fiscal closing checklist is an excellent starting point for a training process. Lastly, the participants should attend your post-close reviews to learn more about the process.

9. Implement a Communication Strategy

Communication throughout the fiscal close is critical to the success of the process. Many companies schedule several checkpoint meetings during the day within critical periods. Other companies hold more formal controller reviews when the financial statements are close to finalization. This is another component of the governance process in which the closing checklist is a key driver for communication with all parties impacting the closing process.

10. Collaborate Across Organizations

For many organizations the reporting process is a mechanical process in which the finance organization is effectively confined to operational silos. The disconnect between the finance organization and the process makes it impracticable to share best practice and to respond efficiently to change. This in turn has implications for the effectiveness of the fiscal close since change, whether externally imposed or internally induced, is a constant feature of the group reporting cycle.

The key objective of collaboration is to remove organizational and geographic barriers in the fiscal close process so that structured and unstructured information can flow unimpeded along the entire length of the closing process. For example, a change to a chart of account line, accounting policy, or an updated account definition or submission deadline should be instantly broadcast to everyone in the finance function that needs to know. Similarly, difficulty implementing a new group instruction or performance measure, or perhaps a query over the interpretation of an accounting standard or group policy, should be widely available to assist knowledge exchange and the propagation of best practice.

But collaboration is not merely confined to the communication of quantitative and unstructured qualitative information—important as this is. Collaboration also extends to the management of the process itself, such as the prior approval of a change to the chart of accounts, the digital signature on a compliance statement, or the rejection of a management commentary and explanation of variances.

Recognizing the importance of collaboration is crucially important since process improvements can be identified with the input of others. Areas that can be simplified and even automated can also be highlighted to achieve a faster fiscal close.

11. Involve Other Functional Areas

Now that financial reporting, controls and compliance are company-wide requirements, there is a need for the finance function to collaborate with other functional areas of the organization, such as internal audit and investor relations, as well as other stakeholders, such as the external auditors. Auditors can provide ideas for enhancing fiscal close processes by providing suggestions for areas of additional review throughout the process.

12. Implement Metrics

The end-to-end process from period close through fiscal close and ultimately the production of the annual report and accounts should be measured to determine cycle times and error rates to identify areas for improvement. Metrics and trends can identify areas for process improvements as well as possible general ledger anomalies. Approaches to metrics programs are provided in the Fiscal Close Dashboard, the Controller's Dashboard, and the Detailed Fiscal Close Scorecard later in this book.

All finance and accounting professionals know that speed and accuracy are vital for the fiscal close. The ability to close the books, consolidate results, and publish statutory accounts in ever-decreasing timescales has become something of a corporate obsession for the last several years as evidenced by such terms as the *virtual close* and the *accelerated close*. These approaches will be explored later in this toolkit.

To support the governance process for the fiscal close, I recommend the implementation and communication of the following components. As previously discussed, communication of all closing requirements is critical during the fiscal close to ensure the completeness of data and accurate financial reporting results.

- **Policies and procedures:** Establishing rules and defining requirements for accounting activities can lead to standardized processes and help mitigate the risk of accounting errors and the need for management adjustments.
- **Transferring knowledge:** Providing ongoing training to all participants to ensure that policies and procedures for the fiscal close process are well understood and followed consistently.
- **Well-established Roles and responsibilities:** Defining tasks and dependencies when ambiguities exist between functional areas can help clarify key activities and decision points. This can help increase the efficiency of a close process by reducing duplication of effort and ensure the effective utilization of resources.
- **Closing Checklists and Calendars:** Implementing a close calendar with well-defined roles and responsibilities can provide finance with the ability to identify dependent sources of information for key activities and track

progress against milestones. Examples of closing checklists and calendars are provided throughout this toolkit.

- **Fiscal close scorecard and metrics:** Defining and tracking key close metrics report results and key trends that can be reported and remediated in a post-close review process are suggested later in this book.

CHAPTER FIVE

The Transaction Accumulation, Reconciliation, and Sub-Ledger Close

THE TRANSACTION ACCUMULATION, RECONCILIATION and Sub-Ledger Close phase of the fiscal close is depicted in the diagram below. This is the first phase of the fiscal close process and focuses on gathering the results of financial transactions that have occurred for the period.

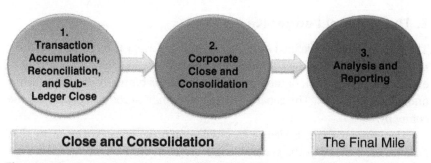

Phase 1: The Transaction Accumulation, Reconciliation, and Sub-Ledger Close

The goal of this phase of the closing process is to ensure the proper transaction accumulation, reconciliation, and sub-ledger close. During this phase, companies need to adhere to the standards established by accounting bodies and regulatory and legal requirements. The following process components are included:

1. The Trial Balance
2. The General Ledger
3. The General Ledger Reconciliation Process

1. Trial Balance

The trial balance is a report produced at the end of an accounting period. It lists the ending balance in each general ledger account. The report is primarily used to ensure that the total of all debits equals the total of all credits, which means that there are no unbalanced journal entries in the accounting system that would make it impossible to generate accurate financial statements.

Even when the debit and credit totals stated on the trial balance equal each other, it does not mean that there are no errors in the accounts listed in the trial balance. For example, a debit could have been entered in the wrong account, which means that the debit total is correct, though one underlying account balance is too low and another balance is too high. For example, an accounts payable clerk records a $100 supplier invoice with a debit to supplies expense and a $100 credit to the accounts payable liability account. The debit should have been to the utilities expense account, but the trial balance will still show that the total amount of debits equals the total number of credits.

The trial balance can also be used to manually compile financial statements, using accounting systems that create the statements automatically.

2. The General Ledger (GL)

The general ledger is defined as the fiscal record of every transaction of a company. Commonly, it is referred to as the "books" of the company. In the general ledger, record each of the transactions twice as both a subtraction (debit) and addition (credit). The general ledger is the main accounting record of the company.

Consequently, general ledger reconciliation is the process of ensuring that accounts contained in the general ledger are correct. In short, reconciliation makes sure you place the appropriate credit and debit in the associated accounts. Seemingly simple, this process requires an experienced bookkeeper when applied to small companies. Complicated applications require the support of a trained CFO or equivalent controller. In either situation, a general ledger reconciliation policy must be implemented to ensure consistency.

In the general ledger, record each of the transactions twice as both a subtraction (debit) and addition (credit). The general ledger is the main accounting record of the company. Consequently, general ledger reconciliation is the process of ensuring that accounts contained in the general ledger are correct.

3. The GL Account Reconciliation Process

The account reconciliation definition is the process of assuring that bank statements equal what a company expects from their internal accounting statements. It is required with every business that keeps financial statements. To explain simply, account reconciliations are making sure a checkbook balance matches bank statements.

Taken to the next level, account reconciliation best practices include the following

- Collecting relevant account data like invoices
- Checking account balances and correcting these balances
- Finding discrepancies
- Controlling policy to prevent discrepancies

Account reconciliation procedures can be either simple or extremely complex depending on the size and scope of a company. Set up a reconciliation statement or reconciliation report in a spreadsheet, with the trial balance at the top of one column and the balance you will be comparing it to in the other column. Enter reconciling items below the appropriate balance and label it. When the sum of the two columns equals, then the account is reconciled.

As a best practice, all balance sheet accounts should be reconciled monthly. For audit purposes, general accounting requires balance sheet account reconciliations be submitted based on the schedule below.

Reconciliation for the FY19 Period Ending	Due
September 31, 2018	October 19, 2018
December 31, 2018	January 18, 2019
March 31, 2019	April 19, 2019
May 31, 2019	June 21, 2019
June 30, 2019	TBD

General ledger reconciliation is one of the key procedures to maintain timely and accurate bookkeeping for businesses. A reconciled general ledger, completed according to GAAP principles of accounting, is the cornerstone to understanding your company's fiscal status, spotting incidences of theft, and pinpointing inaccuracies in your records.

The general ledger is the complete record of every fiscal transaction your company undertakes. When we say we're "balancing the books," the general ledger is what we're referring to. The important thing to remember is that each transaction must have an equal and opposite transaction. This means each transaction is recorded once as a debit and once as a credit.

Other financial statements, including cash flow statements, revenue sheets, and expense reports, are also important, but the general ledger is the comprehensive statement of all your company's fiscal activity.

BEST PRACTICE 5: COMPLETE GENERAL LEDGER RECONCILIATIONS

A reconciliation completed by an accountant or bookkeeper accomplishes many goals as listed below:

- Provides a basis to check all other financial statements for accuracy
- Offers a complete, accurate record of your company's fiscal activity
- Helps you spot accounting anomalies indicating fraud or theft within 30 days of their occurrence
- Helps you identify excessive spending so you can make adjustments and address the appropriate corrective action

Sometimes general ledger accounts will not have a subsidiary ledger to reconcile to. The cash account is the prime example of this. In this case, the cash balance in the general ledger will be reconciled to the monthly bank statement.

This process is becoming increasingly automated, so bank reconciliations will not be discussed here. Occasionally general ledger account balances must be reconciled to an outside statement. For instance, a general ledger rent deposit account must be reconciled to the bank statement to account for any interest the deposit has been accruing.

ACCOUNTING BODIES

The accounting bodies that provide the guidance and rules for accounting transactions to ensure the integrity of results and to preserve the integrity of securities markets are included in the table below.

Accounting Bodies Impacting the Fiscal Close Process
■ **SEC (Securities and Exchange Commission)** – Primary mission: Protect investors and maintain the integrity of the securities markets.
■ **FASB (Financial Accounting Standards Board)** – Develops accounting standards (GAAP) – Responsible for major accounting pronouncements, which include standards and interpretations, fiscal accounting concepts, technical bulletins, and providing emerging issues task force statements
■ **AICPA (American Institute of CPAs)** – Provides input regarding accounting standards – Develops auditing standards (Auditing Standards Board—GAAS) – Peer review
■ **GASB (Governmental Accounting Standards Board)** – Develops standards for governmental accounting
■ **International Accounting Standards Board (IASB)** – The International Accounting Standards Board is the independent accounting standard-setting body of the IFRS Foundation. The IASB was founded on April 1, 2001, as the successor to the International Accounting Standards Committee.
■ **International Federation of Accountants (IFAC)** – There is narrow divergence in international financial reporting. – There are many similarities between U.S. and international accounting standards. – The concern is that international standards may not be as rigorous as U.S. standards.

OTHER REGULATORY REQUIREMENTS

About the Sarbanes Oxley Act of 2002 (SOX)

The implementation of SOX added the following requirements for publicly traded companies.

- Created PCAOB (Public Company Accounting Oversight Board)
- Established new roles for audit committees and auditors

- Established criminal penalties for wrongdoers and protection for whistle-blowers
- Created new financial reporting and auditing requirements
- Biggest piece of accounting/regulatory legislation since 1933–34.

About the PCAOB

PCAOB is a private-sector organization driven by SOX to oversee the auditors of public companies. Similar to the FASB, the PCAOB must receive approval from the SEC prior to implementing standards. PCAOB has the responsibility for:

- Rulemaking
- Financial reporting, standards, disclosure, etc.
- Auditing, attestation, QC, and ethics
- Inspections and enforcement

Rule-Based versus Principle-Based Accounting

The SEC is recommending that U.S. accounting should move more toward a principle-based approach. The FASB is also moving in the direction of principle-based standards. And in support of the IFRS, international accounting standards usually follow a principle-based approach.

Rule-Based Approach

This is an old approach to recording accounting transactions. FASB and its predecessors for many years have attempted to contemplate virtually every application of the standard. A rule-based approach is based on the letter of the law rather than the spirit of the law and is extremely detailed and rigid with no room for new business trends and market innovations.

Principle-Based Approach

This approach is currently favored to facilitate quick responses to new trends. The principle-based approach is flexible and provides room for interpretation in terms of addressing "trends" not defined when standard was implemented. This approach is more objectives-oriented than the rule-based approach and requires financial reporting to reflect the economic substance of the transaction.

CHAPTER SIX

Introduction to the Standards of Internal Control

I NTRODUCTION: THE STANDARDS OF internal control are provided for key processes within the fiscal close. Examples of standards are provided for the transaction accumulation, reconciliation, and sub-ledger close, the corporate close and consolidation process, and the reporting and analysis process.

The discussion usually moves toward ownership—finance versus operations. A major accomplishment for any company's business controls program would be to communicate and implement a consistent definition or approach to standards of internal control to reduce risk during the fiscal close process and to ensure accurate financial reporting as outlined in each standard.

An attempt at such a definition is: An internal controls program is an initiative that is managed within each operating unit. Management is committed to the program and is held accountable for the results and the correction of any deficiencies identified. Management is held responsible to revise and update their business controls program as changes arise within their operating units as well as identify regulatory compliance requirements.

Standards of internal control as defined by a company's internal controls program can be addressed at the strategic and tactical levels. The components at the strategic level include architecture, policy definition, program integration, and planning and metrics.

The tactical or transaction level is where the strategic direction is implemented. This is the operating or auditable level. The sum of the efficiencies of the operating units within a company is equal the company's total operating efficiency.

To ensure the success of a company and to ascertain that the appropriate controls are in place, as well as improve efficiency and productivity, it is important to integrate and leverage all controls expertise and efforts to reduce risk.

BEST PRACTICE 6: IMPLEMENT AN INTERNAL CONTROLS PROGRAM

The following components support a strong foundation of control that can ensure transactions are correctly reconciled and the sub-ledger is closed in a timely and seamless manner.

1. **Understand the operating unit.** A key component of an internal controls program is ensuring that the control points and responsibilities of the operating unit are understood and compliance tests are in place to adequately address each aspect of the unit and its impact on the fiscal close.
2. **Ensure there is management commitment.** Another key component of a program is senior management commitment. This is crucial to the ongoing support and success of a program. It is demonstrated by full management understanding of the value-added of a business controls program and is not merely a commitment because a program is something "we have to implement" or because there is an upcoming audit.
3. **Develop a program that represents the operating unit.** The program should have a firm base of existing audit and control programs with customized programs to address specific aspects and control points of the operating unit. The program needs to be updated as the business environment changes.
4. **Form an Internal Controls Team.** One way to ensure that all aspects and control points of the business are adequately addressed is to form a team from each organization within the operating unit. The team should have a chairperson and hold meetings on a regular basis. A standard agenda includes the review of deficiency findings, status of compliance testing, and plans.

5. **Plan and schedule controls testing.** Although an internal controls program should be flexible to address the changing business environment, a quarterly plan and schedule of tests helps to work around peak periods of activity like the fiscal close.
6. **Complete the controls testing.** Completing the testing means answering the questions on the test, interviewing members of the organization, sampling transactions, and possibly expanding the scope of the test. Most of the testing work will focus on the review of transaction audit trails.
7. **Develop deficiency findings.** A deficiency finding is a factual statement of a problem without judgment or conclusion and should be quantified where possible. Findings should address the root cause of the problem and identify "what is really broken."
8. **Develop a remediation plan.** A corrective action plan is a business controls team and/or management plan that addresses the status of findings on an ongoing, scheduled basis. The plan needs to include:
   - Finding reference number
   - The corrective action
   - Commitment date
   - Actual date the correction occurred
   - Status
   - Test scheduled
   - Test completed, corrected, or retesting recommended

   Recurring findings should be reviewed on an ongoing basis to determine if a process change is needed. Additionally, a review of findings or identified control weaknesses should be included in each scheduled test for the operating unit.
9. **Follow up and retest the finding.** Corrected findings needed to be verified by following up and retesting the issue by the review of audit trails, process changes, and sampling transactions after the correction took place to ensure that the control weakness is properly addressed.
10. **Conduct management review.** Ongoing management review of business controls program results indicates management commitment and strengthens the accountability in each operating unit.
11. **Conduct ongoing training.** Business controls training is key to the operating unit's understanding of components and requirements (e.g. fiscal close roles and responsibilities).
12. **Provide quarterly and year-end business control statements.** Year-end compliance statements reflect management commitment and

accountability. Quarterly and year-end processes require the preparation of control assertions and should have the goal of measuring the adequacy of their programs as required by SOX 302 and 404.

In summary, the inclusion of the above components in an internal controls program results in an adequately controlled environment with clear accountability for all transactions. All operating units are responsible for providing accurate and timely financial results.

ENSURING SUCCESS

The success of an internal controls program is dependent on ongoing management commitment as an operating requirement that will be measured with the operating unit held accountable. Suggestions to ensure the commitment are as follows:

- Include status of internal controls programs and the results of testing in ongoing operational reviews with the status of corrective action plans.
- A methodology for measuring a program should not only be the internal audit rating, but possibly the numeric results of a controls self-assessment or quality assessment based on a score of 0–100% to be included with the SOX 302 and 404 results.
- Include internal control results in operating unit management performance reviews.
- One of the key components of an internal control program is the clear understanding of the business or the operating unit's responsibilities. A method of determining these responsibilities is to identify where the business fits under the business control umbrella. The umbrella addresses integrating all company control activities into one program. Within the operating unit, this approach avoids redundancy and ensures that key control activities are addressed in the same formality and framework. As an example, a company's business controls umbrella could include the following components:
  - Company Business Ethics and Code of Conduct
  - Elements of Business Controls
  - Foreign Corrupt Practices Act (FCPA)
  - Quality
  - Master Data Reviews (e.g. Supplier, Material and Customer)

- Business Continuity Planning
- Balance Sheet Reviews
- Internal Audit Programs
- Controls Self-Assessment (CSA) Processes
- Employee Health and Safety (EH&S)
- Security
- Purchasing
- Budgeting and Planning

CHAPTER SEVEN

Roles and Responsibilities
During the Fiscal Close

NTRODUCTION: TODAY, AN ACCOUNTING executive's role is expanding to include more responsibilities as management understands the impact on the company. With oversight of all accounting activities, business processes and financial reporting, the accounting executive's position yields a solid organization-wide view of the company.

While an executive's and controller's role may differ somewhat in small versus large organizations and in private versus public companies, overall the controller is usually viewed as an accounting leader for the organization. Some organizations may refer to the controller as the chief accounting officer (CAO) while others may have a separate position for this role. Government and non-profit organizations may refer to the controller as the "comptroller."

In some smaller organizations, the controller may assume the responsibilities usually held by the chief financial officer (CFO) at larger companies. And a large public organization may have divisional, functional, regional, subsidiary, and business unit controllers. These positions still have fiscal closing responsibilities for their respective areas and frequencies.

TACTICAL RESPONSIBILITIES

	Description of Activity	Frequency	Responsibilities
	Run the final payroll for the fiscal period	Monthly	Payroll Administrator
	Run accrual report	Monthly	Payroll Administrator
Payroll	Prepare payroll accruals	Monthly	General Ledger or Corporate Accounting Specialist
	Reconcile hours for the month and notify IT	Monthly	Payroll Administrator

	Description of Activity	Frequency	Responsibilities
	Process final customer billings	Monthly	Accounts Receivable (AR) Lead
	Verify cash posted (from bank/cash reconciliation)	Monthly	Corporate Accounting Manager
Accounts Receivable	Verify all accounts receivables have been posted to the GL	Monthly	AR Lead
	Process intercompany receivables	Monthly	AR Lead
	Review and approve accounts receivable reconciliations (customer and intercompany)	Monthly	Controller

	Description of Activity	Frequency	Responsibilities
	Verify all accounts payable (AP) transactions have been posted to the GL	Monthly	AP Lead
Accounts Payable	Prepare and process intercompany payables	Monthly	Assistant Controller
	Review and approve accounts payable reconciliations (customer and intercompany)	Monthly	Assistant Controller

	Description of Activity	Frequency	Responsibilities
	Run monthly inventory receiving reports for all inventory locations	Monthly	Assistant Controller
	Run monthly inventory production usage reports for all locations	Monthly	Assistant Controller
Inventory	Calculate monthly inventory adjustments	Monthly	Assistant Controller
	Send divisional/plant inventory reports to all locations	Monthly	Assistant Controller
	Verify all physical inventory certifications are received from all divisions and plants	Monthly	Assistant Controller
	Review cost variance analysis report for all inventory locations	Monthly	Corporate Controller

	Description of Activity	Frequency	Responsibilities
	Request the benchmark, percent complete detail, trend analysis, and summary reports from all divisions	Monthly	GL Specialist
	Receive and distribute percent complete summary reports from each division to COO, president, and CEO	Monthly	GL Specialist
	Verify payroll, AR, and AP have been closed for the month	Monthly	Assistant Controller
Revenue	Finalize job costs	Monthly	Cost Accounting
	Reconcile/billings roll-forward	Monthly	Cost Accounting
	Run the final (work-in-process) WIP report	Monthly	Financial Reporting Manager
	Dual reporting process	Monthly	Financial Reporting Manager/Corporate Controller
	Set up monthly revenue recognition reports for all divisions	Monthly	Financial Reporting Manager
	Input estimated sales, cost, and margins for each division	Monthly	Financial Reporting Manager

	Description of Activity	Frequency	Responsibilities
	Input actual costs and billings from the final WIP report	Monthly	Financial Reporting Manager
	Review the information/ calculations for each outstanding customer job/project over a specified dollar amount	Monthly	Financial Reporting Manager
Revenue	Review the monthly journal entry adjustment for each division	Monthly	Financial Reporting Manager
	Process adjusting journal entries	Monthly	GL Specialist
	Reconcile and compare calculations, trends, and journal entries	Monthly	Financial Reporting Manager/Corporate Controller
	Review the percent complete calculations and journal entries	Monthly	Corporate Controller

	Description of Activity	Frequency	Responsibilities
	After AP is closed for the month, run the fixed asset report	Quarterly	GL Specialist
	Verify all entries to the applicable fixed assets accounts are valid	Quarterly	GL Specialist
Fixed Assets	For assets placed in service for the quarter, move from CIP accounts to Capital accounts	Quarterly	GL Specialist
	For assets placed in service for the quarter, move to capitalization status	Quarterly	GL Specialist
	Run the Depreciation Expense Reports for all locations	Quarterly	Financial Reporting Manager
	Reconcile the Asset and Accumulated Depreciation accounts for each location	Quarterly	Financial Reporting Manager

EXECUTIVE RESPONSIBILITIES

	Description of Activity	Frequency	Responsibilities
Pre - Close Activities	Review (communication) of closing calendar—discuss public filings/management decisions/efficiency improvements and their impact on the upcoming close	Monthly	CFO/ Financial Reporting Manager/Corporate Controller
	Assure communication of any updates to policies/procedures during the month	Monthly	Financial Reporting Manager/Corporate Controller
	Refer to 12A—Closing Schedule Template: Standard Process Closing Checklist	Monthly	Financial Reporting Manager/Corporate Controller/Business Unit Controllers

	Description of Activity	Frequency	Responsibilities
Monthly Close Activities	Finalization of the percent complete reports (reconciliation of the percent complete revenue recognition calculations)	Monthly	Corporate Controller
	Prepare and review general ledger (GL) journal entries	Monthly	Financial Reporting Manager/Business Unit Controllers
	Trial balance review	Monthly	Financial Reporting Manager/Business Unit Controllers
	Fiscal close workpaper preparation	Monthly	Financial Reporting Manager/Business Unit Controllers
	Prepare and review the financial close consolidation process	Monthly	Financial Reporting Manager
	Finalization of postings to the trial balance	Monthly	Financial Reporting Manager
	Consolidation verification	Monthly	Financial Reporting Manager
	Finalize consolidation	Monthly	Financial Reporting Manager
	Transfer of files for CFO review to the shared drive	Monthly	Financial Reporting Manager/Corporate Controller

	Description of Activity	Frequency	Responsibilities
	Financial review meeting (CFO/FRM/CC)	Monthly	CFO/Financial Reporting Manager/Corporate Controller
	Internal financial schedule	Monthly	CFO/Financial Reporting Manager/Corporate Controller
Financial Reporting	Percent complete reports	Monthly	CFO/ Financial Reporting Manager/Corporate Controller
	Financial package preparation	Monthly	Financial Reporting Manager
	Financial package distribution	Monthly	Financial Reporting Manager
	Financial certification	Monthly	Division Managers
	Complete quarter-end closing checklist	Quarterly	Financial Reporting Manager
	Complete year-end closing checklist	Annual	Financial Reporting Manager

CHAPTER EIGHT

The General Ledger and Trial Balance

NTRODUCTION: TO SIMPLIFY AND focus on a fast closing process, many finance and accounting executives find that they can execute a trial balance by reducing the number of cost centers within their companies. They also focus on reducing the number of general ledgers and may consider implementing shared services or financial management centers to streamline the consolidation process as DEC did in the late 1980s.

The general ledger contains an entry for every transaction ever made within a business. The general ledger's first entry should be the one of the business's transactions, and it should be updated as often as necessary to ensure that every single future transaction is recorded.

Since the general ledger holds all of the information regarding every single transaction in the business's history, it is the core of all of the business's accounting activity. Balance sheets and income statements are both derived from information contained in the general ledger. Each entry records the following information:

- The date of the transaction
- The balance of the transaction
- A description of the transaction

Entering this information is referred to as *posting* a general transaction and the entry itself is referred to as a *post*.

The general ledger may consist of smaller sub-ledgers, or accounts. Examples of commonly used sub-ledgers are accounts receivable sub-ledgers and accounts payable sub-ledgers. Each transaction either posts only in the general ledger or in both the sub-ledger and the general ledger.

When a general ledger is set up for the first time, the value of the starting balance and the balances of all of the sub-ledgers should be carefully determined. The worth of a business's assets, such as cash and equipment, for example, should be included in the starting balance of the asset sub-ledger.

A business's general ledger should be updated to include new transactions as often as necessary to prevent the process from becoming cumbersome. Sometimes, a particular sub-ledger should be updated more often than another sub-ledger. Most accounting software accommodates the general ledger process with integration to transaction processes and reporting.

CHAPTER NINE

The Common Chart of Accounts

NTRODUCTION: AMERICAN PRODUCTIVITY AND QUALITY CENTER (APQC) data shows that organizations with widespread adoption of a standard chart of accounts can shave about two days off of the time to complete their monthly consolidated financial statements, compared with organizations that have low adoption of this approach. The consistent use of names and identification numbers based on the standard chart of accounts means finance teams spend less time guessing and bridging gaps, so they can get information to decision-makers faster.

The chart of accounts provides the fundamental structure that underpins internal and external reporting within an organization. In order to ensure consistent, timely information is delivered to internal and external information users, it is essential that all finance staff understand how the chart is to be used and ensures that each account is reconciled according to corporate policy,

The number of accounts is determined by the size and complexity of a company. Additionally, the number of accounts will correlate directly to the number of general ledgers utilized by the organization.

BEST PRACTICE 7: IMPLEMENT A COMMON CHART OF ACCOUNTS

Introduction: A chart of accounts is a list of all accounts in the general ledger tracked by a single accounting system which is designed to capture fiscal information to make good fiscal decisions. Each account in the chart is assigned a unique identifier, typically an account number. Each account in the chart is classified into one of five categories: (1) Assets, (2) Liabilities, (3) Equity, (4) Income, and (5) Expenses.

All general ledger accounts should have a descriptive account title and account number. This sample policy and procedure defines the methodology for assigning and maintaining the company's chart of accounts. This sample applies to all general ledger accounts utilized by the corporate accounting department.

Chart of Accounts Organization: The chart of accounts is the backbone of any fiscal system. Transactions are coded with values representing distinct elements, each capturing a different aspect of the fiscal transactions. Each account should be assigned titles and numbers that indicate specific ledger accounts.

Each account will be given a short title description that is brief but that allows the reader to quickly ascertain the purpose of the account. Accounts will be arranged in the same sequence in which they appear in the company's financial statements, within the following account ranges:

Assets	1000–1999
Liabilities	2000–2999
Equity	3000–3999
Revenue	4000–4999
Expenses	5000–5999

Account Numbering: Each account will be numbered using a four-digit sequence. In an account number, the location and the value of each digit shall have a specific meaning. Below is a general description of the meaning of the numbers in the company's chart of accounts.

Note: Many enterprise resource planning (ERP) systems automatically provide the numbering process for general ledger accounts using a similar approach as described in this tool.

First Digit (_XXX): The first digit indicates the major classification of the account in the general ledger. The value of the digit indicates whether it is an asset, liability, owner's equity, or other kind of account (i.e. 1000 indicates asset account).

Second Digit (X_XX): The second digit indicates a sub-classification of a major account and the value of the digit indicates a specific sub-classification (i.e. 1100 indicates cash and marketable securities accounts).

Third Digit (XX_X): The third digit indicates a further sub-classification of each major account classification and the value of the digit indicates the specific sub-classification (i.e. 1110 indicates cash account).

Fourth Digit (XXX_): The fourth digit is used to provide a more detailed classification of the account and the value of the digit indicates a specific classification (i.e. 1111 indicates petty cash account).

SAMPLE CHART OF ACCOUNTS

ASSETS
1100 – CASH AND MARKETABLE SECURITIES
1111 Cash in Checking
1112 Petty Cash
1120 Marketable Securities
1200 – RECEIVABLES
1210 Notes Receivable
1220 Accounts Receivable
1230 Interest Receivable
1240 Allowance for Uncollected Accounts
1300 – INVENTORY
1310 Raw Materials
1320 Work In Process
1330 Finished Goods
1500 – PREPAID EXPENSE ACCOUNTS
1510 Prepaid Insurance
1520 Prepaid Taxes
1530 Deposits
1600 – OTHER CURRENT ASSETS
1700 – FIXED ASSET ACCOUNTS
1710 Land
1720 Buildings
1722 Machinery and Equipment
1724 Furniture and Fixtures
1726 Vehicles
1728 Leasehold Improvements
1790 Accumulated Depreciation, Buildings
1792 Accumulated Depreciation, Machinery and Equipment
1794 Accumulated Depreciation, Furniture and Fixtures
1796 Accumulated Depreciation, Vehicles
1798 Accumulated Depreciation, Leasehold Improvements

1800 – INTANGIBLE ASSET ACCOUNTS
1810 Goodwill
1820 Patents
1900 – OTHER ASSET ACCOUNTS
Liabilities
2100 – CURRENT LIABILITY ACCOUNTS
2110 Notes Payable
2120 Accounts Payable
2130 Wages and Salaries Payable
2135 Long-Term Debt Due Within One Year
2140 Interest Payable
2150 Dividends Payable
2160 Payroll Taxes Payable
2170 Property Taxes Payable
2180 Income Taxes Payable
2181 Federal Income Taxes Payable
2182 State Income Taxes Payable
2300 – LONG-TERM LIABILITY ACCOUNTS
2310 Bank Loan
2320 Mortgage Payable
Owner's Equity Accounts
3100 – Common Stock
3200 – Preferred Stock
3300 – Paid-in-Capital in Excess of Par Value
3400 – Treasury Stock
3900 – Retained Earnings
3910 Dividends
Sales Accounts
4010 – Sales Product A
4011 – Sales Returns and Allowances Product A
4020 – Sales Product B
4021 – Sales Returns and Allowances Product B
4030 – Sales Product C
4031 – Sales Returns and Allowances Product C
Cost of Sales and Departmental Expense Accounts
5010 Cost of Materials Product A
5020 Cost of Materials Product B
5030 Cost of Materials Product C
5090 Material Price Variance
Utilize the accounts below when applicable. Accounts are designated as follows:
5XXX – Cost of Sales
6XXX – Administration Expense Accounts
7XXX – Sales Expense Accounts
X100 – Salaries
X110 – Employer Taxes

X120 – Employee Benefits
X200 – Telephone
X210 – Utilities
X220 – Postage and Delivery
X230 – Supplies and Small Equipment
X240 – Dues and Subscriptions
X250 – Travel
X260 – Meals and Entertainment
X310 – Rent, Building
X320 – Rent, Equipment
X330 – Repairs and Maintenance
X340 – Depreciation
X350 – Amortization
X410 – Insurance
X420 – Property Taxes
X430 – Licenses
X510 – Consulting Services
X520 – Legal Fees
X530 – Accounting Fees
X540 – Seminars and Conferences
X550 – Bank Fees
X610 – Advertising and Promotions
X620 – Printing Costs
Other Expense Accounts
9110 – Interest Income
9120 – Dividend Income
9190 – Miscellaneous Income
9210 – Interest Expense
9220 – Penalties
9290 – Miscellaneous Expense

CHAPTER TEN

Cost Centers

INTRODUCTION: A COST CENTER often represents a department or key function within a company. The manager and employees of a cost center are responsible for costs incurred but are not responsible for revenues or investment decisions that impact the company. As an example, a manufacturer's cost centers include each of its production departments as well as the manufacturing service departments such as the maintenance department or quality control department. Other examples of cost centers include the human resource department, the information technology (IT) department, the accounting department, and so on.

Cost centers are usually not limited to departments. There might be several cost centers within a department. For example, each assembly line within a manufacturing company could be assigned a cost center. Even a special production, new product, packaging machine, or media events could have a cost center. Cost centers are usually associated with the topic of decentralization, responsibility accounting, and planning and control.

Many companies have established business rules to initiate a cost center and require that each cost center has an annual budget and monthly forecast. The business rules will mandate controller's approval for each new cost center and that there is a headcount requirement of 5 to 10 people with project annual spending of $100,000.00 to $500,000.00. These requirements will be dependent upon the size of the company.

As an additional best practice, some companies review the number of cost centers assigned to a department or division to determine if some cost centers can be consolidated.

A cost center is often a department within a company. Some companies may assign a cost center to a large project that should also be tracked with project accounting tools and reporting. Another key component of an organization's cost structure is the cost allocation strategy and the policies and procedures that support this strategy. Cost center rules and the cost allocation strategy will be presented within this tool.

A **cost center** is also considered to be a defined area, machine, or person to whom direct and indirect costs are allocated. A cost center is also defined as a distinctly identifiable department, division, or unit of an organization whose managers are responsible for all its associated costs and for ensuring adherence to its budgets. It is also called cost pool or expense center.

A **profit center** is a distinctly identifiable department or unit that contributes to the overall fiscal results of a firm. Where adequate cost accounting systems are in place, profit centers are given responsibility to target certain percentages of the total revenue and are given adequate authority to control their costs to achieve those targets.

A **revenue center** is a distinctly identifiable department, division, or unit of a firm that generates revenue through sale of goods and/or services. For example, rooms department and food-and-beverages department of a hotel are considered to be its revenue centers.

BEST PRACTICE 8: DEFINE BUSINESS RULES FOR ESTABLISHING COST CENTERS

Introduction: As a recommendation, define and communicate rules for establishing cost centers. I've found that a large number of cost centers can create bottlenecks during the fiscal closing process. Budgets and forecasts are often established for each individual cost center, which can bog down the closing process and create the need for unnecessary reporting. Refer to Chapter 29, "Budgeting and Forecasting."

Cost Center Business Rules

---

1. **Responsibilities:** The manager and employees of a cost center are responsible for its costs but are not responsible for revenues or investment decisions.
2. **Cost Centers in Manufacturing:** A manufacturer's cost centers include each of its production departments as well as the manufacturing service departments, such as the maintenance department or quality control department. Other examples of cost centers include the human resource department, the IT department, the accounting department, and so on.
3. **Application of Cost Centers:** Cost centers are not limited to departments. There might be several cost centers within a department. For example, each assembly line could be a cost center. Even a special machine could be a cost center.
4. **Cost Center Rules for Departments:** The most common type of cost center is at the department level in the company. Accounting, marketing, and information technology are cost centers that do not usually relate to the direct production of goods and services.
5. **Cost Pools:** Some companies may use cost pools, which is a method of pooling nonproduction costs by each production facility. This cost center contains only the nonproduction costs by each facility, rather than an applied amount of total corporate overhead.
6. **Indirect Cost Centers:** Indirect cost centers include security, maintenance, or utilities not related to the production of goods or services. These types of support cost centers are grouped together in a total production overhead amount.
7. **Overhead:** Each cost center is a subunit of the production overhead amount. These costs are tracked so the support cost centers may be applied to the actual cost of the goods or services.
8. **Applying Costs:** To apply the cost center amounts to goods and services, the total overhead amounts are applied using a production cost driver, such as machine hours or labor hours. Overhead costs are applied to production goods to ensure that some of these costs may be recouped through sales.

BEST PRACTICE 9: DEFINE ALLOCATION RISKS

Introduction: According to Philip Boken, Gary Callaghan, and Eric Williams of Protiviti, as the economy moves toward recovery, businesses continue to be under pressure to plan for and achieve profitability goals. Accordingly, companies that have traditionally directed their energies toward top-line growth have increased their focus on cost. While cost management is often an operations-driven responsibility, finance is playing a growing role in supporting the capture and analysis of the associated data.

With the renewed focus on cost, organizations are refreshing their awareness of the impact of indirect costs on both margin and the bottom line.

Consequently, they are developing a better understanding of the processes that support the capture, application, and reporting of their indirect cost allocations. Experience shows that an effective allocation solution creates the foundation necessary to both identify and drive out inefficiencies, resulting in better margins, an improved bottom line, and increased cash flow. In many cases, though, the more sophisticated the allocation methodology, the greater the downstream impact on financial reporting processes. Efficiency of the fiscal close cycle is at risk of being compromised when striving to achieve effective indirect cost-allocation reporting.

In many cases, the allocation of indirect costs to business units, functional areas, or products can be overly complex, time-consuming, and inconsistently applied, limiting the value the process provides to the organization. This shortfall in value can come about for a variety of reasons:

1. Allocation strategies for indirect costs are developed without input from key process stakeholders.
2. Allocation strategies are understood, but are out-of-date and/or not reflective of the current business environment.
3. Heavy reliance on manual allocation procedures and workarounds causes bottlenecks, rework, and delays during critical times (e.g. during the fiscal close cycle).
4. Technology is used ineffectively.

Ultimately, flaws in the allocation process can lead to irrelevant, inaccurate, and/or untimely information about indirect costs. When defining and implementing allocation strategies, leading organizations are taking the time to consider the entire allocations process, including the impact of the capture, analysis, and reporting of allocation information during the close cycle. By striking a balance between reporting requirements and efficiency, operations managers and finance can identify opportunities for improvement while not placing an additional burden on the close cycle.

Finance, facilities, human resources (HR), and information technology (IT) representatives are typically responsible for operationalizing and administering the allocations process, often operating separately from other relevant process owners (e.g. business analysts, budget directors, product managers, and business unit [BU] leaders). If the methodology does not fully consider the broad business drivers, process dependencies, and impacts of the allocation process, the organization will likely continue to struggle to appropriately interpret charges to its cost centers. This disconnect can impede the ability of the organization to forecast key metrics accurately and manage budget fluctuations, and can increase the risk of poor decision making by relying on incomplete, incorrect, or faulty data.

COMMON ALLOCATION CHALLENGES

- **Inconsistent application of costs:** A lack of standardization in determining cost pools and drivers sets the stage for inconsistent application of allocations among BUs or functional areas. Process owners may frequently find themselves challenging the validity of certain allocations, and finance is continually placed in the position of having to defend the rationale for how allocations have been applied.
- **Impact on budgeting/forecasting:** Finance organizations are often constrained in providing timely and reliable forecast data and guidance to relevant process owners. Process owners need to understand the calculations and inputs that drive changes within their forecast, and they need clarity on how those estimates compare to previous periods. In addition, the budgeting and forecasting processes need to be consistent with the methods employed to allocate indirect costs to the individual businesses. By developing and retaining a deep understanding of the flow of actual costs and ensuring consistent application of the methodologies, process owners can simplify the integration of actual costs with their forecast analysis.
- **Irrelevant information:** The allocation process needs to provide relevant information to the process owners in order to help drive desired behaviors. Key performance indicators should include indirect cost metrics generated by the allocation process. Otherwise, resource-consuming allocations may provide interesting but ultimately irrelevant information.
- **Post-allocation support:** Finance organizations may not be properly structured to provide support to the process owners relative to the shared indirect costs. As costs fluctuate and/or the dynamics of the enterprise change, finance should be in a position to provide the analytical support needed to comprehend how changes to the business affect indirect cost allocations.

The allocation process neither begins nor ends with the application of allocations during the fiscal close. Allocation-related issues materialize both (a) early in the process—as organizations pull together their profit forecast—and (b) in later stages when actual results are compared to budget and the allocation methodology comes under scrutiny.

- **Precision:** Finance organizations need to ensure that cost allocations are processed accurately. Offline calculations present the greatest concern due to the risk of human/spreadsheet error and lack of transparency. Even automated processes present risks to accuracy if not administered appropriately.
- **Lack of corporate direction:** Accounting and IT departments need to have senior-level sponsorship relative to the allocation of costs. Organizations that lack these frameworks can spend significant time arbitrating internal debates over specific allocations. Such debates are often left unresolved, and can resurface on a regular basis, further compromising efficiency.
- **Lack of training and support:** Training for allocation solutions (both process and technology) often does not receive appropriate priority. As a result, process owners can be ill-equipped to interpret data and typically require substantial support from the often resource-constrained finance and IT departments to maintain the process.
- **Timing:** The charging of indirect costs across the organization can be time-consuming, even where automated solutions have been deployed. In many situations, the allocation of indirect costs occurs late in the close cycle. Since allocations can be a multistep effort of cascading dependencies, by the time the final reports with allocations are included, it may be too late for the process owners to react.
- **Multiple allocations solutions:** The existence of multiple solutions, within and across technologies (e.g. spreadsheets and ERP systems) can present further complexities and inefficiencies. This can cause additional confusion for process owners in understanding the allocation calculations.

Companies with appropriate supporting technologies either are not utilizing them for their intended purpose or have not properly implemented them. Many still rely on spreadsheets or other "offline computing tools" to administer at least a portion of the allocations process, further increasing the risk of error and internal control failure.

Current technologies offer many benefits that can support and help to sustain an efficient and effective cost allocation process. Many fiscal systems have integrated functionality that allows allocations to be performed in tighter time frames with greater and more verifiable accuracy.

Appropriate application of technology can increase the repeatability and predictability of the cost allocations process. Most notably, allocation drivers can be centrally maintained, providing a more effective support mechanism for analysis of actual results.

Developing an awareness of the challenges specific to an organization's allocations process is an important first step in designing, implementing, and sustaining meaningful improvements. The following six symptoms may be indicative of improvement opportunities:

1. Lack of a formal allocation strategy/policy (or lack of adherence to existing policies)
2. Lack of alignment with relevant process owners pertaining to the accuracy and validity of cost allocations
3. Lack of horizontal ownership for allocation processes and technology
4. Inconsistent allocation methodologies
5. Multiple allocations performed on multiple systems and spreadsheets
6. Disparate, aging, non-scalable systems

BEST PRACTICE 10: IMPLEMENT AN INDIRECT COST ALLOCATION METHODOLOGY

<u>Introduction:</u> Organizations can benefit by taking the time to plan how best to implement an indirect cost allocation methodology. Various considerations should be made when doing so:

1. **"How much of what, why, and when?"** These are questions that can and should be answered by an organization's allocations strategy. This strategy should encompass the allocation policy, the appropriate allocation drivers, and a periodic review of the allocation solution(s) and their relevance.
2. **Allocations policies:** Successful organizations invest time in developing policies that both guide and align activities across businesses and functions on the expectations for fiscal stewardship. A properly designed policy should set the tone for the entire organization regarding the approach and methodology for the cost allocations process to:
   ▪ Provide proper guidance on which costs are to be allocated and when.
   ▪ Allow for consistent application of cost pools and drivers for each allocation.
   ▪ Establish linkages to the budgeting and forecasting cycle.
   ▪ Identify the critical systems where cost allocations occur.
   ▪ Identify the key functional support staff and ownership of the process.
   ▪ Provide for communication mechanisms among finance, IT, and process owners to avoid misunderstandings.

- Drive intended results and behaviors by developing and implementing KPIs that incorporate allocation results through individual and team performance metrics.

3. **Appropriate and logical allocation basis:** The development of allocation strategies requires upfront analysis of the drivers and cost pools for each indirect cost. From this, a basis for allocating the indirect costs can be derived. It should be acknowledged that one cost is not the same as another cost. Therefore, the basis for allocation can and will vary from one cost to the next. The al-location basis should be determined using logical relationships between cost pools and drivers, while at the same time balancing the degree of complexity required to perform the allocation.

4. **Ongoing allocations maintenance:** Periodically, cost allocations procedures and design should be challenged, identifying opportunities to add value to the business and improve the efficiency and effectiveness of the solution. Review strategies to ensure that the cost pools allocated are relevant and holistic.

To get started, organizations can begin with a current-state diagnosis, developing both the case for change and a roadmap for improvement:

- A review of corporate strategy to determine if appropriate indirect cost guidance and policies have been established
- Development of a comprehensive allocation strategy for indirect costs to ensure that accurate and relevant key performance metrics are produced
- Assessment of the current state of the allocation landscape (e.g. types of allocations, departments involved, and methodologies for cost pools and drivers)
- Review of the budgeting and forecasting procedures to identify gaps between the existing process and future indirect cost allocation requirements
- Evaluation of current technological capabilities to identify options for optimizing existing tools versus implementing new applications

To address the increased need for timely information regarding profitability and performance, organizations are increasingly relying on finance to provide value-added insights beyond the traditional fiscal close.

When addressing the most common issues associated with the cost allocation process, organizations can realize tangible impact on the efficiency, timeliness, and accuracy of the related processes. By working together with the business managers, finance can play a key role in helping the organization ensure that the most relevant cost data is captured and compiled so that the resulting information is adding value to the decision-making process.

Focusing on a combination of people, process, and systems levers allows organizations to drive greater transparency and consistency into the information they use for decision making and ultimately realize greater value from their reporting cycle.

CHAPTER ELEVEN

The Journal Entry Process

NTRODUCTION: THERE CAN EASILY be dozens or even hundreds of journal entries created during a single reporting period. With so many being created, it is difficult to wade through them all to see if critical entries are being made every month and if they are using the same accounts from period to period. If not, the reported fiscal results will be extremely inconsistent. For example, if a wage accrual entry is only made sporadically, the reported level of wage expense will increase when the entry is used and decline when it is not.

To fix this problem, begin with a standard checklist of journal entries to be completed as part of the closing. The checklist should include a checkbox or space for initials to indicate completion, the approximate timing of the entries, and a reference number to show the name of the journal entry template as it is stored in the accounting system.

Most closing processes require the use of some journal entries, and frequently a great many of them. Because some of these entries can be complex, there is a high likelihood that some account numbers or dollar figures will be entered incorrectly.

Another common problem is transposing entries, so debits are recorded as credits and vice versa. These errors are difficult to spot and always time-consuming to correct. If not found, they can have a significant impact on reported fiscal results.

BEST PRACTICE 11: STREAMLINE RECURRING JOURNAL ENTRIES

Introduction: One solution is to use the recurring journal entry feature in accounting software. This allows users to record a journal entry with all account numbers and dollar figures, and then state the number of accounting periods over which it shall be in effect. The system will take matters from there, automatically recording journal entries in succeeding periods until entries have been recorded for the full range of designated months. In the interim, the accounting staff has a reduced workload, which can make a small dent in the length of the closing process.

The recurring entry is best used for transactions that have no chance of requiring adjustments over the period when they are preloaded to run, such as the amortization of a specific value for a designated period. It can also be used for large journal entries where some changes are likely each month, but revising the recurring entry is still less time-consuming than using a template. An example is a depreciation expense entry where there are continuing updates to dollar values in the entry based on asset additions and dispositions.

When using recurring entries, it is useful to create a printed list of all such entries and compare it to the entries appearing in the general ledger each month. This step ensures that all recurring entries are running that are supposed to run. Also, consider inspecting in detail any recurring entry that is in its final month of activation. These entries may require slight adjustments so that the total value of a series of recurring entries matches the goal amount. For example, if the objective of a series of recurring entries was to amortize an initial value of $12,003 over 12 months, the monthly entry may have been $1,000, which leaves an extra $3 to adjust in the final recurring entry in order to completely eliminate the initial value.

CHAPTER TWELVE

Spreadsheet Controls

BEST PRACTICE 12: ADDRESS SPREADSHEET RISKS AND IMPLEMENT CONTROLS

Risk 1: Unskilled Users

Spreadsheet training is not just for beginners. In fact, lack of adequate training will result in poor-to-mediocre spreadsheet results, such as improper referencing, linking to other spreadsheets, or using inaccurate formulas to master complex calculations.

Risk 2: Lack of Guidelines for Spreadsheet Preparation

If the policies and procedures to mitigate spreadsheet risks are inadequate, errors will become more common and lack of consistency will show up in internal control audit reports. Therefore, the style, content, and accountability for spreadsheets should be documented in the organization's policies and procedures or in the spreadsheet used.

Also, a current inventory of spreadsheets used to prepare complex tasks or financial statements will help ensure where adequate documentation is needed. In addition, documentation needs to be kept up-to-date and include who was responsible for preparing or updating the spreadsheet or policy.

Risk 3: Data Entry and Recycling

People are creatures of habit, which is one reason why spreadsheets are reused from year to year. Unfortunately, after cutting and pasting information, the spreadsheet might not work the way it did before—formulas can be damaged, links can be broken, or cells can be overwritten. To help mitigate spreadsheet recycling risks, the accounting staff needs to make sure the information added to the spreadsheet is as good as the expected output by:

- Saving input data separately from the active spreadsheet used for calculations
- Using a control total (i.e. a result obtained by subjecting a set of data to an algorithm to check the data at the time the algorithm is applied) to prevent errors in formulas totaling columns of data, numbers, or dollars
- Using self-checks, like a hash or batch total, to verify that formula results are accurate
- Using an automatic tool to stop errors from creeping into spreadsheets
- Verifying that spreadsheet templates are not changed accidentally by using password protection

Risk 4: Spreadsheet Errors

Phone calls, chatty coworkers, and coffee breaks and lack of focus can cause errors in spreadsheets. A recent PricewaterhouseCoopers (PwC) study shows that up to 91% of sophisticated spreadsheets contain errors. Unfortunately, if auditors know there are spreadsheet errors, so do fraudsters. For example, inadequate spreadsheet controls may lead to errors, misstatements, and possibly fraud.

One way to reduce the number of spreadsheet errors and to help mitigate fraud is to limit access to files. A spreadsheet is no different than other software, so access to spreadsheet information should be limited to persons on a need-to-know basis, which can help to deter fraudsters. Furthermore, storing important spreadsheets in an access-limited server can protect information from prying eyes. If open-access file storage is used, implementing password-limited access makes sense with these spreadsheets. Locked access to certain cells also can protect valuable formulas from tampering. It is critical to take backups of spreadsheets several times during the fiscal close.

Risk 5: Loss of Data

As a general rule, it's always easier to retrieve information from a backup file than redo the entire spreadsheet. The auto-save function in the spreadsheet software is a reliable means for preventing accidental loss of data in the event of errors or system malfunctions.

 ## BALANCING RISKS WITH CONTROLS

Whether an organization is large or small, spreadsheets were an overlooked risk by many people until Sarbanes Oxley mandated spreadsheet controls compliance in Section 404. Flexibility, ease of use, and transferability are a few of the advantages of electronic spreadsheets.

CHAPTER THIRTEEN

Checklists for the Transaction Accumulation, Reconciliation, and Sub-Ledger Close

THIS SECTION CONTAINS A series of checklists for the Transaction Accumulation, Reconciliation, and Sub-Ledger Close process.

CHECKLIST 1: TRANSACTION ACCUMULATION AND FISCAL CLOSE CHECKLIST

Introduction: Our first checklist defines the tasks and areas of review that will help to ensure that transactions are accumulated properly to accommodate a faster fiscal close.

Transaction Accumulation and Fiscal Close Checklist	
1. Complete Closing Adjustments	
Area of Review	**Examples of Transactions and Activities**

Review Automatic Payments	▪ Review automatic payments, which include the following transaction types:
	  ▪ Bank Drafts
	  ▪ Recurring Payments
	  ▪ Adjustments

Transaction Accumulation and Fiscal Close Checklist	
1. Complete Closing Adjustments	
Transactions Not Entered	▪ Ensure that the following transactions are properly entered in the applicable accounting systems:
	▪ Invoices
	▪ Sales Commissions
	▪ Royalties
	▪ Warranties
	▪ Intercompany Transactions
Transaction Errors—Transactions Not Entered in the Correct GL Account	▪ Review the following transactions for errors that will impact the correct statement of fiscal information:
	▪ Invoices
	▪ Sales
	▪ Payroll
	▪ T&E
	▪ Accounts Payable
	▪ Inventory Adjustments
Infrequent Transactions	▪ Customer returns
	▪ Voided, corrected, or reissued payroll checks and bonuses
	▪ Tax refunds
	▪ Supplier refunds
Inventory Adjustments	▪ Corrections are identified as a result of cycle counting and physical inventory processes.
Project Adjustments and Allocations	▪ Adjustments resulting from the project accounting process are identified.
Payroll Process Adjustments	▪ Adjustments resulting from the payroll process needed to properly reflect payroll expenses are identified.
Adjustments for Taxes	▪ Sales Taxes
	▪ Payroll Taxes
	▪ Franchise Taxes
Fixed Assets	▪ Complete the correction of depreciation entries.
	▪ Complete corrections resulting from a fixed assets physical inventory.
Loan Payments	▪ Review the allocation of interest and principle.
Aged Accounts (AR) Receivables	▪ Review aging for uncollectible AR balances and update reserves.
	▪ Complete AR write-offs if appropriate.
Accruals	▪ Complete AP accruals.
Journal Entries (JEs)	▪ Finalize JEs as a result of controller and management reviews.

2. Accumulation of Financial Information	
Revenue and Cost of Goods Sold	▪ Ensure information is correct and complete.
Project Accounting	▪ Ensure that project status and expenses are properly reflected for the fiscal period.
Payroll	▪ Ensure that payroll expenses are properly stated for the fiscal period.

3. Reconciliation	
Bank Statements	▪ Ensure that bank statements are properly reconciled and all variances are identified and addressed.
Petty Cash	▪ Ensure that petty cash accounts are accurately reconciled and all variances are identified and addressed.
Accounts Payable (AP)	▪ All AP sub-ledger activity is reconciled with the general ledger.
Accounts Receivable (AR)	▪ All AP sub-ledger activity is reconciled with the general ledger.
Credit Card Statements	▪ Determine that all employee credit card statements have been reconciled and submitted. All non-business charges are identified and action is taken.
Equity Accounts	▪ Ensure that all equity accounts are properly stated for the fiscal period.
Loans	▪ Ensure that all loan balances are properly stated for the fiscal period.
Inventory	▪ Validate inventory balances and ensure that corrections are identified as a result of cycle, counting and physical inventory processes.
Fixed Assets	▪ Validate fixed asset account balances and ensure that corrections are identified as a result of physical inventory processes.
Other Assets and Liabilities	▪ Ensure that other assets and liabilities account balances are properly reconciled and stated.

4. Payroll Closing Checklist	
1. Is documentation for new hires complete?	Y/N
2. Are hourly rate and salaries correct and reported correctly?	Y/N
3. Are hours reported correct?	Y/N
4. Are overtime rates correct?	Y/N
5. Are payroll deductions and tax withholding correct?	Y/N
6. Are garnishment orders up to date?	Y/N

4. Payroll Closing Checklist	
7. Have bonuses been paid with the correct withholdings?	Y/N
8. Are employee receivables correctly reported?	Y/N
9. Have payroll metrics been reported for the period, and have process issues been identified and corrected?	Y/N
10. Are unemployment payments and reports handled accurately?	Y/N
11. Are payroll expenses charged to the correct project?	Y/N

5. Review	
General Ledger Coding Consistency	▪ Is the transaction coded completely and to the right account?
Expense Classification	▪ Do expenses need to be reclassed?
Project Classification	▪ If project codes are used, is the coding accurate for all transactions?
Backup Documentation	▪ Is the backup documentation in order?
Transaction Authorization	▪ Are authorizations reviewed and complete?
Reasonableness of Transactions	▪ Do the transactions look reasonable?

6. Financial Reporting	
1. Finalize the trial balance.	Y/N
2. Complete profit and loss Statement.	Y/N
3. Complete sales reports.	Y/N
4. Complete the balance sheet.	Y/N
5. Finalize the aged accounts receivable.	Y/N
6. Finalize project accounting reports.	Y/N
7. Complete budget, forecast, and actual comparisons.	Y/N
8. Identify significant account variances.	Y/N
9. Identify missing supplier and employee checks.	Y/N
10. Close the fiscal period.	Y/N
11. Create backups.	Y/N

 ## CHECKLIST 2: FISCAL YEAR-END CLOSE SAMPLE SCHEDULE

Introduction: This checklist proposes a sample schedule for a fiscal year-end closing process. The key milestones and tasks are identified with the required dates for completion.

Fiscal Year-End Close Schedule	
1. Changes to company organization structure due to corporate financial reporting	Workday Minus 7
2. Vendor invoices and employee expense reports due to the accounts payable department by 5:00 p.m.	Workday Minus 6
3. Intercompany charge cutoff (except charges calculated as a percent of revenue)	Workday Minus 5
4. Foreign exchange rates loaded into the accounting system	Workday Minus 1
5. Preliminary operating expense reports available	Workday 1
6. Expense accruals and re-classes due to general ledger by 12:00 p.m.	Workday 2
7. Revenue and commissions entered and closed	Workday 3
8. Division controllers sign off on expenses by 12:00 p.m.	Workday 4
9. Final operating expense reports distributed	Workday 4
10. Revenue and expense accounts closed by 12:00 p.m.	Workday 4
11. Balance sheet reconciliations due to the general ledger reporting group	Workday 10
12. Unaudited fiscals released (except at each quarter-end, when fiscals are available after the earnings press release)	Workday 10

CHECKLIST 3: ACCOUNTS PAYABLE ROLES AND RESPONSIBILITIES YEAR-END CHECKLIST

Introduction: This checklist is provided to ensure that accounts payable transactions are accumulated accurately and in a timely manner to ensure a smooth year-end close.

Accounts Payable Roles and Responsibilities Checklist

1. Establish a calendar or schedule that contains all the deadlines and cut offs. Provide all appropriate team members with a copy of the schedule.
2. Remember that those who file T&E reimbursement requests need this fiscal year-end cutoff information, too.
3. Review your 1099 supplier information to make sure it is complete. Review your supplier master file for missing TINs and try to obtain as many as possible. We suggest an annual Tax Identification Number (TIN) matching process prior to completing your 1099 process.
4. Consider scheduling calls to business units and/or departments in mid-December to ensure they are aware of the requirements for the fiscal year-end closing process.
5. Review year-end policy and procedures and update the documentation if required.
6. Assign specific year-end related tasks to appropriate team members.
7. Review vacation schedules to ensure adequate staffing, particularly in the week between Christmas and New Year's Day.

Accounts Payable Roles and Responsibilities Checklist

8. Determine what routine tasks (if any) can be delayed in order to comply with year-end closing requirements.
9. Make sure that all invoices that have been received are entered into your ERP system.
10. Review recurring payments to ensure that they will fall into the correct accounting period. Ensure all routine journal entries are completed in a timely manner.
11. Establish the proper procedures for accruing amounts due for invoices that are not received by the end of the year. Consider closing schedules of your key suppliers during the holiday period.
12. Adjust any prepaid items, such as insurance, that should be expensed. Journalize any other accruals for year-end that won't be paid until the following calendar year.
13. Review all invoices received shortly after the new year has begun to determine when the goods were received or services performed to ensure that the accrual is made for the correct amount.
14. Schedule the production, review, and archival of year-end reports.

CHECKLIST 4: RECONCILIATION TEMPLATE

Introduction: This checklist is provided as a standard template for the monthly balance sheet account reconciliation process.

Balance Sheet Reconciliation

Preparer: _____   Reviewer: _____
Department: _____   GL #: _____
Fund #: _____   GL Description: _____
Date: _____   Currency: _____
Account Definition: _____

{A} Dept Subledger Account Balance:
Account #

Total Subledger Balance $ _____ -   A

{B} General Ledger Balance:
Account #

Total General Ledger Balance $ _____ -   B

{C} Variance: $ _____ -   C = B - A

{D} Reconciling Item

Date   Contact   Explanation/status of item :

Total Explained Variance $ _____   D

Unreconciled Balance (Should be zero): $ _____   C - D

CHAPTER FOURTEEN

Sample Policies for the Transaction Accumulation, Reconciliation, and Sub-Ledger Close

NTRODUCTION: THE FOLLOWING SECTION provides sample policies to be considered for the Transaction Accumulation, Reconciliation, and Sub-Ledger Close process. The following policies are included:

1. Account Reconciliation Policy
2. Accounts Payable Accruals
3. Spreadsheet Controls

 POLICY 1: ACCOUNT RECONCILIATION POLICY

Introduction: This policy establishes the standards for ensuring that the company performs account reconciliations in compliance with management's objectives, generally accepted accounting principles (GAAP), and internal control requirements.

The purpose of this policy is to define the requirements for balance sheet reconciliations, and to communicate those requirements to those responsible for completing the reconciliations.

It is a key responsibility of all divisional and functional finance and accounting directors/controllers to monitor their balance sheets to ensure that these financial statements accurately reflect business results. This responsibility should be accomplished by implementing and following a formal process which ensures that all balance sheet accounts are reconciled regularly and in a timely and consistent manner. (Refer to Tool 12, "Closing Schedule Templates.")

i. General Policy

In general, an account is considered reconciled if documentation is provided that the account balance accurately reflects the underlying asset, liability, or equity position of the company as of the reconciliation date. All variances must be identified for the accounting period with a detailed explanation for all the details of the variance as well as an action plan to address the resolution of the issue with roles and responsibilities assigned.

The account reconciliation compares a general ledger balance with the detail-level sub-ledger, which should support the general ledger account balance. As an example, the "sub-ledger" may be a bank statement, an aging analysis, a spreadsheet, or another form of detailed documentation. Both the general ledger balance and the sub-ledger balance should be reconciled to an "adjusted" balance (i.e., what the balance should be) since there may be errors in the general ledger, the sub-ledger, or both. In addition, the reconciliation identifies the source of any differences between the general ledger and sub-ledger's balances and the reconciler's plan for eliminating the variances as noted above.

Many accountants make the mistake of providing only an analysis of the activity in the general ledger. This does not constitute reconciliation and is not considered the appropriate supporting documentation and will not be accepted by internal or external auditors.

ii. Assignment of Balance Sheet Accounts

Each balance sheet account is assigned to an individual. Ownership responsibility is assigned to the person who has the most knowledge and control of the account (unless internal control considerations dictate otherwise) as well as the accounting skill to prepare the reconciliation. Additionally, each balance sheet account should have an "approver" assigned to ensure proper segregation of duties.

iii. Reconciliation Procedural Steps

1. On the XXth business day of each month, a summary of the status of all balance sheet account reconciliations will be prepared by the general ledger group in the form of a metric, which will be emailed to the reconciliation preparers, their managers, and senior financial management. Alternatively, the reconciliation preparers may be required to obtain the account reconciliation form from a corporate repository such as SharePoint.

2. Each account should be reconciled monthly, unless an exception is approved by the corporate finance and corporate controller. Examples of exceptions may be a low dollar value or percentage of variances over XX months or quarters for certain types of balance sheet accounts.

3. All clearing and miscellaneous accounts should be reconciled on a monthly basis due to the propensity of the occurrence of fraud in these accounts.

4. The reconciliation should be done in a standard format that has been approved by the corporate controller.

5. The reconciliation should indicate the general ledger balance at the end of the month and identify each item comprising the difference, if any, between the actual general ledger and what the general ledger balance should have been (the "adjusted" figure).

6. The reconciler should identify the corrective steps taken to clear each reconciling item (note the journal entry number, etc.) or provide a commitment date when the item will be cleared. Reconciling items should be cleared within one month.

7. The reconciliation should indicate the sub-ledger balance at the end of the month and identify each item comprising the difference, if any, between the actual sub-ledger balance and what the sub-ledger balance should have been (the "adjusted" figure).

8. The reconciler should identify the corrective steps taken to clear each reconciling item. Items in the sub-ledger that are unidentified and require further research should be listed in a separate section of the form. An account containing such items is unreconciled and the amount of the unidentified items will be identified as the "unreconciled amount" at the bottom of the reconciliation. A commitment date should be provided indicating when the items will be researched and the sub-ledger (and/or the general ledger) corrected.

9. A copy of the sub-ledger should be attached to the reconciliation form. The sub-ledger should contain enough information such that the reasonableness of each item's inclusion in the sub-ledger is apparent. If the nature of the account is such that the account does not represent a group of detail items, the appropriate support is a detailed calculation of the proper account balance.

10. The exact nature of the supporting documentation will vary account by account and will be mutually determined by the reconciler and the general ledger group. The reconciler should maintain sufficient documentation to support each item comprising the balance in the sub-ledger. A representative from the general ledger group may request to review the documentation from time to time. The reconciler should be prepared to explain, for each item, when it will be relieved and how.

11. The number of reconciling items and the absolute value of these reconciling items should be computed at the bottom of the reconciliation. These data will be used to track total reconciling items in the company and their dollar value as a measure of the quality of the company's account reconciliations.

12. A copy of every approved reconciliation should be submitted to the general ledger group via email by the XXth business day of the following month or placed in the designated SharePoint folder.

13. Periodically, the finance and accounting management team may review the results of balance sheet of the reconciliations within a formal Quarterly Balance Sheet Review Process.

POLICY 2: ACCOUNTS PAYABLE ACCRUALS

Introduction: All expenses shall be captured to the greatest degree possible in the period that they are incurred. Proper internal controls will be in place to ensure that only valid and authorized payables are recorded in financial statements and paid to the correct supplier.

This sample policy and procedures is intended to provide guidelines for recording and issuing payments for accounts payable transactions. This procedure applies to all purchases and includes the reimbursement of travel and expense reports.

Documentation

1. Upon receipt of a vendor invoice, the invoice will be date stamped and forwarded to the appropriate accounts payable processor. A match between the vendor invoice, original purchase order (PO), and packing slip/receiving report will be performed in order to form a voucher package. If a match is unable to be processed, the invoice will be placed on hold until matching issues are resolved with the appropriate process owners.

   Note: Most enterprise resource planning (ERP) systems perform the matching process automatically and will "block" the invoice if a match does not occur.
2. All invoices must be reviewed to ensure:
   a. Proper authorization of the PO.
   b. Quantities shown shipped or delivered on the invoice are the same as those found on the packing slip and/or receiving report.
   c. Pricing is in alignment with the PO pricing.
   d. Any discrepancy will be investigated prior to payment.

Recording and Payment

1. The voucher package will be coded with the appropriate general ledger accounts and vendor number.
2. The voucher will then be batched with other voucher packages and entered into the accounts payable system weekly and posted to the accounts payable sub-ledger. The voucher packages will be temporarily filed alphabetically by vendor name, in the unpaid invoice files, to await payment.
3. On a weekly basis, invoices will be selected within the system for payment according to their payment terms. All discounts offered by vendors should be taken advantage of during this process.
4. A listing of all invoices to be paid (insert report name here) will be printed and reviewed by the accounts payable manager and/or controller. Upon approval, checks will be printed. The checks will subsequently be matched to the voucher package. Checks over $X will be submitted to the corporate controller (or other designated individual) for signing.

Manual Checks

1. Manual checks for the purchase of goods and services will not be processed. All purchases requiring an advance of funds should be paid through the use of the company's purchase card/petty cash fund.

Accrued Expenses

1. At the close of each month, accrual procedures are needed to ensure that all expenses related to that month are properly included in the Company's financial statements. Accrued expenses represent amounts due for services or benefits that the company has received but have not yet been paid. Accrual process shall be accomplished in a timely and accurate manner and must be in compliance with all applicable fiscal and accounting standards.
2. In determining what accruals should be made, the following should be considered:
   - The expense must have been incurred during the month being closed; that is, the product or service must have been received on or before the last day of the month in order to qualify as an expense.
   - Only expenses >$X will be accrued.
3. Types of expense to be accrued can include:
   a. Advertising
   b. Commissions
   c. Interest
   d. Payroll and payroll taxes
   e. Rent
   f. Utilities

Property and Business Taxes

1. Payables and accrued liabilities shall be recorded at face value plus or minus any interest premium or discount and other appropriate adjustments. The payable amount can be determined from the billing received and should be verified against purchase orders/requisitions, contract terms or any other appropriate documents prior to recording liability.
2. When actual values are not available, recorded value should be based on best available estimates. Estimates should be based on current market price, past history, and a comparison of prior periods.

▦ POLICY 3: SPREADSHEET CONTROLS

Introduction: This policy pertains to the entire population of desktop financial applications that include Excel and Access databases and any other user developed/maintained fiscal applications or tools outside of the company's general information technology control environment. These applications and tools will collectively be referred to as "spreadsheets" in this policy document.

This policy requires the user of spreadsheets to implement and maintain internal controls over spreadsheets commensurate with their specific use, fiscal significance of the account, or process with which the spreadsheet is associated and its complexity. Each significant spreadsheet (defined below) must be assigned an owner accountable for the control standards.

Overview: Spreadsheets are integral components of the company's information and decision-making framework currently supporting fiscal and business operations. This has come about due to the ease, flexibility, and efficiency with which spreadsheets have empowered end-users to meet a broad array of business requirements without requiring involvement of the traditional IT organizations.

The uses of spreadsheets can generally be split into the following three categories:

1. **Financial reporting:** Spreadsheets used to directly determine fiscal statement transaction amounts or balances that are subsequently posted to the general ledger, create or support the financial reports and disclosures, or act as a key control within the financial reporting process, e.g. balancing and or reconciliation of significant accounts
2. **Analytical:** Spreadsheets used to support management's decision-making process
3. **Operational:** Spreadsheets used to facilitate tracking and monitoring of workflow to support operational processes, such as listing of open claims, unpaid invoices, or other information

The control standards defined in this policy will be required for *all* significant spreadsheets (defined below) and are strongly recommended for all other spreadsheets.

Identification of Significant Spreadsheets: Determining significance requires management's judgment and typically involves a risk assessment of both quantitative and qualitative factors. A *significant spreadsheet* is a key spreadsheet within the financial reporting process with a heightened level of complexity. Key spreadsheets are those spreadsheets that:

1. Directly impact or provide support in the **initiation, authorization, recording, processing,** and **reporting** of fiscal transactions and disclosures; and
2. Directly impact or provide support in those financial reporting processes that are in scope; and
3. Where control breakdowns within the spreadsheet could give rise to a greater than remote likelihood of a misstatement in financial statements that is more than inconsequential.

Spreadsheets with a heightened level of complexity are those spreadsheets that are:

1. Complex computational models used to calculate fiscal statement amounts using formulas and based on a number of inputs (e.g. reserves and valuations); or
2. Systems of record used as an "application" system to record and process transactions; or
3. Transporters of data used as a type of "middleware" to transport transactional or fiscal data between systems, between individuals, or between systems and individuals (e.g., used to upload transaction data into the general ledger). [If the subsystems are independently reconciled to the general ledger, then this may be viewed as lower/moderate risk.]

Examples of spreadsheets where a heightened level of complexity *is not* present:

- Summation/basic mathematics: Used to perform basic add-ups and calculations of numbers as part of a process
- Presentation: Used to display information, graphically or in various reporting formats, for management review and analysis (e.g. to facilitate tracking, reporting, and monitoring of results of fiscal or operational activity)
- Data repository: Used as a type of database to store data (e.g. used to store customer details, name, address, etc.)
- Decision support: Used to support analytical review and management decision-making (e.g. to calculate rates and determine if a rate is above or below fair market value)

Spreadsheet Controls: This policy addresses two categories of controls for spreadsheets, depending on the use, significance, complexity, and management's overall risk assessment of the spreadsheet:

1. Control standards that are similar to those in place within our general information system control environment are encouraged for all spreadsheets and are required for all *significant spreadsheets* based on management's overall assessment as follows:

Management's Overall Risk Assessment of Material Error	Control Standards Required
High	1. Input and Output Validation Controls 2. Version/Logic Documentation 3. Restricted Access 4. Data/Security Integrity Controls 5. Change Controls and Testing
Low	1,2, and 3 Above
Minimal	N/A—Significant spreadsheets are considered at least low risk.

2. Best Practice Guidelines are encouraged for significant spreadsheets and all other spreadsheets.

 ## CONTROLS STANDARDS

1. **Input and output validation:** Spreadsheets should have built-in, documented controls for ensuring that data is input completely and accurately, either manually or by system interfaces, by performing tests such as reconciliations, batch totals, and using formulas to foot and cross-foot totals. Printing out the spreadsheets input cells and reviewing for accuracy can effectively validate data. A spreadsheet user's output validation controls may include multi-period comparative analytical reviews of account balances generated from the spreadsheet with any unusual or unexpected fluctuations investigated, corroborated, and documented.
2. **Version/logic documentation:** Spreadsheets should include a documentation sheet that identifies its purpose, name, location, owner, version, date last modified, description of its logic and fundamental calculations/results, operating instructions, and summary description

of built-in controls. For each hardcopy printing, standard headers and footers should be used that identify the current name, version, date, and time.

3. **Restricted access:** Spreadsheets should be placed on a secured corporate server, as opposed to a personal hard drive, and access to the spreadsheet should be restricted to only those individuals with a legitimate business need to access the file. Spreadsheets may also be password protected to provide additional security for high-risk or sensitive contents.

4. **Data/security integrity:** Spreadsheets should lock and protect all key cells that calculate, summarize, or contain a formula that should not change. This also applies to any standard data that is utilized in the current calculations.

5. **Change controls and testing:** Changes to spreadsheet logic should be separately logged, described, tested, and documented. The change log should describe why it was changed and what was changed, and it should reference the version number of the current spreadsheet. With each significant logic or formula change, the spreadsheet should be tested with a formal signoff by an independent individual documenting that the change in logic is functioning as intended before moving it into production.

 ## BEST PRACTICE GUIDELINES

Structure/Design

1. Separate inputs from calculations and results. Separating inputs, calculations, and results, either on the same spreadsheet or on multiple spreadsheets, makes it easier to understand and reduces the risk that inputs are overlooked or that calculations are overwritten with data.

2. Separate the data input areas into two sections: data you change regularly and data you change irregularly. Use colors or shading cells that contain data input. Input area should not contain formulas.

3. When using the sum function ensure that the range to be summed always contains a blank cell at either end of the range. This ensures that when rows or columns are added, the formula maintains its integrity.

4. When a critical value is contained in a formula in one or more cells (e.g. interest or tax rate), put it in a separate cell and refer to this cell in the formula.

5. Try to avoid complex formulae. Break complex formulae into smaller components to make it easier to understand, change, or edit.

6. Use each column for the same purpose throughout the spreadsheet. Spreadsheets should have a consistent layout.
7. Use only one formula for each row or column. This will result in quicker development, more effective testing, and better documentation.

Training

8. Managers should ensure that all spreadsheet users attend a training course covering both the basic and moderately advanced control functions addressed in the Standards and Additional Guidelines set forth in this policy.

General

9. Keep a catalog or inventory of spreadsheets in use in your department. At a minimum, a catalog of significant spreadsheets should be kept and updated regularly.
10. Develop a consistent spreadsheet naming convention for each department. Every time you change the logic of a spreadsheet, change the name to reflect the change and remember to keep a copy of at least the prior two versions for backup.
11. Prior to using a spreadsheet to develop a new highly complex fiscal calculation application, engage the IT department to discuss and evaluate the merits of developing your new tool in an application system with a more formalized information technology control environment.

CHAPTER FIFTEEN

Process Narratives for the Transaction Accumulation, Reconciliation, and Sub-Ledger Close Process

 PROCESS NARRATIVE 1: JOURNAL ENTRY (JE) PROCESS

Introduction: This section provides examples of process narratives for the key processes within the Transaction Accumulation, Reconciliation, and Sub-Ledger Close process. This information can be used to improve internal controls and business process. Improvements to current internal controls and business processes will support a faster closer process. Here is the process narrative for the Journal Entry (JE) process.

Process Activity Description

1. **Month-End Journal Entry Preparation and Posting:** JEs are prepared to post fiscal transactions to the applicable ERP system general ledger. The JE workflow process has predetermined approval limitations. Upon manual approval of journal entry, accountant begins journal entry workflow process by uploading journal entry into the workflow process.
2. **Data Entry:** The accountant enters JE data into the template.

Process Activity Description

3. **Records Management:** The accountant attaches the copy to the original JE, created from the template, and the transaction is filed according to the company's file management process.
4. **Month-End Checklist:** The accountant enters document number into the month-end checklist, which is reviewed by management for completion and accuracy.

 ## PROCESS NARRATIVE 2: MANAGEMENT APPROVAL OF JOURNAL ENTRIES

Introduction: This section provides examples of process narratives for the key processes within the Transaction Accumulation, Reconciliation, and Sub-Ledger Close process. This information can be used to improve internal controls and business processes that impact the accurate processing of transactions and ultimately the fiscal close. Improvements to current internal controls and business processes will support a faster closer process. Here is the process narrative for the management approval of JEs.

Process Activity Description

1. **Approval Tiers:** The management approval of JEs is facilitated through the workflow system. The approval levels are tiered and approvals are organized by dollar amount and management levels. The recommended tiers of approval are as follows: Tier 4 $100,000,000.01–$99,999,999,999.99, Tier 5 $25,000,000.01–$100,000,000, Tier 6 $10,000,000.01–$25,000,000, and Tier 7 $0–$10,000,000. Directors have approvals for Tier 5. Beyond those levels, journal entries are approved by the vice-president of general accounting.
2. **Preparation and Submission:** The accountant prepares the JE and compares to supporting documentation for accuracy. The accountant submits a hardcopy of the JE to the applicable manager for review.
3. **Management Approval:** The manager approves by initials and dates the JE and returns to accountant for upload into the ERP system's workflow.
4. **Workflow Process:** The accountant uploads the entry into the workflow and begins the approval and posting process. The manager receives a JE approval notification.
5. **JEs Not Approved:** If the entry is not approved by the manager, the accountant makes appropriate revisions to the entry based on the results and recommendations from the management review.
6. **Additional Approvals:** If additional approval is needed, approval notifications are sent to the next tier levels for approval. If the JE is not approved, the workflow process starts all over again.
7. **GL Posting:** The approved JE is posted to the GL.

PROCESS NARRATIVE 3: OTHER CURRENT AND LONG-TERM ASSETS

Introduction: This section provides examples of process narratives for the key processes within the Transaction Accumulation, Reconciliation, and Sub-Ledger Close process. This information can be used to improve internal controls and business process. Improvements to current internal controls and business processes will support a faster closer process. Here is the process narrative for Other Current and Long-Term Assets.

Process Activity Description

1. **Monthly Reconciliations:** The accountant performs monthly reconciliations for asset accounts in the Other Current Asset section of the balance sheet. The Other Current Asset section includes six subcategories: A/R Non-Trade, Other Receivables, Prepaid Expenses, Retail Inventory, Employee Advances, and Other Current Assets. The purpose of this reconciliation process is to ensure the accuracy of the Other Current Asset accounts as reported in the General Ledger through identifying, investigating, validating, and verifying the adequacy of the account activity and supporting documentation.

2. **Responsibility:** General ledger accounts are the responsibility of the specific business unit that owns the account.

3. **New GL Accounts:** The designated accountant determines whether there are any new accounts in the GL or any reactivated unassigned existing accounts by generating activity reports and year-to-date balance reports immediately after month-end GL close. If new GL accounts or reactivated accounts are noted, the accountant researches the entries to determine whether the activity was recorded to the correct account. The accountant determines if new activity is correctly recorded.

4. **Miss-posted Activity:** If the accountant determines that the activity was mis-posted, a request for a correction is made to the appropriate department, or, if necessary, the accountant proposes the correction.

5. **Account Assignment:** If the accountant determines that the activity was appropriately posted to the account, the manager is notified so that the account is assigned for reconciliation. The manager assigns the account to a reconciler based on the account range and account type.

6. **Understanding the Assigned GL Account:** Obtain an in-depth understanding of the nature of the account, including the type of transactions that post to the account and the sources of the entries by reviewing the account history and supporting documentation.

7. **Account Activity:** Determine how the account is supported by reviewing the accompanying supporting documentation (contract, amortization schedule, invoices, trial balance upload, wire transfers, bank statement, check, etc.). Determine the type and frequency of activity which should post to the account by reviewing the journal entry history, including the supporting documentation.

8. **Account Balance:** Determine the nature of the account balance (debit, credit, zero, eliminating) and document in the reconciliation package.

9. **Company Codes:** Determine which company codes and profit centers are normally used for the account by reviewing previous journal entry postings and associated support.

Process Activity Description
10. **Contact Information:** Obtain contact information by company code for those responsible for providing explanations/supporting documentation or otherwise knowledgeable with the account from the journal entry preparer or other sources.
11. **Documentation:** Review the associated asset account in relation to the valuation allowance account by reviewing the reconciliation for the related asset or the source documentation of the asset.
12. **GAAP:** Review the associated short-term/long-term portion of the asset to ensure proper classification in accordance with GAAP.
13. **Zero-Balance Accounts:** Determine whether all previously assigned accounts that are expected to have a zero balance (zero balance accounts) remain a zero balance.
14. **Variances:** Determine if there are any variances between the applicable ERP system and other accounting systems. If a variance exists, research the cause of the system discrepancy and the steps taken to resolve the issue.
15. **Reconciliation of Variances:** Reconcile current month's beginning GL balance from the applicable ERP system to the previous month's reconciled ending balance. If a variance exists between the beginning GL balance and the previous month's reconciled balance, research and document the cause of the discrepancy. Verify GL activity in the applicable ERP system and the detail transaction reports. If variances exist between the activities reported, research and document the cause of the system discrepancy and the steps taken to resolve the issue.
16. **International Activity:** Identify international activity and segregate from domestic activity.
17. **Monthly Trend Analysis**: Calculate percentage of monthly change and monthly dollar amount change.
18. **Monthly and Quarterly Fluctuations:** Identify monthly and quarterly fluctuations based on the preliminary account review assessment noted above. Analyze whether the balance increased/decreased as expected or if the account remained constant when the balance should have moved (or vice versa). As an example, significant fluctuations are defined as variances in excess of 10% over the prior period balance and over $500,000 in value. If the fluctuation is greater than 10% and $500,000, investigate and document the explanation for the fluctuation as well as any other unexpected fluctuations.
19. **Supporting Documentation:** Collect available supporting documentation from the appropriate contact/department and determine whether the documentation is sufficient to support the account activity.
20. **Investigation:** Investigate activity and account balances that are different than expected based on the preliminary account review above (e.g. if the activity or balance is normally a debit, but has a credit entry or balance, entry or balance does not eliminate, an abnormal company code or profit center is used, or clearing accounts do not net out). Contact entry owner or referred party for explanation of abnormal entries based on account analysis. Determine whether the account activity posted to the account is appropriate.

Process Activity Description

21. **Incorrect Entries:** If the entry was not appropriate, determine if another group will make the requested correction or if it is appropriate to propose a journal entry to correct the inappropriate entries. If a journal entry is proposed and the general ledger is open for the period being reconciled, submit the entry to the appropriate person authorized to initiate the journal entry process through the applicable ERP system.

22. **Closed GL:** If the general ledger is closed for the period being reconciled and the proposed adjustment is significant, submit to the appropriate director for review and approval. For quarter-end or year-end close, a significant post-close adjustment is defined as an adjustment in excess of $500,000. If not a quarter-end or year-end close, only proposed post-close adjustments in excess of $5 million are presented at the controller's close meeting. All limits are reviewed periodically by management.

23. **Closed GL—Significant Adjustments:** If the general ledger is closed for the period being reconciled, proposed adjustments which are significant are reviewed and approved by the appropriate director. The approval for posting to the closed period is determined at the controllers' close meeting by the corporate controller and then the person authorized to initiate the journal entry process in the applicable ERP system is given special authorization to post such entries to the closed period. For quarter-end or year-end close, a significant post-close adjustment is defined as an adjustment in excess of $500,000. If not a quarter-end or year-end close, only proposed post-close adjustments in excess of $5 million are presented at the controller's close meeting. All limits are reviewed periodically by management.

24. **Closed GL—Insignificant Adjustments:** If the general ledger is closed for the period being reconciled, proposed adjustments that are not significant are posted in the subsequent period. For quarter-end or year-end close, a significant post-close adjustment is defined as an adjustment in excess of $500,000. If not a quarter-end or year-end close, only proposed post-close adjustments in excess of $5 million are presented at the controller's close meeting. All limits are reviewed periodically by management.

25. **Follow-up:** Follow-up to verify the requested adjustment or proposed journal entry was correctly made.

26. **Allowance Accounts:** Determine whether the allowance account balance is reasonable when compared to the related asset account and that the allowance is calculated in accordance with the company guidelines or as set by management. Reasonableness is evaluated in accordance with the company policy/guidelines. If the allowance account is not reasonable as compared to the related asset account, research and document the cause and course of action taken or recommendation made for correcting the account.

Process Activity Description

27. **Accurate Classification:** Verify the short-term (or long-term) portion of the asset is accurate when combined with the opposite portion of the asset based on the contract or other adequate supporting documentation and review for proper classification in accordance with GAAP. Request a resolution or adjustment if there are variances between calculation of the short-term and long-term asset accounts and ensure the proper adjustment was made.

28. **Supporting Documentation:** Attach the supporting documentation for account activity listed in the monthly transaction detail report, which includes a copy of invoice, trial balance, schedule, aging reports, roll-forwards, wires, checks, and other reconciliations. Include a copy of proposed journal entries and the supporting documentation for each entry in the reconciliation.

29. **References:** Cross-reference the reconciliation folder using the company's standardized referencing system. Date and label each report for tracking purposes in the event of balance changes. Note any issues of outstanding/missing documentation and include the nature of the documentation and expected date of availability. Update reconciliation when documentation is received and re-submit for manager review.

30. **Outstanding Documentation:** If outstanding/missing documentation is not received by the expected date of availability, follow-up with the appropriate party and update the issue accordingly. Log any other outstanding issues in manager review.

31. **Submission of Completed Reconciliations:** The accountant submits the completed reconciliation to the manager for review and approval within five business days after the final GL close date.

32. **Manager Review:** The manager reviews all completed reconciliations to verify the accuracy and completeness by ensuring that reconciling items have been properly disclosed, variance explanations are reasonable, necessary corrections are proposed, and the supporting documentation is adequate and included in the reconciliation or the availability is appropriately referenced.

33. **Review and Approval:** If the manager notes any questions or issues, the accountant should address accordingly and resubmit to the manager for review and approval. Upon final approval, the manager signs where indicated.

34. **Record Keeping:** The reconciler retrieves the approved reconciliation folder from the manager and files in the appropriate department filing cabinet and saves the approved electronic reconciliation file to the shared drive.

PROCESS NARRATIVE 4: OTHER CURRENT AND LONG-TERM LIABILITIES

Introduction: This section provides examples of process narratives for the key processes within the Transaction Accumulation, Reconciliation, and

Sub-Ledger Close process. This information can be used to improve internal controls and business process. Improvements to current internal controls and business processes will support a faster close process. The following narrative describes Other Current and Long-Term Liabilities.

Process Activity Description

1. **Reconciliation Process:** The general accounting department reconciles all significant accounts as determined by general accounting management on a monthly basis and prepares a reconciliation folder for each identified account. The accountant is responsible for preparing the reconciliation analysis, including opening and closing balances for general ledger accounts, identifying issues, providing status of items being resolved, and providing supporting documentation required for adjustments. Additionally, account balance variance analysis is performed for each account. The analysis is designed to assist in identification of unusual or unexpected balances and activity that may indicate a specific risk of material misstatement or deficiencies in controls. General accounting performs monthly, quarterly, and annual account balance variance analysis, identifying and investigating significant fluctuations, providing explanations for significant fluctuations, and submitting explanations for review and approval. General accounting ensures that the review and approval of the reconciliation effort is performed independently of the preparation.

2. **Management Review:** The manager reviews monthly, quarterly, and annual account reconciliations to determine accuracy of account balances and whether the company's liabilities are reasonably stated and are in accordance with GAAP. The manager reviews all GL accounts within Other Current and LT Liabilities and makes sure that each account has been assigned to be reconciled and that each account has been properly classified to ensure the information is rolled into the appropriate line item. If a new account has been established, the manager determines which accountant should be the reconciler depending on the technical complexity and the quantity of transactions posting to the account.

3. **Account Assignment:** The manager assigns identified domestic accounts to general accounting accountants to perform reconciliations for the accounts. For newly assigned accounts, the accountant performs a preliminary account review.

4. **Understanding the Assigned Account:** Obtain an in-depth understanding of the nature of the account including the type of transactions that post to the account and the sources of the entries by reviewing the transaction detail history and supporting documentation. This process also serves to verify the account has been properly classified and ensures that the information is rolled into the appropriate line item.

5. **Supporting Documentation:** Determine how the account is supported by reviewing the accompanying supporting documentation (contract, invoices, wire transfers, bank statements, check requests, etc.).

Process Activity Description

6. **Account Activity:** Determine the nature of the account balance (debit, credit, zero) and document on the lead sheet in section A of the reconciliation folder. Determine the type and frequency of activity which should post to the account by reviewing the transaction detail history, including the supporting documentation. Determine which company codes and profit centers are normally used for the account by reviewing transaction detail history and associated support.

7. **Contact Information:** Obtain contact information by company code for those responsible for providing explanations/supporting documentation or otherwise knowledgeable with the account from the journal entry preparer.

8. **GL Differences:** If there are differences, the accountant reviews the applicable ERP system and determines which report is incorrect and contacts the application support team. The application support team makes the appropriate system adjustments to correct the reporting issue and ensure that it ties back to the General Ledger (the applicable ERP system).

9. **Prior Period Ending Balances:** The accountant compares the prior period reconciliation's ending balances to current period beginning balances to ensure there have been no changes since the last month's reconciliation process. If there are differences, the accountant determines why and records adjustments needed to the reconciliation to bring it back into balance with the GL.

10. **Account Fluctuations:** To identify significant fluctuations early in the reconciliation process, the accountant performs month over month, quarter over quarter, and year over year account balance variance analysis. Significant fluctuations are defined as variances in excess of 10% over the prior period balance and over $500,000 in value.

11. **Investigation:** The accountant investigates significant fluctuations by obtaining supporting documentation from the applicable ERP system, and/or the field contacts.

12. **Reporting:** The accountant prepares a report explaining the significant fluctuations and includes the report in the reconciliation binder for management review.

13. **Supporting Documentation:** The accountant obtains supporting documentation for material monthly activity transactions from the applicable ERP system, and/or the field contacts. Support documentation includes items such as trial balances, vendor schedules, invoices, other schedules, agreements, etc. The accountant should pull enough documentation to support 90% of the accounts balance. Obtain clarification of validity and accuracy of the transactions from the field contact or supporting documentation. Determine if the supporting documentation correctly validates the journalized transaction by reviewing schedules, invoices, and agreements and verifying they agree with journalized transaction.

Process Activity Description

---

14. **Account Activity:** Determine if the account activity posted to the account is consistent with the normal account activity in nature and amount as defined in the preliminary account review. Determine if the monthly account activity posted to the account is inclusive of all account activity. This can be determined by comparing the account's prior months' activity run rates and verifying similar transactions previously recorded in the account continue to be recorded. This knowledge is acquired from reviewing prior reconciliations or other communications to the accountant. The accountant's review of account activity includes analysis of estimates of accruals, true-ups to actual payments, or any other dispositions of the accrual.

15. **Missing and Invalid Activity:** If activity is missing, the accountant makes inquiries of the responsible parties to get an understanding of why the adjustments were not made and when the adjustments will be made. For invalid or missing entries, an adjusting journal entry is proposed and processed through the JE process.

16. **Quarterly Reviews:** Quarterly, review the associated short-term/long-term portion of the liability to ensure proper classification in accordance with GAAP.

17. **Reclassification:** If there are short-term portions in long-term that need to be reclassified, an adjusting journal entry is proposed and processed through the JE process.

18. **Reconciling Items:** Reconciling items not requiring an adjusting entry (i.e. immaterial or timing differences) should be clearly identified. Supporting documents for all proposed adjustments and reconciling items should be placed in the reconciliation folder.

19. **Account Reconciliation Process:** The accountant prepares a reconciliation that shows line item detail by transaction description. This reconciliation shows the beginning balance, the monthly activity, for all 12 months, classified by transaction description, vendor, etc., the resulting ending balance, reconciling items, and the reconciled balance. Reconciling items are the transactions needed in the account to properly reflect the liabilities of the company.

The accountant prepares a standardized account reconciliation which includes account description, accounting methodology, a listing of account contacts, a listing of posting sources and reporting information sources, the account's normal balance (debit or credit), and the reconciliation rating (low, medium, high). The account rating is determined by the complexity of the account and the transaction level within the account.

The accountant compiles the reconciliation reports and supporting documentation. The accountant reviews the long-term trends to identify missing transactions or unusual trends, such as unrelieved balances or continually increasing balances that are not detected by the month-over-month analysis.

20. **Reconciliation Approval:** The accountant obtains final approval for the reconciliation from management. The accountant obtains supporting documentation and prepares proposed journal entry. The accountant submits the proposed entry to management for review and approval.

Process Activity Description

21. **Journal Entries:** If the journal entry is not correct, the accountant makes corrections to the proposed journal entry and resubmits the proposed entry and supporting documentation to management for review. Accountant sends proposed entry and related documentation to the appropriate operations group for processing and makes reference to this step in the reconciliation binder. If a journal entry is proposed and the general ledger is open for the period being reconciled, the accountant processes the journal entry.

22. **Closed GL—Significant Adjustments:** If the general ledger is closed for the period being reconciled, proposed adjustments which are significant are reviewed and approved by director. The approval for posting to the closed period is determined at the controllers' close meeting by the corporate controller and then the person authorized to initiate the journal entry process through the applicable ERP system is given special authorization to post such entries to the closed period. For quarter-end or year-end close, a significant post-close adjustment is defined as an adjustment in excess of $500,000. If not a quarter-end or year-end close, only proposed post-close adjustments in excess of $5 million are presented at the controller's close meeting. All limits are reviewed periodically by management.

23. **Closed GL—Not Significant Adjustments:** If the general ledger is closed for the period being reconciled, proposed adjustments which are not significant are posted in the subsequent period. For quarter-end or year-end close, a significant post-close adjustment is defined as an adjustment in excess of $500,000. If not a quarter-end or year-end close, only proposed post-close adjustments in excess of $5 million are presented at the controller's close meeting. All limits are reviewed periodically by management.

24. **Due Date for Reconciliations:** On a monthly basis the accountant delivers his account reconciliation folders to his manager upon completion. Reconciliations are due five business days after the final GL closing date.

25. **Reconciliation Review:** Manager reviews reconciliation and verifies accuracy of accruals and account trending, determines if the liability is current or long-term, and determines if the liability should be recorded at present value (PV). Review all sections of the reconciliation to make sure that all amounts have been cross-referenced, in both directions, to supporting documentation.

CHAPTER SIXTEEN

Standards of Internal Control for the Transaction, Accumulation, Reconciliation, and Sub-Ledger Close Process

STANDARDS OF INTERNAL CONTROL 1: JOURNAL ENTRY (JE) PROCESS

Introduction: These standards of internal control define the control objectives, risks, control assertions, control activity title, and frequency to ensure that good controls are in place for the Journal Entry process. And to ensure a timely and accurate fiscal close, these standards are used throughout the process. Note the segregation-of-duties controls, the review processes, and communication processes at the controllers' close meetings as control activities.

Control Objective	Risk	Control Assertion	Control Activity Title	Control Activity	Frequency
1. Ensure that journal entry is reviewed and approved by manager.	Amounts reflected in transactions are not accurately posted to the general ledger, resulting in misstatement.	Completeness Valuation	JE Approval	All journal entries are written up and given to the accounting manager for approval before they are uploaded and posted to the general ledger.	Transaction Based
2. Ensure proper approval, complete and accurate recording, and verification.	An incorrect amount is posted, or the incorrect account number is used, resulting in material misstatements of the financial statements.	Completeness Valuation	JE Approval Within the Applicable ERP System Workflow	Management reviews all journal entries and posts them within the applicable ERP system separately from the preparer. This allows for final review that the correct accounts and amounts have been posted as well as a final separation of duties to ensure that the financial statements are fairly presented.	Transaction Based
3. Ensure all monthly recurring entries are posted to the ledger prior to the close of the current period.	If not posted, then material misstatements of the financial statements could occur.	Completeness Valuation	Management Review (Segregation of Duties)	Management reviews month-end checklist for completion to ensure all monthly recurring entries are posted to the general ledger.	Monthly

STANDARDS OF INTERNAL CONTROL 2: MANAGEMENT APPROVAL OF JOURNAL ENTRIES

Introduction: These standards of internal control define the control objectives, risks, control assertions, control activity title, and frequency to ensure that good controls are in place for the Approval of Journal Entries. And to ensure a timely and accurate fiscal close, these standards are used throughout the process. Note the segregation-of-duties controls, the review processes, and communication processes at the controllers' close meetings as control activities.

Control Objective	Risk	Control Assertion	Control Activity Title	Control Activity	Frequency
1. Ensure that journal entry is reviewed and approved by the assigned level of management.	Amounts reflected in transactions are not accurately posted to the general ledger, resulting in the misstatement of the company's financial results.	Existence/ Completeness	Management Review	Manager review of journal entries and documentation. Management reviews work of staff to ensure that all journal entries have been properly prepared, the correct GL account has been used, and the journal entry is posted to the proper period.	Daily
2. Ensure that journal entry is reviewed and approved by the assigned level of management.	If not posted, then material misstatements of the financial statements could occur.	Existence/ Completeness	Management Approval	Manager approval of JE in the ERP system. If the journal entry does not have a manager's signature, the entry is not approved. If all of the documentation is correct, then the manager will approve, which will post the entry to the financial statements.	Daily
3. Ensure that journal entry is reviewed and approved by the assigned level of management.	If not posted, then material misstatements of the financial statements could occur.	Existence/ Completeness	Director Approval	Any journal entries over a certain amount must go up to the next tier in management to be properly approved.	Daily

STANDARDS OF INTERNAL CONTROL 3: OTHER CURRENT AND LONG-TERM ASSETS

Introduction: These standards of internal control define the control objectives, risks, control assertions, control activity title, and frequency to ensure that good controls are in place for the Other Current and Long-Term Assets accounts. And to ensure a timely and accurate fiscal close, these standards are used throughout the process. Note the segregation-of-duties controls, the review processes, and communication processes at the controllers' close meetings as control activities.

Control Objective	Risk	Control Assertion	Control Activity Title	Control Activity	Frequency
1. Ensure accurate classification of accounts and adequate coverage of account balances are identified for reconciliation.	Significant accounts and transactions could be left unreconciled, presenting the possibility of material misstatements of GL balances and financial statements. Significant accounts and transactions could roll up into the wrong financial statement line item.	Completeness Presentation & Disclosure	Account Classification and Assignment	The manager reviews all GL accounts within Other Current and Long-Term Assets and makes sure that each account has been assigned to be reconciled and that each account has been properly classified to ensure the information is rolled into the appropriate line item. If a new account has been established, the manager determines which accountant should be the reconciler depending on the technical complexity and the quantity of transactions posting to the account.	Monthly
2. Ensure that all account activity has been captured for analysis.	Inconsistent data reported by the different sources of data could result in errors requiring adjustment.	Completeness Valuation or Allocation	System Report Comparison	The accountant compares the activity query to the applicable ERP system detail report for specific account and determines if all account activity has been captured in each report.	Monthly

Control Objective	Risk	Control Assertion	Control Activity Title	Control Activity	Frequency
3. Ensure all journal entries resulting from prior period reconciliation process were posted to correct account and no post-closing adjustments were made after completion of the prior-period reconciliation.	Incorrect posting of prior-period activity could result in unreconciled current-period beginning balances, resulting in errors requiring adjustment.	Completeness Valuation or Allocation	Prior-Period Balance Confirmation	The accountant identifies the prior-period-ending account balance from the prior month's reconciliation and compares the amount to current-period beginning balance.	Monthly
4. Ensure significant fluctuations in account balances are identified and supported by relevant documentation.	Errors or irregularities in an account balance may go undetected, unreconciled, or uncorrected due to lack of segregation-of-duties controls. This may result in potential misstatements.	Valuation or Allocation Existence or Occurrence Rights and Obligations	Investigation of Significant Fluctuations	The accountant reviews account balance variance analysis, comparing current-period balance to prior-period balance(s), and identifies all accounts with fluctuations exceeding established thresholds. The variance analysis reviewed by accountant is filed in the standard reconciliation binder.	Monthly

Control Objective	Risk	Control Assertion	Control Activity Title	Control Activity	Frequency
5. Ensure that the recorded balance is complete and accurate and supported by appropriate documentation.	Inadequate supporting documentation for a transaction underlying an account balance could represent or result in an error or irregularity that goes undetected.	Existence or Occurrence Rights and Obligations Valuation or Allocation	Transaction Support Analysis	The accountant reviews supporting documentation, including schedules, invoices, agreements, etc. and verifies the information supports the journalized transaction amounts.	Monthly
6. Ensure that the recorded balance is inclusive of all activity for the period.	Incomplete transactions may be recorded or transactions that have occurred during the period may not be recorded or may be recorded incorrectly.	Completeness	Transaction Analysis	Determine if the monthly account activity posted to the account is inclusive of all account activity. This can be determined by comparing the account's prior months' activity run rates and verifying similar transactions previously recorded in the account continue to be recorded. This knowledge is acquired from reviewing prior reconciliations or other communications to the accountant. The review of account activity includes analysis of estimates of accruals, true-ups to actual payments, or any other dispositions of the accrual.	Monthly

Control Objective	Risk	Control Assertion	Control Activity Title	Control Activity	Frequency
7. Reconciliations are complete and accurate and prepared in a timely manner.	Errors or irregularities in an account balance may go undetected, unreconciled, or uncorrected due to lack of segregation-of-duties controls. This may result in potential misstatements.	Completeness Existence or Occurrence Valuation or Allocation	Reconciliation Preparation	The accountant prepares a reconciliation which shows line item account detail by transaction description. This reconciliation includes the beginning account balance, the monthly activity, for all 12 months, classified by transaction description, vendor, etc., and the resulting ending balance. The schedule then discloses reconciling Items, which are the transactions needed to be recorded in the account to properly reflect the account balance at period end.	Monthly
8. Ensure that the recorded balance is complete and accurate and unusual trends are understood and addressed.	Errors or irregularities in an account balance may go undetected, unreconciled, or uncorrected due to lack of segregation-of-duties controls. This may result in potential misstatements.	Completeness Valuation or Allocation	Trend Analysis	The accountant reviews the reconciliation to identify long-term unusual trends, potentially missing transactions, or potentially undetected incorrect postings.	Monthly

Control Objective	Risk	Control Assertion	Control Activity Title	Control Activity	Frequency
9. Ensure significant proposed entries are presented to controllers' close for posting in current period.	Significant adjustments will not be reflected in the proper period.	Completeness	Director Review of Significant Adjustments for the Controllers' Close Review and Meeting	If the general ledger is closed for the period being reconciled, proposed adjustments which are significant are reviewed and approved by director. The approval for posting to the closed period is determined at the controllers' close meeting by the corporate controller and then the person authorized to initiate the journal entry process through the applicable ERP system is given special authorization to post such entries to the closed period. For quarter-end or year-end close, a significant post-close adjustment is defined as an adjustment in excess of $500,000. If not a quarter-end or year-end close, only proposed post-close adjustments in excess of $5 million are presented at the controller's close meeting. All limits are reviewed periodically by management.	Monthly

Control Objective	Risk	Control Assertion	Control Activity Title	Control Activity	Frequency
10. Management is provided with adequate, timely, and accurate information to enable them to discharge their responsibility.	Errors or irregularities in an account balance may go undetected, unreconciled, or uncorrected due to lack of segregation-of-duties controls. This may result in potential misstatements.	Completeness Existence Rights and Obligations Valuation or Allocation Presentation and Disclosure	Manager Review and Approval of Reconciliation	For segregation-of-duties controls, the manager performs a review of the reconciliation. The review entails the following: 1. Verify accuracy of accruals, account trending. 2. Verify accurate classification (long term vs. current). 3. Review account reconciliation detail—do schedules foot and tie, are reconciling items disclosed and supported, are JEs proposed, are variances explained adequately? 4. Review and approve any journal entries. 5. Completion of manager review is evidenced by comments provided and if applicable, manager signoff on the account reconciliation.	Monthly

Control Objective	Risk	Control Assertion	Control Activity Title	Control Activity	Frequency
11. Reconciliations are complete and accurate and prepared in a timely manner.	Errors or irregularities in an account balance may go undetected, unreconciled, or uncorrected due to lack of segregation-of-duties controls. This may result in potential misstatements.	Completeness Valuation or Allocation	Monitor/ Update Resolution of Reconciling Items	Updated items are cleared to show that outstanding items have been resolved and approved within the account reconciliation.	Non-Routine

STANDARDS OF INTERNAL CONTROL 4: OTHER CURRENT AND LONG-TERM LIABILITIES

Introduction: These standards of internal control define the control objectives, risks, control assertions, control activity title, and frequency to ensure that good controls are in place for the Other Current and Long-Term Liability accounts. And to ensure a timely and accurate fiscal close, these standards are used throughout the process. Note the segregation-of-duties controls, the review processes, and communication processes at the controllers' close meetings as control activities.

Control Objective	Risk	Control Assertion	Control Activity Title	Control Activity	Frequency
1. Ensure accurate classification of accounts and adequate coverage of account balances are identified for reconciliation.	Significant accounts and transactions could be left unreconciled, presenting the possibility of material misstatements of GL balances and financial statements. Significant accounts and transactions could roll up into the wrong financial statement line item.	Completeness Presentation and Disclosure	Account Classification and Assignment	Manager reviews all GL accounts within Other Current and LT Liabilities and makes sure that each account has been assigned to be reconciled and that each account has been properly classified to ensure the information is rolled into the appropriate line item. If a new account has been established, the manager determines which accountant should be the reconciler depending on the technical complexity and the quantity of transactions posting to the account.	Monthly
2. Ensure that all account activity has been captured for analysis.	Inconsistent data reported by the different sources of data could result in errors requiring adjustment.	Completeness Valuation or Allocation	System Report Comparison	The accountant compares specific account details and determines if all account activity has been captured in each report.	Monthly

Control Objective	Risk	Control Assertion	Control Activity Title	Control Activity	Frequency
3. Ensure all journal entries resulting from prior period reconciliation process were posted to correct account and no post-closing adjustments were made after completion of the prior-period reconciliation.	Incorrect posting of prior-period activity could result in unreconciled current-period beginning balances, resulting in errors requiring adjustment.	Completeness Valuation or Allocation	Prior Period Balance Confirmation	The accountant identifies the prior-period-ending account balance from the prior month's reconciliation binder and compares the amount to current-period beginning balance.	Monthly
4. Ensure significant fluctuations in account balances are identified and supported by relevant documentation.	Errors or irregularities resulting from large variances in account balances may not be detected or understood.	Valuation or Allocation Existence or Occurrence Rights and Obligations	Investigation of Significant Fluctuations	The accountant reviews account balance variance analysis, comparing current-period balance to prior-period balance(s), and identifies all accounts with fluctuations exceeding established thresholds. For all such accounts, accountant obtains supporting documentation and/or the field contacts to support the balance(s). The variance analysis reviewed by accountant is filed in the standard reconciliation binder.	Monthly

Control Objective	Risk	Control Assertion	Control Activity Title	Control Activity	Frequency
5. Ensure that the recorded balance is complete and accurate and supported by appropriate documentation.	Inadequate supporting documentation for a transaction underlying an account balance could represent or result in an error or irregularity that goes undetected.	Existence or Occurrence Rights and Obligations Valuation or Allocation	Transaction Support Analysis	Accountant reviews supporting documentation, including schedules, invoices, agreements, etc. and verifies the information supports the journalized transaction. Supporting documentation is referenced or placed in reconciliation binder.	Monthly
6. Ensure that the recorded balance is inclusive of all activity for the period.	Incomplete transactions may be recorded or transactions that have occurred during the period may not be recorded or may be recorded incorrectly.	Completeness	Transaction Analysis	Determine if the monthly account activity posted to the account is inclusive of all account activity. This can be determined by comparing the account's prior-months' activity run rates and verifying similar transactions previously recorded in the account continue to be recorded. This knowledge is acquired from reviewing prior reconciliations or other communications to the accountant. The accountant's review of account activity includes analysis of estimates of accruals, true-ups to actual payments, or any other dispositions of the accrual.	Monthly

Control Objective	Risk	Control Assertion	Control Activity Title	Control Activity	Frequency
7. Reconciliations are complete and accurate and prepared in a timely manner.	Errors or irregularities in an account balance may go undetected, unreconciled, or uncorrected, resulting in potential misstatements.	Completeness Existence or Occurrence Valuation or Allocation	Reconciliation Preparation	The accountant prepares a reconciliation that shows line item account detail by transaction description. This reconciliation includes the beginning account balance, the monthly activity, for all 12 months, classified by transaction description, vendor, etc., and the resulting ending balance. The schedule then discloses reconciling Items, which are the transactions needed to be recorded in the account to properly reflect the account balance at period-end.	Monthly
8. Ensure that the recorded balance is complete and accurate and unusual trends are understood and addressed.	Errors or irregularities in an account balance may go undetected or unreconciled, resulting in potential misstatements.	Completeness Valuation or Allocation	Trend Analysis	The accountant reviews the reconciliation to identify long-term unusual trends, potentially missing transactions, or potentially undetected incorrect postings.	Monthly

Control Objective	Risk	Control Assertion	Control Activity Title	Control Activity	Frequency
9. Ensure significant proposed entries are presented to controllers' close for posting in current period.	Significant adjustments will not be reflected in the proper period.	Completeness	Director Review of Significant Adjustments for Controllers' Close	If the general ledger is closed for the period being reconciled, proposed adjustments that are significant are reviewed and approved by the director. The approval for posting to the closed period is determined at the controllers' close meeting by the corporate controller and then the person authorized to initiate the journal entry process through the applicable ERP system is given special authorization to post such entries to the closed period. For quarter-end or year-end close, a significant post-close adjustment is defined as an adjustment in excess of $500,000. If not a quarter-end or year-end close, only proposed post-close adjustments in excess of $5 million are presented at the controller's close meeting. All limits are reviewed periodically by management.	Monthly

Control Objective	Risk	Control Assertion	Control Activity Title	Control Activity	Frequency
10. Management is provided with adequate, timely and accurate information to enable them to discharge their responsibility.	Errors or irregularities in an account balance may go undetected, unreconciled, or uncorrected, resulting in potential misstatements.	Completeness Existence Rights and Obligations Valuation or Allocation Presentation and Disclosure	Manager Review and Approval of the Reconciliation	Manager performs a review of the reconciliation folder. Review entails the following: 1. Verify accuracy of accruals, account trending. 2. Verify accurate classification (long term vs. current). 3. Review account reconciliation detail—do schedules foot and tie, are reconciling items disclosed and supported, are JE's proposed, are variances explained adequately? Review and approve any journal entries.	Monthly
11. Reconciliations are complete and accurate and prepared in a timely manner.	Errors or irregularities in an account balance may go undetected, unreconciled, or uncorrected, which may result in potential financial misstatements.	Completeness Valuation or Allocation	Monitor/ Update Resolution of Reconciling Items	Update the reconciliation as items are cleared to show that outstanding items have been resolved and sign off on the account reconciliation.	Non-Routine

CHAPTER SEVENTEEN

Corporate Close and Consolidation

NTRODUCTION: THE FISCAL CLOSING process represents a key corporate governance process and the ultimate set of controls over fiscal results. While transactions represent the results of operations, it is up to the finance and accounting organization to execute control reviews and analysis processes to validate transactional information, identify potential errors or misstatements, and put the seal of approval on financial results during the corporate close and consolidation processes.

The Corporate Close and Consolidation process includes the close of business or operating units and includes the completion of the adjusted trial balance and the first pass of consolidated financial statements. This process is highlighted in the diagram below.

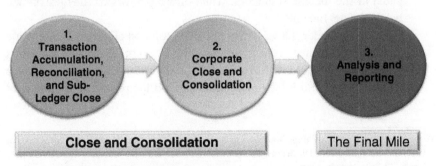

Phase 2: Corporate Close and Consolidation

For many organizations, the number of information interfaces, period-end journal entries, validation and analysis activities, and consolidation of results equates to several hundred sequential steps performed to close the books, ideally in the fewest number of days possible in order to release results on a timely basis.

Typically, the word *consolidated* appears in the title of a fiscal statement, as in a consolidated balance sheet. A consolidation of a parent company and its majority-owned (more than 50% ownership or "effective control") subsidiaries means that the combined activities of separate legal entities are expressed as one economic unit. The presumption is that consolidation as one entity is more meaningful than separate statements for different entities.[i]

DIFFERENCES BETWEEN IFRS AND U.S. GAAP THAT IMPACT THE R2R PROCESS

Generally accepted accounting principles (GAAP) or International Financial Reporting Standards (IFRS) are used to prepare financial statements. Both methods are legal in the United States, although GAAP is most commonly used. The main difference between the two methods is that GAAP is more "rules-based," while IFRS is more "principles-based." Both have different ways of reporting asset values, depreciation, and inventory, to name a few. These examples provide a flavor of impacts on the financial statements and therefore on the conduct of businesses;

- **Consolidation:** IFRS favors a control model, whereas U.S. GAAP prefers a risks-and-rewards model. Some entities consolidated in accordance with FIN 46(R) may have to be shown separately under IFRS.
- **Statement of income:** Under IFRS, extraordinary items are not segregated in the income statement, while under U.S. GAAP they are shown below the net income.
- **Inventory:** Under IFRS, LIFO (a historical method of recording the value of inventory, a firm records the last units purchased as the first units sold) cannot be used while under U.S. GAAP companies have the choice between LIFO and FIFO (a common method for recording the value of inventory).

---

[i] Richard Loth, "Twelve Things You Need to Know About Financial Statements," Investopedia. Last modified April 19, 2019. Accessed March 20, 2019. https://www.investopedia.com/articles/basics/06/fiscalreporting.asp.

- **Earnings-per-share:** Under IFRS, the earnings-per-share calculation does not average the individual interim period calculations, whereas under U.S. GAAP the computation averages the individual interim period incremental shares.
- **Development costs:** These costs can be capitalized under IFRS if certain criteria are met while it is considered as "expenses" under U.S. GAAP.[ii]

HOW OFTEN ARE NEW IFRS PRONOUNCEMENTS ISSUED?

International Financial Reporting Standards (IFRS) and pronouncements are issued as needed to reflect emerging accounting issues and changing business practices to ensure financial reporting accurately reflects the substance of business transactions. The last new standard was established in 2009, and every year the IASB publishes revisions to existing standards and interpretations. The IASB also is presently engaged in working through a number of issues, which may lead to changes in the following areas (in priority order):

- Consolidations
- De-recognition
- Fair value measurements
- Liability and equity distinctions
- Financial statement presentation
- Post-retirement benefits
- Revenue recognition
- Leases
- Financial instruments
- Intangible assets

IS IFRS, AS ISSUED BY THE IASB, THE SAME FOR ALL COMPANIES AND INDUSTRIES, IN ALL COUNTRIES?

IFRS, as issued by the IASB, provides a common set of accounting principles to be used by all companies in all industries and in all countries. It specifically

---

[ii] The American Institute of CPAs (AICPA), "Is IFRS That Different from U.S. GAAP?" Accessed January 17, 2019. https://www.ifrs.com/overview/General/differences.html.

refers to the body of authoritative literature issued by the IASB, which has not been changed or customized to incorporate local GAAP practices of any individual country. It also contains some specific standards that apply only to certain industries, such as mining or real estate. However, in some countries that have adopted IFRS, local accounting standards have been commingled with IFRS, thus creating deviations from IFRS as issued by the IASB. Accordingly, even though a country has adopted IFRS, there may be differences in the application of IFRS to certain topics, which can vary by country. Deviations from IFRS as issued by the IASB can impact the comparability of financial statements of companies that are in the same industry, but prepare their financial statements under International Financial Reporting Standards as uniquely adopted by their country. Thus, while IFRS as issued by the IASB is the same for all companies and industries in all countries, in practice, IFRS around the world can vary by country and industry.

WHAT IS THE PRINCIPAL STANDARD GOVERNING CONVERSION TO IFRS?

IFRS 1, "First-Time Adoption of International Financial Reporting Standards," must be used by an organization during its initial conversion from local GAAP to IFRS. IFRS 1 generally requires full retrospective application of IFRS effective at the reporting date of an organization's first IFRS-compliant financial statements. However, there are certain optional exemptions and mandatory exceptions to the requirement for retrospective application.

These exemptions and exceptions cover standards that in practice have proven to be too difficult to apply retrospectively or would likely result in a cost exceeding any benefits to users. As the exemptions in IFRS 1 are optional, companies can elect to retroactively apply relevant International Financial Reporting Standards to these areas at the time of conversion, provided they can accurately calculate their effect. An organization may take advantage of optional exemptions in any or all of the following areas:

- Business combinations
- Fair value or revaluation as deemed cost for property, plant and equipment, and other assets
- Employee benefits

- Cumulative translation differences
- Compound fiscal instruments
- Assets and liabilities of subsidiaries
- Associates and joint ventures
- Share-based payment transactions
- Insurance contracts
- Changes in existing decommissioning, restoration, or similar liabilities
- Arrangements containing leases
- Fair value measurement of fiscal assets and liabilities at initial recognition
- Service concession arrangements
- Borrowing costs
- Investments in subsidiaries, jointly controlled entities, and associates

The following exemptions to retroactive application of International Financial Reporting Standards are mandatory and cannot be presented retrospectively by an organization at the reporting date of its first IFRS-compliant financial statements:

De-recognizing of fiscal assets and fiscal liabilities
Hedge accounting
Estimates
Non-controlling interests
Assets classified as "held for sale" and discontinued operations

Organizations implementing IFRS should refer to IFRS 1 often during the conversion process for guidance on specific conversion exemptions, exceptions, and required disclosures and reconciliations.

DOES IFRS USE THE SAME FINANCIAL STATEMENTS AS THOSE REQUIRED UNDER U.S. GAAP?

Currently, U.S. GAAP and IFRS use similar statements as part of a complete set of financial statements and require accrual-based accounting. The general content and presentation of the financial statements under IFRS is comparable to U.S. GAAP.

The following table provides a comparison of the required components for a complete set of financial statements under IFRS and U.S. GAAP:

IFRS Financial Statements	U.S. GAAP Financial Statements
Statement of fiscal position	Balance sheet
Statement of income	Income statement
Statement of comprehensive income	Other comprehensive income and accumulated other comprehensive income*
Statement of changes in equity	Statement of changes in shareholders' (stockholders') equity
Statement of cash flows	Statement of cash flows
Notes to financial statements	Notes to financial statements

*The component of other comprehensive income and accumulated other comprehensive income is commonly combined with the income statement or the statement of changes in stockholders' equity, but may be presented as a separate statement.

As part of the convergence effort, the FASB and IASB are currently working on a joint project established under a Memorandum of Understanding that would not only synchronize the financial statements required under U.S. GAAP and IFRS, but would also radically change financial reporting and presentation as it currently exists.

HOW WILL IFRS IMPACT INTERNAL CONTROL REPORTING AND CERTIFICATION UNDER THE SARBANES OXLEY ACT OF 2002?

The transition to IFRS will not affect the internal control reporting and executive certifications required of U.S. registrants under the Sarbanes Oxley Act. However, the change in accounting principles and methods under IFRS, as compared to U.S. GAAP, will require an updated assessment of the effectiveness of internal control over financial reporting. As IFRS is implemented, changes in accounting policies, business processes, accounting methods, and information systems will occur. These changes will require an assessment of the underlying risks and controls, just as in the past when complying with Sarbanes Oxley. The IFRS transition requires an update of the documentation supporting management's conclusions around ICFR design effectiveness and of the test plans supporting a conclusion on ICFR operating effectiveness. The extent of this update is dependent on the extent of the IFRS transition itself. Because of the involvement of the external auditor(s), management needs to plan for completing the IFRS transition in time to enable completion of the Section 404 compliance and attestation process. This planning requires careful attention by both the IFRS transition team and the Sarbanes Oxley PMO or compliance group.

CHAPTER EIGHTEEN

The Number of Consolidation Points

I NTRODUCTION: SIMPLY STATED, CONSOLIDATION means regrouping fiscal data for a company's segments and subsidiaries into a set of accounting records—as if these records were the financial statements of a single company. For example, if a U.S.-based multinational operates in 50 countries and has 20 subsidiaries in various parts of the world, fiscal consolidation requires adding up fiscal data for all 20 subsidiaries and presenting a single set of corporate financial statements.

Remember my example at DEC where multiple general ledgers were impacting the cycle time for the fiscal close. The implementation of financial management centers significantly reduced the consolidation points and added speed and accuracy to the closing process.

Financial statement consolidation serves three purposes. First, it helps regulators review all decisions that a company's top management makes and ensures that these decisions comply with regulations and industry practices.

For example, the Securities and Exchange Commission (SEC) may review the activities of a U.S.-based company in Venezuela. Second, it allows investors to gauge a firm's market share, competitive standing, and business performance. Third, it helps a company's top leadership evaluate the economic health of the company and identify nonperforming areas, countries, or segments.

Financial consolidation can be complicated or simple, but, for chief fiscal officers, the overriding goal is always the same: faster and more efficient closes with quick visibility to accurate results.

The need for fiscal consolidation varies significantly by organization and typically depends on how often consolidation occurs, as well as the number and disparateness of corporate entities and data systems. Regardless of the specific requirements, user and expert advice can help companies optimize their fiscal close processes by reducing time and effort. Checkpoints can be added along the way to ensure additional data accuracy.

BEST PRACTICE 13: AUTOMATE THE CONSOLIDATION PROCESS

Many companies have moved their finance and accounting processes to ERP systems but still depend on spreadsheets for the corporate consolidation process. During the consolidation process, collaboration, review, and visibility to the results are critical throughout the process. Version control can be an issue spreadsheets can break, and formulas can be overridden.

BEST PRACTICE 14: INCLUDE THE PEOPLE WHO IMPACT THE CLOSE

As financial management software products have become more robust, they allow for more users to participate in processes like fiscal consolidation. With clear roles and responsibilities and defined accountability, the owners of the data can respond to queries and make corrections during the closing process. However, as more people become involved in the closing process, it's important to define segregation of duties and system access controls, and ensure communication during the close process.

BEST PRACTICE 15: CREATE CONSISTENT CLOSING SCHEDULES

A closing schedule should be implemented within all levels of the organization to ensure that every department understands their role in the closing process. Many companies start by developing a process map of the fiscal close at the corporate level and then identify the departments that impact the process.

BEST PRACTICE 16: CONSIDER FISCAL CLOSE PROCESS IMPROVEMENTS

1. Eliminate steps that have little or no value.
2. All subsystems are electronically posted to the general ledger by the end of the first day. Post transactions on a real-time basis. Every time you post a transaction in accounts payable, also post it on the general ledger, or have the ability to match accounts payable to the general ledger every day.
3. Allocations booked prior to the close and based on budget or prior period. Move your cost allocations off the monthly cycle by going to fixed-rate, budgeted rates or prior month.
4. No reclassifications or manual correcting entries unless material. Move toward the automatic consolidation of multiunit results.
5. Forecasting treated outside the close process. Move the forecasting process away from the close period.

CHAPTER NINETEEN

The Number of Closing Cycles

NTRODUCTION: THE NUMBER OF cycles is dependent on the complexity of the process and number of systems used. The number of closing cycles is also driven by system functionality and the number of passes needed to complete the consolidation process. Lastly, a controller or CFO may require an additional cycle to review and analyze fiscal results and review accuracy before the statements are created.

BEST PRACTICE 17: REDUCE THE NUMBER OF CLOSING CYCLES

The number of closing cycles should be reviewed to determine if the driver is a process weakness or the creation of an additional review step that could be included in the close process. The controller should also understand that each additional closing cycle is adding additional time to the overall cycle time to complete the end-to-end process. Lastly, a delay in the close process increases the risk for misstating fiscal results and possible fiscal statement fraud.

CHAPTER TWENTY

Post-Closing Entries

 ## FINANCIAL CLOSING STRATEGIES

Two overlapping strategies are often at work when organizations have fast monthly, quarterly, and annual accounting closes. These strategies are:

- **Invest in robust information technology systems:** Companies that follow this strategy have enterprise resource planning (ERP) and business process management systems in place. Then, these businesses share information across a single and unified accounting and fiscal system that features standardized datasets and processes and centralized consolidations.
- **Implement best practices:** Managers reorganize processes or tweak procedures inside the accounting and finance function so that their staffs produce accounting information in ways that are faster, smarter, better, and cheaper. With this approach, the operative dynamic is continuous improvement with managers regularly monitoring and adjusting each component of a close so that efficiency and value rise.

1. Procedural Best Practices

- Use accruals to shorten the close.
- Cross-train staff and document processes.
- Create templates for recurring reports.
- Reduce investigation levels.

- Minimize journal entries during the closing process.
- Eliminate or minimize manual data-entry.

2. Management Best Practices

- Establish clear and regular close communication.
- Develop and monitor close performance metrics.
- Establish clear accountability for closing tasks in a closing schedule and enforce deadlines. Continuously improve closing processes.
- Assign responsibility for resolving discrepancies.

BEST PRACTICE 18: DEVELOP BUSINESS RULES FOR POST-CLOSING ENTRIES

As soon as an error is found, it must be corrected. How you correct the error under GAAP depends on the type of error, the number of fiscal periods the error affects, how the error affects fiscal statement presentation, and whether the error is a counterbalancing entry.

To straighten out these mistakes and give the recipients of the financial statements accurate data for ratio analysis, you have to ask yourself these three questions:

1. **What is the type of error?** Determine the type of error.
2. **What do you need to do to fix it?** Sometimes a simple journal entry is enough. Other times, a direct correction to retained earnings for a prior-period adjustment is on the accounting menu.
3. **Do the financial statements have to be restated?** Restatement means previously issued financial statements are revised to correct the error. If the error is material or prior-period financial statements are shown with the current year, restatement of the financial statements is a must.

CHAPTER TWENTY ONE

Communication and Accountability

INTRODUCTION: COMMUNICATION IS A key component of the closing process since it's important to determine if there are any significant issues or problems that need immediate attention or escalation rather than wait until the last few days or hours of the cycle.

Enterprise organizations usually hold controller meetings during each closing cycle to make sure that the process is going smoothly. The meetings are managed by the corporate controller and the closing checklist is used to determine the status of the process.

An issue tracker is also maintained to document any problems that arise during the close. All issues should be assigned to a single person with a date for completion. The tracker is reviewed during the post-close review and analyzed for recurring themes such as systems, process, training, and staffing issues.

Key Point: You'll see the controller's meeting mentioned as an additional control in the process narratives and standards of internal control provided in this toolkit. Here is the structure for the controller's meeting.

Controller Meeting Agenda

1. Discharge of Liabilities Subject to Compromise (LSTC)
   - Monthly Highlights
   - Roll-Forward
2. Balance Sheet Analysis

3. Significant Account Fluctuations
4. Material Account Variances
5. Post-Closing Entries Recommended
6. Asset Impairment Status
7. Disclosure Items
8. Issue Tracker
   ▪ New Issues
   ▪ Closed Issues
9. Process Improvement Opportunities and Themes

FISCAL CLOSE POSTMORTEM MEETINGS

The *Journal of Accountancy* recommends holding a postmortem meeting immediately after the close is completed. This post-close meeting should be focused on reviewing issues, successes, and key performance indicators (KPIs). It should include a discussion that helps the organization learn from its fiscal close practices and make improvements to the process.

The fiscal close process should be managed like a cross-functional project with key business partners. Unlike a onetime project, improvements can be achieved and successes measured every 30 days. Input from all participants is important, and the organization's responsiveness to issues is critical to becoming a learning organization.

The post-close meetings should encourage a culture of learning and sharing of best practices. Meetings should be run efficiently by publishing each day's agenda in advance and providing all necessary reporting available (issues being tracked, financial system report execution updates, logistic updates) that enables financial close participants to check and report on the status of their individual progress. The controller's meeting agenda can be used as starting point, but the postmortem meetings should be focused on process, people, and systems and areas for improvement.

CHAPTER TWENTY TWO

Financial Statement Assertions

I NTRODUCTION: FINANCIAL STATEMENT ASSERTIONS, also referred to as management assertions, are the explicit or implicit assertions
made by a company regarding the fundamental accuracy of information
contained in its financial statements.

Financial statement assertions can be viewed as a company's official
statement that the figures in its financial statements, such as the balance sheet
and income statement, are a truthful presentation of its assets and liabilities in
accordance with the applicable standards for recognition and measurement of
such figures.

The Public Company Accounting Oversight Board (PCAOB) states that "in
representing that the financial statements are presented fairly in conformity
with the applicable financial reporting framework, management implicitly or
explicitly makes assertions regarding the recognition, measurement, presentation, and disclosure of the various elements of financial statements and related
disclosures."[i]

The table in the following section provides the requirements for the financial statement assertion process.

---

[i] PCAOB, "Auditing Standard Number 15." Accessed March 20, 2019. https://pcaobus.org/
Standards/Auditing/Pages/Auditing_Standard_15.aspx.

FINANCIAL STATEMENT ASSERTION REQUIREMENTS AND APPLICATION

1. **Existence/Occurrence:** The assertion of existence is the assertion that the assets, liabilities, and shareholders' equity balances appearing on a company's financial statements actually exist as stated at the end of the accounting period that the fiscal statement covers.

Application:

- **Existence – balance sheet focused** – Assets, Liabilities, and Ownership Interests (Equity) exist as of the statement date and balances have a real-world counterpart (i.e. customers, suppliers, employees).
- **Safeguard Assets** – Access to assets and critical documents that control their movement are suitably restricted to authorized personnel. Often covered as part of segregation-of-duties review.
- **Occurrence** – Income statement focused – Transactions and events that have been recorded actually occurred and pertain to the entity.

2. **Completeness:** The assertion of completeness is an assertion that the financial statements made are thorough and include every item that should be included in the statement for a given accounting period.

For example, the completeness of transactions included in a fiscal statement means that all transactions included in the statement occurred during the accounting period that the statement covers, and that all transactions that occurred during the stated accounting period are included in the statement. The assertion of completeness also states that a company's entire inventory, even inventory that may be temporarily in the possession of a third party, is included in the total inventory figure appearing on a fiscal statement.

Application:

- **Completeness** – All transactions and events that should have been recorded have been recorded.
- **Cutoff** – Transactions and events have been recorded in the proper fiscal period.

3. **Rights and Obligations:** The assertion of rights and obligations is a basic assertion that all assets and liabilities included in a fiscal statement belong to the company issuing the statement. The rights and obligations assertion states that the company owns and has the ownership rights or usage rights to all recognized assets. In regard to liabilities, it is an assertion that all liabilities listed on a fiscal statement are liabilities of the company and not the liabilities of a third party.

Application:

- **Rights** – The entity holds the rights to the assets.
- **Authorization** – Transactions are executed in accordance with management's general and specific authority.
- **Obligations** – Liabilities recorded are the obligation of the entity.

4. **Accuracy and Valuation:** The assertion of accuracy and valuation is the statement that all figures presented in a fiscal statement are accurate and based on proper valuation of assets, liabilities, and equity balances.

For example, the assertion of accurate valuation regarding inventory states that inventory is valued in accordance with the International Accounting Standards Board's IAS 2 guidelines, which requires inventory to be valued at the lower figure of either cost or net realizable value. The fiscal assertion of accuracy and valuation states that the different components of a fiscal statement, such as assets, liabilities, revenues, and expenses, have all been properly classified within the statement.

Application:

- **Valuation** – Amounts based on estimates and judgments are in accordance with U.S. GAAP.
- **Allocation** – Costs are allocated from the balance sheet to the income statement in the proper period (e.g. depreciation and amortization).
- **Accuracy** – Amounts recorded are mathematically accurate.

5. **Presentation and Disclosure:** The final fiscal statement assertion is that of presentation and disclosure. This is the assertion that all appropriate information and disclosures regarding the company's fiscal statement are included in the statement, and that all the information presented in the statement is presented in a fair and clear manner that facilitates ease of understanding the information contained in the statement.

Application:

- **Classification** – This component is fiscal statement focused, and the assertion states transactions and events have been recorded in the proper accounts.
- **Understanding** – This component is disclosure driven (generally footnotes) and asserts that fiscal information is appropriately described and understandable to users.

CHAPTER TWENTY THREE

Checklists for the Corporate Close and Consolidation Process

CHECKLIST 5: CORPORATE CLOSE AND CONSOLIDATION

Introduction: This checklist recommends the process steps, applicable business unit, frequency, and responsible party for the tasks within the corporate close and consolidation process.

	Corporate Close and Consolidation					
	Period Ending_____					
	CONSOLIDATION:					
Steps:	Description	Applicable Business Unit	Fre-quency	Responsible Party	Initial and Date Completed	Comments
1.0	Prepare Consolidation Spreadsheets for the new month	Corporate	Monthly	Financial Reporting Manager		
2.0	Print and review each Division Trial Balance	Corporate	Monthly	Financial Reporting Manager		

Steps:	Description	Applicable Business Unit	Fre-quency	Responsible Party	Initial and Date Completed	Comments
3.0	Enter each company's trial balance to the Consolidation Spreadsheet	Corporate	Monthly	Financial Reporting Manager		
4.0	Verify entry by balancing and reviewing the trial balance for each division	Corporate	Monthly	Financial Reporting Manager		
5.0	Prepare Adjustments and Elimination entries	Corporate	Monthly	Financial Reporting Manager		
6.0	Prepare Adjustments and Elimination entries	Corporate	Monthly	Financial Reporting Manager		
7.0	Prepare Adjustments and Elimination entries	Corporate	Monthly	Financial Reporting Manager		
8.0	Enter Adjustments and Elimination entries into the Consolidation Spreadsheet	Corporate	Monthly	Financial Reporting Manager		
9.0	Verify the Consolidation Spreadsheet check items are correct	Corporate	Monthly	Financial Reporting Manager		
10.0	Enter the income tax and minority journal entries	Corporate	Monthly	Financial Reporting Manager		
11.0	Verify tax rate matches CFO estimate	Corporate	Monthly	Financial Reporting Manager		

CHECKLIST 6: EXECUTIVE-LEVEL CLOSING CHECKLIST

Introduction: This checklist provides the process steps, applicable business unit, frequency, and responsible party at the executive level for the tasks within the corporate close and consolidation process.

	Executive-Level Closing Checklist					
	Period Ending _____					
	PRE-CLOSE ITEMS:					
Steps:	Description	Applicable Business Unit	Fre-quency	Responsible Party	Initial and Date Completed	Comments
1.0	Review (communication) of closing calendar - discuss public filings/ management decisions/ efficiency improvements and their impact on the upcoming close	Corporate	Monthly	CFO/Financial Reporting Manager/ Corporate Controller		
2.0	Assure communication of any updates to policies/ procedures during the month	Corporate	Monthly	Financial Reporting Manager/ Corporate Controller		
3.0	Refer to Closing Schedule Template: Standard Process Closing Checklist	All Business Units	Monthly	Financial Reporting Manager/ Corporate Controller/ Business Unit Controllers		

		MONTHLY CLOSE ITEMS:				
Steps:	Description	Applicable Business Unit	Frequency	Responsible Party	Initial and Date Completed	Comments
1.0	Finalization of the % complete reports (reconciliation of the % Complete Revenue Recognition calculations)	Corporate	Monthly	Corporate Controller		
2.0	Refer to General Ledger (GL) Journal Entry Checklist	All Business Units	Monthly	Financial Reporting Manager/ Business Unit Controllers		
2.1	Trial balance review	All Business Units	Monthly	Financial Reporting Manager/ Business Unit Controllers		
2.2	Workpaper preparation	All Business Units	Monthly	Financial Reporting Manager/ Business Unit Controllers		
3.0	Refer to Financial Close Consolidation Checklist	Corporate	Monthly	Financial Reporting Manager		
4.0	Finalization of postings to the Trial Balance	Corporate	Monthly	Financial Reporting Manager		
4.1	Consolidation verification	Corporate	Monthly	Financial Reporting Manager		

Steps:	Description	Applicable Business Unit	Fre-quency	Responsible Party	Initial and Date Completed	Comments
5.0	Finalize - Consolidation	Corporate	Monthly	Financial Reporting Manager		
6.0	Transfer of files for CFO review to the shared drive	Corporate	Monthly	Financial Reporting Manager/ Corporate Controller		

REPORTING ITEMS:						
Steps:	Description	Applicable Business Unit	Fre-quency	Responsible Party	Initial and Date Completed	Comments
1.0	Financial Review meeting (CFO/FRM/CC)	Corporate	Monthly	CFO/Financial Reporting Manager/ Corporate Controller		
1.1	Internal financial schedule	Corporate	Monthly	CFO/Financial Reporting Manager/ Corporate Controller		
1.2	Percent complete reports	Corporate	Monthly	CFO/Financial Reporting Manager/ Corporate Controller		
2.0	Financial package preparation	Corporate	Monthly	Financial Reporting Manager		
3.0	Financial package distribution	Corporate	Monthly	Financial Reporting Manager		
4.0	Financial certification	All Business Unit	Monthly	Division Managers		
5.0	Refer to Quarter-End Closing Checklist	Corporate	Quarterly	Financial Reporting Manager		
5.0	Refer to Year-End Closing Checklist	Corporate	Annual	Financial Reporting Manager		

CHECKLIST 7: TWENTY CRITICAL AREAS TO REVIEW AT YEAR-END

Introduction: Many experienced controllers and finance professionals have been through the fiscal year-end process countless times and rely on their accounting system and controls to lead them through the process. To help augment the closing processes, this checklist provides specific transactional and business process areas to address during the fiscal year-end process.

- Assist with the planning process for the fiscal year-end close.
- Ensure roles and responsibilities are assigned.
- Determine if manual checks and balances need to be added to automated controls.
- Establish schedules and timelines.

Twenty Critical Areas to Review at Year-End

1. Accrue any year-end costs associated with payroll and post to payroll expense and payroll liabilities.
   a. Review your fringe benefits to ensure they are accurately reported for the year.
   b. Ensure all your employee information is correct for year-end reporting (W2, W3, 940, and 941).
2. Ensure all your outstanding invoices are posted by the year-end close date.
3. Adjust outstanding receivables that are deemed to be uncollectible against bad debt expense and review if any should be sent to an outside collection agency for assistance.
4. Review your 1099 supplier information to make sure it is complete. We suggest an annual Tax Identification Number (TIN) matching process prior to completing your 1099 process.
5. Complete reconciliations of all general ledger and sub-ledger accounts.
6. Conduct a physical inventory count and record adjustments within inventory.
7. Adjust any prepaid items, such as insurance, that need to be expensed.
8. Journalize any other accruals for year-end that won't be paid until the following year.
9. Calculate and record amortization, depreciation, and any other necessary year-end adjusting journal entries.
10. Review your asset and expense balances to ensure that all fixed assets have been accurately recorded for any purchases or selling of assets.
11. Update any changes in employee or sales tax rates for the new year.
12. Ensure any prepaid deposits received from clients throughout the year are adjusted to earned revenue.
13. Review and update the business plan to include changes anticipated for the upcoming year as needed.
14. Initiate the budget process for the following year if not done previously.

Twenty Critical Areas to Review at Year-End

15. Prepare year-end reports, and the applicable W2, W3, 940, 941, 1096, 1099 forms and remit to appropriate parties.
16. Check to see if any local licensing or permits need to be filed with year-end data.
17. Review standardized transactions to ensure they are still applicable for the following year.
18. Review your year-end reports, which should include:
    a. Profit and Loss Statement
    b. Balance Sheet
    c. Accounts Receivable Aging
    d. Accounts Payable Aging
    e. Budgeted vs. Actual
19. Ensure you have a process to back up your data along with a business continuity plan.
20. Implement a year-end schedule with well-defined roles and responsibilities and consideration for holiday time off.

CHECKLIST 8: THE YEAR-END FINANCIAL STATEMENT CHECKLIST

Introduction: The year-end financial statements are the most important reports that controllers issue. They will be used for tax preparation, future reference, and decision making more than any other monthly reports prepared.

The Year-End Financial Statement Checklist

1. Does my general ledger bank balance reconcile to the bank statement?
2. Are there any accounts receivables that are worthless and should be written off?
3. Is my balance in Allowance for Bad Debts a reasonable estimate of potential write-offs?
4. Is the company's inventory balance correctly stated?
5. Are there inventory items that cost more than they are worth and should be written down to their market value?
6. Does the company still have all the fixed assets reported?
7. Is depreciation correctly recorded for those fixed assets still in the company's possession?
8. Did I amortize goodwill and franchise fees?
9. Are there any prepaid items that need to be adjusted, such as prepaid insurance?
10. Have all assets been reviewed for accuracy?
11. Have we recorded all of our payables?
12. Do the payroll tax liabilities coincide with our quarterly reports?
13. Do the balances in the notes payable accounts (loans) agree with what the banks say we owe?
14. Are there other debts that have not been included on the books?
15. Are there debts on the books that no longer exist because of forgiveness or oversight?

CHECKLIST 9: THE YEAR-END TRANSACTION CHECKLIST

Introduction: As a timely refresher we are providing a simple checklist of items that you should consider for each business process impacting the consolidation of fiscal transactions when ensuring the completeness and correctness of your year-end financial statements.

1. Adjustments

- ❏ Automatic payments (bank drafts and adjustments)
- ❏ Transactions not yet entered: invoices, bills, sales commissions, and royalties
- ❏ Transactions entered or coded incorrectly: invoices, bills, sales, payroll
- ❏ Infrequent transactions: returns, voided, corrected or reissued paychecks, tax payments, vendor refunds
- ❏ Inventory adjustments
- ❏ Job adjustments or allocations
- ❏ Payroll adjustments
- ❏ Adjustments for taxes: sales tax, payroll taxes, franchise taxes, etc.
- ❏ Fixed assets: depreciation entries
- ❏ Loan payments: allocating interest and principle
- ❏ Aged accounts receivable: any to be written off as uncollectible
- ❏ Accruals
- ❏ Any questions the client might bring up that would lead to a journal entry

2. Integration

- ❏ Revenue and cost of goods sold/inventory entry
- ❏ Job costing
- ❏ Payroll (here you may have several weekly entries to post)
- ❏ Suggest change to Intuit systems where applicable

3. Reconcile

- ❏ Bank statement additions and corrections to cash accounts
- ❏ Petty cash
- ❏ Accounts receivable
- ❏ Credit card statements
- ❏ Equity accounts

- ❑ Loans
- ❑ Accounts payable
- ❑ Inventory
- ❑ Fixed assets
- ❑ Any other asset or liability accounts

4. Review

- ❑ General ledger coding consistency: Is the transaction coded completely and to the right account?
- ❑ If a class is used, is it complete for all transactions?
- ❑ If job or project number is used, is it complete for all transactions?
- ❑ Is the backup documentation in order?
- ❑ Are authorizations complete?
- ❑ Do the transactions look reasonable?

5. Payroll

- ❑ Is documentation for new hires and terminated employees complete?
- ❑ Is the hourly rate or salary amount correct?
- ❑ Are hours accurate for hourly employees?
- ❑ Is overtime paid at the agreed-upon rate?
- ❑ Are deductions taken?
- ❑ Are taxes figured correctly?
- ❑ Are payroll deposits made on time?
- ❑ Are there any court orders that need to be followed?
- ❑ Is tax taken out of bonus checks?
- ❑ Are there any checks that are paid directly to employees?
- ❑ Are employee loans accounted for and collected?
- ❑ Are expense reports in order and coded properly?
- ❑ Are payroll reports filed timely (quarterly)?
- ❑ Are state unemployment payments and reports handled accurately?
- ❑ Are all transactions booked correctly?

6. Reports

- ❑ Reports by job, project, or class
- ❑ Budget vs. actual reports if applicable
- ❑ Generate task list from report analysis
- ❑ General ledger

❑ Missing check number report
❑ Voided/deleted transactions
❑ Audit trails
❑ Payroll reports
❑ Ledgers from any accounts that need special review

CHECKLIST 10: THE YEAR-END PAYROLL PROCESS CHECKLIST

Introduction: Here is a simple checklist of items for the year-end payroll process that will impact the consolidation of fiscal transactions when ensuring the completeness and correctness of your year-end financial statements.

1. Check employee and employer data

1. Verify the employer and employee data that is used in processing your quarterly tax reports and W2s.
2. To which employees does the "retirement plan" indicator in Box 13 of Form W2 apply?
3. Confirm that employee names and Social Security numbers are in the correct format.
4. The IRS may impose a penalty for each Form W2 with a missing or incorrect Social Security number or employee name.
5. Ensure that deceased employees are properly coded.

2. Check wage, tax, and benefits data

1. Confirm that deferred compensation plan type is correct and verify employee contribution amounts.
2. Check that Group-Term Life Insurance adjustments have been updated and submitted.
3. Ensure that other special tax items have been updated and submitted, such as Other Compensation, Third-Party Sick Pay, Employee Business Expense Reimbursements, Taxable Fringe Benefits, Tip Allocation information, and Dependent Care Benefits.
4. Verify the employer state unemployment insurance tax rate and taxable wage limit for each state.
5. Compute uncollected Social Security and Medicare taxes for retirees and former employees.

6. Verify that withholding has been made properly, or withhold from the final paycheck for taxable fringe benefits. These may include:
   - Group-term life insurance in excess of $50,000
   - Third-party sick pay (Is the third party issuing a W2?)
   - Personal use of company vehicle
   - Nonqualified moving expense reimbursements
   - Company-provided transportation or parking
   - Employer-paid education not related to the employee's job
   - Non-accountable business expense reimbursements or allowances
   - Bonuses
   - Non-cash payments
7. Check for required backup withholding; verify amounts.
8. Determine whether Earned Income Credit (EIC) coding has been submitted properly.
9. Review discrepancies such as negative quarter and/or year-to-date fields and qualified pension coding discrepancies.
10. Verify the employer's new state unemployment insurance tax rate and taxable wage limit for each state where the employer has workers.
11. Verify new state disability insurance rate and taxable wage limit, where applicable.
12. Test reasonableness of Social Security tax withholding (multiply total wages less excess wages by 6.2%).
13. Verify the reasonableness of employer's matching Social Security tax.
14. Test reasonableness of Medicare withholding (multiply total wages by 1.45%).
15. Double-check the reasonableness of employer's matching Medicare tax.
16. Test reasonableness of state unemployment insurance tax (verify taxable wages and multiply by the employer experience rate).
17. Compare payroll register totals to Form W3 totals.
18. Compare Forms W2 to state and local report totals.
19. Compare total wages reported for each tax; reconcile any differences.
20. Does reported taxes from Form W3 equal tax deposits (total of Forms 941)?
21. Check contributions to and distributions from Section 125 (cafeteria) plan for child care and for medical care reimbursements.
22. Check for excess contributions to qualified plans, including 401(k), 403(b), and SIMPLE plans, especially for highly compensated employees.
23. Check for required tip allocations for tipped employees.

24. Ensure that any employee tax and/or taxable blocks have been removed, if not desired for the new year.
25. Verify that employee requests for fringe benefit deduction changes for the new year have been applied.
26. Confirm the settings and clearing of special accumulators for the new year.

3. Check for special procedures

1. Schedule any special bonus payrolls for the current year.
2. Request any special reports needed for year-end.
3. Ensure adequate payroll supplies to complete the year and to begin the new year, including blank checks, payroll forms, and blank Forms W2.
4. Determine whether all adjustments are applied or that an adjustment payroll has been scheduled.
5. Remind employees to fill out a new Form W4 if their situation has changed.
6. Obtain new Forms W5 for Advance Earned Income Credit (EIC) for the new year.
7. Confirm that all "manual" checks written during the year have been accounted for and updated in the system.
8. Determine that all voided or reversed paychecks have been accounted for in the system.

4. Check employee and employer indicative data

1. Review discrepancies such as missing addresses and missing or invalid Social Security numbers.
2. Check the "purge" coding of any terminated employees who should be removed from the database.
3. Ensure that terminated employees have zero balances for loans, garnishments, vacation, and sick time. These discrepancies were uncovered while preparing for the last payroll of the calendar year and should be corrected or adjusted.

5. Check for special procedures

1. Schedule any special bonus payrolls.
2. Verify that the new year month-end close-out dates are accurate.
3. Verify that management reports for the new year are scheduled, and will include the correct weeks and process.

Confirm that for the new year the schedule of pay dates, period-ending dates, and quarter closing dates, are as intended and do not fall on holidays or weekends.

CHAPTER TWENTY FOUR

Sample Policies for the Corporate Close and Consolidation Process

 ## POLICY 4: FISCAL CLOSE AND CONSOLIDATION PROCESS

Introduction: This policy provides guidelines for the monthly, quarterly, and year-end fiscal statement close process, including key tasks and responsibilities, and applies to the fiscal statement close process. This policy is focused on the tasks and responsibilities of the general ledger (GL) and financial reporting departments but also includes a discussion of required inputs from other corporate departments as well as finance and accounting personnel.

The fiscal close shall be designed to provide reasonable assurance that the fiscal records of the company include all material transactions and such transactions are properly recorded in accordance with generally accepted accounting principles (GAAP). Additionally, such transactions will be reported on in a time frame that is adequate to provide timely and relevant information for both internal management purposes and to meet Securities and Exchange Commission (SEC) reporting deadlines.

Fiscal Close Schedules

The applicable accounting department shall maintain a detail listing of tasks to be completed by the general ledger accounting manager and accounts receivable manager during each monthly, quarterly, and year-end close cycle. The schedule shall be of sufficient detail to describe critical tasks.

The schedule will change as changes in the business or other circumstances dictate.

1. For example, if the company enters into new types of transactions or new lines of business, the close schedule is to be updated to reflect any new tasks that need to be completed as a result of these changes.
2. Each task shall be assigned a due date along with a responsibility. Due dates will be monitored during the close process to ensure that tasks are completed on time and, if tasks are being delayed, that communication of those delays is made to appropriate parties.

Fiscal Close Process

The completed close schedule shall be reviewed at the end of each close cycle by the managing director of accounting, GL accounting manager, and accounts receivable (AR) manager to determine if there are items that should be added to, deleted from, or changed on the schedule. The roles and responsibilities for specific tasks on the close schedule may change depending on the structure of your company's finance and accounting department as well as the complexity of your closing process.

1. The completed close schedule should indicate the due date of each task along with the completion date. When the completion date is after the due date (i.e. the task was completed late), an explanation will be added to describe the delay.
2. The completion dates will be reviewed to determine if there are tasks that can be completed more efficiently in a post-close review session.

Delays or Errors

Tasks in which delays or errors were encountered will be reviewed to determine the nature of the delay or error. Delays and errors will be formally discussed with the controller or CFO. At the discretion of the controller, delays and/or errors that are recurring, significant, or affect the timeliness of required SEC filings will be discussed with the CFO. The action plan for delays and errors will be as follows:

1. **Delays caused by not receiving timely information from other corporate departments or regional finance personnel:** Such delays will be discussed with the appropriate corporate department head. The discussion will include details of the delay, the effect of the delay on the fiscal close, and what can be done in future periods to eliminate the delay.

2. **System-related delays or errors:** These include delays in the provision of interfaces or incorrect and/or incomplete interfaces and shall be discussed with the chief information officer (CIO) and/or the controller. The discussion will include details of the delay or error, the effect of the delay on the fiscal close, and what can be done in future periods to eliminate the delay or error.

3. **Other errors or delays identified during or after the close process:** Other errors or delays that result from the general ledger reconciliation process may be identified either during or after the close process. Such errors or delays will be discussed with the appropriate manager (i.e. GL manager or AR manager) and appropriate staff as necessary.

4. **Significant errors or delays** will be discussed with the controller at the discretion of the managing director of accounting. All material adjustments made as a result of an error in a reconciliation process will be discussed with the controller. Appropriate action will be taken to ensure similar errors do not occur in the future, including, but not limited to, a formal documented change in procedure, appropriate counseling of staff members, and further monitoring of affected accounts.

Quarter and Year-End Close Cycles

The close schedule for quarter and year-end periods will differ from those of the normal monthly close cycle. Additional time or information may be required in order to provide for the completion of reconciliations and the posting of adjustments, if necessary, in the proper quarter or year-end period. Such differences will be documented on the appropriate quarter or year-end close schedule.

During the quarter and year-end close cycles a list of documentation required by the company's external audit firm will be provided to the managing director of accounting. This documentation, where appropriate, should be prepared in the normal course of the quarter and year-end close cycle so as to provide our independent accountants with the requested information in as timely a manner as possible.

Reporting

The estimated date of report distribution, for both preliminary and final results, will be included on the close schedule. The responsibility for communication of fiscal close–related report completion, changes to any fiscal close reports, and the maintenance of report distribution lists will be held with the internal reporting manager.

THE TIMELY COMMUNICATION OF DELAYS

The timely reporting of fiscal results is necessary for field and corporate personnel for purposes of performing analytics, reporting requirements under contracts, and managing their operations. When it is determined that delays in the close process will result in the delay of the distribution of monthly financial reports to field and corporate personnel, an email will be sent to affected parties by the managing director of accounting as soon as the delay is identified. The communication will provide a brief description of the delay and a new estimation of the report distribution date.

Any concerns regarding the content and/or timing of distribution of fiscal close reports should be communicated to the managing director of accounting.

Documentation of Financial Statement Analysis

An appropriate amount of financial statement analytics will be performed to further provide reasonable assurance that the fiscal records of the company include all material transactions and such transactions are properly recorded in accordance with GAAP. This includes but is not limited to the analyses presented in the Monthly Management Report and those provided in the Policy on P&L Variance review.

1. Any issues identified in such reviews will be addressed by the controller to determine if further adjustments are required.
2. The conclusion on any such adjustments will be formally documented and the documentation will be maintained with the adjustment.

ADJUSTMENTS REQUESTED BY FIELD AND CORPORATE PERSONNEL

During the close process it is sometimes necessary to make adjustments to amounts recorded in the general ledger. All requested adjustments should be accompanied by sufficient documentation to detail the amount and need for the adjustment.

1. Adjustments relating to revenue and/or receivable accounts should be directed to the accounts receivable manager.
2. All other adjustments should be directed to the GL manager.
3. At no time should adjustment requests be sent directly to an accounting staff member without also notifying the appropriate manager or the managing director of accounting.

ADJUSTMENTS BETWEEN PRELIMINARY AND FINAL RESULTS

1. As part of the normal monthly close process, preliminary results are reported to corporate and field personnel. Time is provided for the review of these results and the posting of additional adjustments if necessary. Additionally, from time to time adjustments may be initiated by corporate accounting personnel.
2. Any adjustments made between the distribution of preliminary and final results will be communicated to affected parties so as to provide reconciliation between the financial reports.

"LATE" ADJUSTMENTS

1. Any late adjustments (adjustments made after final reports are distributed) made as the result of a quarter or year-end review and/or audit process will be communicated in a timely manner to affected parties, including the controller, CFO, external reporting, tax, treasury, and fiscal planning departments.
2. The communication of such adjustments will include a description of the adjustment and its effect on the company's financial statements.

Policy Compliance

Adherence to this policy is the responsibility of the managing director of accounting. Any instances of noncompliance will be discussed with the controller.

CHAPTER TWENTY FIVE

Process Narratives for the Corporate Close and Consolidation Process

PROCESS NARRATIVE 5: BALANCE SHEET CONSOLIDATION

Introduction: This process narrative defines the steps for the consolidation of fiscal information for the balance sheet in the Corporate Close and Consolidation process. Roles and responsibilities to ensure good segregation-of-duties controls are identified throughout the process.

Process Activity Description
1. **Consolidated Balance Sheet Model:** The accountant maintains a password-protected model for the company consolidated balance sheet. The model contains worksheets for individual balance sheet line items, which are used for trending and analysis. Finally, the model contains the 10K and 10Q balance sheet formats. These worksheets are used for yearly and quarterly reporting needs.
2. **Balance Sheet Worksheets:** The accountant compares totals on the worksheet to the rounded totals on the balance sheet worksheets (presentations and SEC filings are rounded to $million to ease reporting), for both Assets and Liabilities/Shareholders' Equity, to ensure all ledger activity has been properly captured in the model.
3. **Balance Sheet Totals:** If totals do not match the rounded balance sheet totals, the accountant investigates and resolves any differences.

Process Activity Description

4. **Monthly Closing Package:** The accountant links the model directly to the monthly closing package. This link ensures that the presentation is consistent with the model, and reflects the most up-to-date balance sheet. Any changes that occur to the model will be updated automatically in the close package. The closing package is reviewed with general accounting director for completeness and accuracy. Any adjustments to the presentation are discussed and implemented at this time. The closing package is forwarded to the financial reporting department for inclusion in the monthly controllers meeting presentation.

5. **Variance Analysis:** The accountant coordinates with the General Accounting Asset, Liability, and Cash Managers to obtain variance analysis for any significant variances for individual balance sheet line items. The general accounting managers will use their monthly reconciliations for individual accounts to determine the cause of any variance for a particular balance sheet line item. The cause of the change will then be included in the monthly close package. International variances will be identified as such and are further explained in the closing documentation.

6. **GL Adjustments:** Adjustments to the general ledger are identified based on discussions at the monthly close meeting and the corporate controller's approval.

7. **Comparison of Balance Sheet Totals:** The accountant compares totals to the rounded totals within the balance sheet worksheets (presentations and SEC filings are rounded to $million to), for both Assets and Liabilities/Shareholders' Equity, to ensure all ledger activity has been properly captured in the model. If totals do not match the rounded balance sheet totals, the accountant investigates and resolves any differences.

8. **Balance Sheet and the Monthly Closing Package:** The accountant links the model directly to the monthly closing package. This link ensures that the presentation is consistent with the model, and reflects the most up-to-date balance sheet. Any changes that occur to the model will be updated automatically in the close package.

9. **Post Closing Package:** The post-closing package is reviewed with general accounting director for completeness and accuracy. Any adjustments to the post-closing package are discussed and implemented at this time.

10. **Quarter End:** If the period under review is a quarter end or year end, the director receives Balance Sheet Template from Financial Reporting. The template is pre-populated with prior period balance sheet amounts. The template requests current-period balance sheet by summary line item. The director forwards the template to the accountant.

11. **10Q and 10K Reporting:** The accountant prepares the template based on information from the final balance sheet model. The accountant compares the current 10Q/10K balance sheet worksheet to both the current ledger totals and the previously issued 10Q/10K financials. The accountant ensures that each line item of the current balance sheet matches the ledger and that the prior period balances match the line items from any previously issued 10Q/10K filings. Any issues with previously reported balance sheets are researched and resolved.

Process Activity Description

12. **Approval Process:** The revised balance sheet template is submitted to the director for approval. The director reviews template for completeness and accuracy. The accountant makes changes needed to the template and also updates balance sheet model and resubmits to the director for approval. The director forwards completed template, inclusive of changes, to the financial reporting department. The director determines if adjustments are required based on discussions with the financial reporting department. If adjustments are required, the accountant adjusts the template for the balance sheet model accordingly.

PROCESS NARRATIVE 6: ASSETS HELD FOR SALE DUE TO DISCONTINUED OPERATIONS

Introduction: This process narrative defines the steps for reporting assets held for sale due to discontinued operations as one of the processes within the Corporate Close and Consolidation process. Roles and responsibilities to ensure good segregation-of-duties controls are identified throughout the process.

Process Activity Description

1. **Pending Divestitures:** General Accounting attends weekly meetings with Corporate Development where the current status of any pending divestitures is discussed.
2. **Review of Pending Transactions:** General Accounting reviews all pending transactions to determine if the transaction (1) meets the SFAS No. 144 Assets Held for Sale criteria, and (2) meets the SFAS No. 144 Discontinued Operation criteria. General Accounting is also responsible for tracking all "costs to sell" to ensure that these costs are properly recorded to the "assets held for sale" account in accordance with SFAS No. 144. Finally, General Accounting is responsible for posting the final entry to record the gain/loss on disposal of the "assets held for sale."
3. **Review and Approval:** General Accounting ensures that the review and approval of (1) the conclusions reached relating to meeting the "assets held for sale" and "discontinued operation" criteria, as well as (2) the related journal entries are performed independently of the preparation. The director of general accounting reviews the whitepaper and related journal entries to determine accuracy of proposed entries and the conclusions reached in the whitepaper.

Process Activity Description

4. **Processing:** The information is processed as described within this narrative and compiled in folders for each transaction. Folders typically include: whitepaper, all related journal entries, copy of sale agreements, minutes or delegation of authority approval, and bankruptcy court approval (where applicable). A separate binder includes support for all expenses (i.e. "costs to sell") that have been reclassified to "assets held for sale." General accounting works with corporate development to identify the date that the transaction closes.

If "costs to sell" are identified that have not yet been recorded, general accounting prepares the necessary journal entries to reclassify any "costs to sell" against the carrying value of the "assets-held-for-sale" account (as required by SFAS No. 144). These journal entries are proposed and processed through the JE process. (See Process Narrative 1). The general accounting department works with the treasury and general accounting's cash group to identify all related cash payments (e.g. deposits held in a deposit account, escrow payments held by third parties, and/or other cash payments received at closing). The general accounting department posts a journal entry to record the gain/loss on the divestiture. The entry nets the proceeds received against the amounts in the "assets-held-for-sale" and "liabilities-held-for-sale" accounts. This journal entry is proposed and processed through the JE process. (See Process Narrative 1.)

5. **Assets Held for Sale:** General accounting works with the appropriate group (e.g. property, plant and equipment (PP&E) in the case of the disposal of PP&E, Consolidations in the case of the disposal of a subsidiary, etc.) to ensure that the assets (and any related liabilities) are appropriately reclassified to "assets-held-for-sale." General Accounting reviews related accounts (primarily assets subject to depreciation and amortization) to ensure that depreciation/amortization ceases once the asset is reclassified to "assets-held-for-sale" (as required by SFAS No. 144).

6. **Discontinued Operations:** General accounting works with the appropriate group (e.g. PP&E in the case of the disposal of PP&E, Consolidations in the case of the disposal of a subsidiary, etc.) to ensure the operating results of an asset held for sale are reclassified to "discontinued operations" on the income statement. General accounting and corporate development monitor the divestiture for changes that may affect the conclusions reached. General accounting identifies any "costs to sell" by (1) reviewing engagement letters (investment bankers, lawyers, etc.), (2) discussions with corporate development, and (3) review of certain general ledger expense accounts. If "costs to sell" are identified, General accounting prepares the necessary journal entries each month to reclassify any "costs to sell" against the carrying value of the "assets-held-for-sale" account (as required by SFAS No. 144). These journal entries are proposed and processed through the JE process. (See Process Narrative 1.)

7. **Discontinued Operations Template:** General accounting receives the Discontinued Operations Template from Financial Reporting. The template requests code and summary income statement and balance sheet information for entities identified as discontinued operations. General accounting prepares the template based on information from the "discontinued operations" account on the income statement. Support for this information is obtained from the technical whitepapers for the appropriate transactions.

Process Activity Description

---

8. **Approval Process:** The Discontinued Operations Template is submitted to the director of general accounting for approval. Both general accounting and the director of general accounting review the template for completeness and accuracy. General accounting makes changes to template and resubmits to the director for approval. General accounting forwards the completed template, inclusive of changes, to financial reporting. Determine if adjustments are required based on discussions with the financial reporting group. If adjustments are required, general accounting adjusts template accordingly.

9. **JE Process:** The accountant obtains supporting documentation and prepares proposed journal entry. The accountant submits the proposed entry to the director of general accounting for review and approval. If the proposed journal entry is correct, the accountant determines whether the journal entry is significant. The director of general accounting reviews significant proposed adjusting entries in the controllers' close meeting to determine whether to record the adjustment in the current period or in the next period. This determination is generally based on whether it is a quarterly close.

Accountant processes the journal entry in the upload process. After completing the JE upload process, the accountant logs the entry information into the JE checklist. The accountant places a copy of the JE and support in the Costs to Sell binder for the transaction and forwards to appropriate accounting groups impacted by entry (i.e. General Accounting Asset and Liability Groups, SG&A, Consolidations, Property, etc.). The accountant places a copy of the JE and support in the Divestiture binder for the transaction and forwards to appropriate accounting groups impacted by entry (i.e. General Accounting Asset and Liability Groups, SG&A, Consolidations, Property, etc.)

CHAPTER TWENTY SIX

Standards of Internal Control for the Corporate Close and Consolidation Process

 ## STANDARDS OF INTERNAL CONTROL 5: BALANCE SHEET CONSOLIDATION

Introduction: These standards of internal controls define the control objectives, risks, control assertions, control activity title, and frequency to ensure that good controls are in place for the consolidation of fiscal information for the balance sheet.

Control Objective	Risks	Control Assertion	Control Activity Title	Control Activity	Frequency
1. Ensure that all account activity has been captured in the balance sheet model.	The balance sheet model is incorrect.	Completeness Valuation or Allocation	Comparison of Balance Sheet Model to Applicable Totals	The accountant compares totals on the worksheet to the rounded totals on the balance sheet worksheets (presentations and SEC filings are rounded to $million to ease reporting) for both Assets and Liabilities/Shareholders' Equity, to ensure all ledger activity has been properly captured in the model.	Monthly
2. Ensure that all account activity and post-close adjustments have been captured in the balance sheet model.	The balance sheet model is incorrect.	Completeness Valuation or Allocation	Comparison of Balance Sheet Model to Applicable Totals	The accountant compares totals on the worksheet to the rounded totals on the balance sheet worksheets (presentations and SEC filings are rounded to $million to ease reporting) for both Assets and Liabilities/Shareholders' Equity, to ensure all ledger activity has been properly captured in the model.	Monthly
3. Ensure that 10Q/10K worksheet is consistent with previous 10Q/10K financials.	Current 10Q/10K financials do not tie to ledger or previously issued 10Q/10K financials.	Completeness Valuation or Allocation Presentation and Disclosure	Comparison of Balance Sheet Model and Previously Issued 10Q/10K Financials	If the period under review is a quarter or year end, the accountant compares the current 10Q/10K balance sheet worksheet to both the current ledger totals and the previously issued 10Q/10K financials.	Quarterly

Control Objective	Risks	Control Assertion	Control Activity Title	Control Activity	Frequency
				The accountant ensures that each line item of the current balance sheet matches the ledger and that the prior period balances match the line items from any previously issued 10Q/10K filings. Any issues with previously reported balance sheets are researched and resolved.	Monthly
4. Ensure that all significant variances are supported and explained.	The balance sheet balances cannot be supported.	Completeness Valuation or Allocation Presentation and Disclosure	Analytic Review of Consolidated Balance Sheet	The accountant coordinates with the General Accounting Asset, Liability, and Cash managers to obtain variance analyses for any significant variances for individual balance sheet line items. The general accounting managers will use their monthly reconciliations for individual accounts to determine the cause of any variance for a particular balance sheet line item.	Monthly
5. Ensure completeness and accuracy of the balance sheet model.	The balance sheet model is incorrect.	Completeness Valuation or Allocation Presentation and Disclosure	Director Review of Balance Sheet Model (Segregation of Duties)	The close package/post-close monthly package/10Q-10K balance sheet is reviewed with general accounting director for completeness and accuracy. Any adjustments to the presentation are discussed and implemented at this time.	Monthly

STANDARDS OF INTERNAL CONTROL 6: ASSETS HELD FOR SALE DUE TO DISCONTINUED OPERATIONS

Introduction: These standards of internal control define the control objectives, risks, control assertions, control activity title, and frequency to ensure that good controls are in place for assets held for sale due to discontinued operations.

Control Objective	Risk	Control Assertion	Control Activity Title	Control Activity	Frequency
1. Ensure that all "assets-held-for-sale" and "discontinued operations" are appropriately classified in the balance sheet and income statement, respectively.	"Assets-held-for-sale" and/or "discontinued operations" are not correctly reported in the balance sheet and income statement, respectively.	Existence or Occurrence Presentation and Disclosure Valuation or Allocation	Analysis of New Divestitures	General Accounting evaluates any divestiture to determine if the transaction (1) meets the SFAS No. 144 Assets Held for Sale criteria, and (2) meets the SFAS No. 144 Discontinued Operations criteria.	Transaction Based
2. Ensure that all "assets-held-for-sale" and "discontinued operations" are appropriately classified in the balance sheet and income statement, respectively.	"Assets-held-for-sale" and/or "discontinued operations" are not correctly reported in the balance sheet and income statement, respectively.	Existence or Occurrence Presentation and Disclosure Valuation or Allocation	Director Approval of Technical Whitepaper	Technical whitepaper submitted to director for approval.	Transaction Based

Control Objective	Risk	Control Assertion	Control Activity Title	Control Activity	Frequency
3. Ensure that all "assets-held-for-sale" are appropriately classified in the balance sheet.	"Assets-held-for-sale" are not correctly reported in the balance sheet.	Existence or Occurrence Presentation and Disclosure Valuation or Allocation Completeness	Review of "Assets-Held-for-Sale" Balance Sheet Accounts	General Accounting works with the appropriate group (e.g. PP&E in the case of the disposal of PP&E, Consolidations in the case of the disposal of a subsidiary, etc.) to ensure that the assets (and any related liabilities) are appropriately reclassified to "assets-held-for-sale."	Monthly; Transaction Based
4. Ensure that depreciation/ amortization ceases once an asset has been reclassified to "assets-held-for-sale."	Depreciation/ amortization continues to be recorded despite the asset having been reclassified to "assets-held-for-sale."	Existence or Occurrence Presentation and Disclosure Valuation or Allocation	Review of Depreciation/ Amortization Expense Accounts	General Accounting reviews related accounts (primarily assets subject to depreciation and amortization) to ensure that depreciation/ amortization ceases once the asset is reclassified to "assets-held-for-sale" (as required by SFAS No. 144).	Monthly; Transaction Based
5. Ensure that all "discontinued operations" are appropriately classified in the income statement.	"Discontinued operations" are not correctly reported in the income statement.	Existence or Occurrence Presentation and Disclosure Valuation or Allocation Completeness	Review of "Discontinued Operations" P&L Account	General Accounting works with the appropriate group (e.g. PP&E in the case of the disposal of PP&E, Consolidations in the case of the disposal of a subsidiary, etc.) to ensure the operating results of an asset held for sale are reclassified to "discontinued operations" on the income statement.	Monthly; Transaction Based

Control Objective	Risk	Control Assertion	Control Activity Title	Control Activity	Frequency
6. Ensure that all "costs to sell" have been identified and are appropriately reclassified to "assets-held-for-sale."	"Costs to sell" are (1) either expensed directly to the income statement and not reclassified to "assets-held-for-sale," or (2) costs that meet the definition of "costs to sell" are not reclassified to "assets-held-for-sale."	Existence or Occurrence Presentation and Disclosure Valuation or Allocation Completeness	Review of "Costs to Sell"	General Accounting identifies any "costs to sell" by (1) reviewing engagement letters (investment bankers, lawyers, etc.), (2) discussions with Corporate Development, and (3) review of certain general ledger expense accounts. Those expenses that meet the definition of "costs to sell" as defined by SFAS 144 are reclassified to "assets-held-for-sale."	Monthly; Transaction Based
7. Ensure that journal entries for divestiture are properly recorded.	Journal entries for divestiture are not properly recorded.	Existence or Occurrence Presentation and Disclosure Valuation or Allocation Completeness	Director Approval of Divestiture Journal Entries	The accountant submits the proposed entry to Director of General Accounting for review and approval.	Monthly; Transaction Based

Control Objective	Risk	Control Assertion	Control Activity Title	Control Activity	Frequency
8. Ensure that divestitures are properly presented and disclosed in financial statements.	Divestitures are not properly presented and disclosed in financial statements.	Existence or Occurrence Presentation and Disclosure Valuation or Allocation Completeness	Review of Quarterly Template and Disclosures	General Accounting and Director General of Accounting review Financial Reporting Template and Quarterly Disclosure Checklist for completeness and accuracy.	Quarterly

CHAPTER TWENTY SEVEN

Analysis and Reporting (The Final Mile)

NTRODUCTION: THE BASIC OBJECTIVE of financial reporting is to provide information about economic resources, the claims on these resources, and changes in them that is useful to those making investment and credit decisions and that is useful to present and future investors and creditors in assessing future cash flows to individuals who reasonably understand business and economic activities.

Financial reporting should be straightforward, concise, informative, and understandable, using information that is timely, accurate, and meaningful. The Analysis and Reporting phase is the final mile of the fiscal close and the last cycle in the record to report (R2R) process. The final mile is dependent on the timeliness and accuracy of results from the: (1) Transaction Accumulation, Reconciliation, and Sub-Ledger Close and (2) the Corporate Close and Consolidation phases.

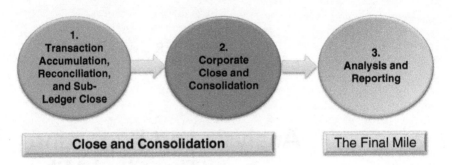

Phase 3: Analysis and Reporting Phase (The Final Mile)

Most companies have a department focused on the financial reporting process. This department is responsible for the preparation, accuracy, and distribution of various internal and external financial statements to management, maintenance of the organization's general ledger, and ensuring that all transactions and documentation comply with U.S. GAAP and IFRS requirements.

Key Point: *Financial reporting* and *financial statements* are terms often used interchangeably in process definitions and discussions. However, in a discussion of fiscal close processes there are some differences between financial reporting and financial statements. Reporting is used to provide information for decision making and analysis. Financial statements are the final products of the financial reporting process.

Generally accepted accounting principles (GAAP) or International Financial Reporting Standards (IFRS) are used to prepare financial statements. Both methods are legal in the United States, although GAAP is most commonly used. The main difference between the two methods is that GAAP is more "rules-based," while IFRS is more "principles-based." Both have different ways of reporting asset values, depreciation, and inventory, to name a few.

CHAPTER TWENTY EIGHT

Internal and External Reporting

I NTRODUCTION: INTERNAL REPORTS PROVIDE a company with the information needed for decision making and business rules. Many internal reporting processes include a comparison of actual financial results with budgets, forecasts, and plans.

The internal reporting process often includes routine reports that provide information on production, sales, labor and payroll, results of operations, schedule of debtors, research and development, and working capital changes.

INTERNAL REPORTING

Internal reporting is a business practice that involves collecting information for internal use. Big firms rely on internal reporting to make a variety of management decisions, and small companies can also benefit from internal reports. In some companies, a specific staff member is charged with internal reporting while in others people complete internal reports as part of their jobs. These reports are not designed to be made public and may include confidential or proprietary company information.

One important area of internal reporting is financial reporting. Financial reports are used to monitor a company's fiscal health and can inform decisions that need to be made about the direction in which a company will be taken. For example, an internal report could reveal that one division spends a lot of money without generating very much revenue and managers could discuss how to make that division more efficient or consider the possibility of closing that division altogether.

Internal reporting can also include reports on employees. These reports can discuss efficiency, job performance, and other aspects of employee activity which may be of concern. Many companies also support whistleblowing activity, encouraging employees to file reports if they suspect that activities may be violating the law or company policy.

Who Are the Users of Internal Financial Reports?

The users of internal financial reports typically include members of the organization's management, fiscal oversight committees, and the organization's governing body. In designing a system of internal financial reporting, those who are responsible for preparing financial reports must take into consideration the specific users or audience for which the financial reports are to be prepared. They must also take into consideration the nature and scope of information that each user or group of users' needs in order to effectively carry out their duties.

For example, the CFO of an organization will likely need financial information that is more detailed in nature and scope than the information needed by the governing board. Additionally, the CFO will likely need specific information regarding the fiscal activities of all areas of the organization's operations, whereas department heads may only need information regarding the fiscal activities of their respective departments.

BEST PRACTICE 19: ASK KEY QUESTIONS TO DEFINE YOUR INTERNAL FINANCIAL REPORTING PROCESS

Introduction: Organizational decision-makers and those charged with fiscal oversight should determine the nature and scope of information they need in order to carry out their respective responsibilities. An effective way to make such a determination is to identify "key questions" for which they will need answers as part of the financial reporting process.

Once the key questions are identified, leaders can evaluate and modify the financial reporting content and format to ensure that the financial reports adequately address the key questions. Following are examples of questions that nonprofit leaders might incorporate into their list of key questions (the list is not intended to be exhaustive):

1. Is the organization's current liquidity sound or strong? On what do we base our opinion? How do we know?
2. Is the trending in the organization's liquidity improving or declining? Elaborate.
3. What is the organization's current balance for cash and other liquid assets overall? What is the balance net of donor-restricted and designated amounts? Provide details.
4. If current accounts payable and other similar liabilities were paid, how many months of cash operating expenses would the current cash and liquid assets balance (net of donor-restricted and designated amounts) cover?
   - How does the answer to this question compare to the organization's objectives?
   - Is there a plan in place to improve the operating cash reserves balance? What is the plan? How are we doing with respect to implementing the plan?
5. Is the organization paying all of its bills on time? How do we know?
6. Has the organization had any trouble in recent weeks or months meeting its cash flow demands? If yes, elaborate.
7. Does the organization expect to have any trouble in the foreseeable future with respect to meeting its cash flow demands? How do we know? If yes, elaborate.
8. Has the organization borrowed any money to fund regular operations or noncapital outlays? If yes, elaborate.
9. Has the organization dipped into donor-restricted or designated cash or investment balances in order to fund operations at any point during the last year? How do we know? If yes, elaborate.
10. What is the current balance of the organization's mortgage or long-term debt?
11. Are debt payments being made in a timely manner, without any difficulty?
12. Are there any specific fiscal covenants contained in the organization's loan agreements that stipulate specific fiscal requirements the organization must meet as a condition of complying with the terms of the loan?

If yes, provide details with respect to the nature of each covenant as well as the organization's compliance with the terms of the covenant.

13. What percentage of the organization's total revenues is being spent on servicing the organization's debt?
    - How does the answer to this question compare with organization's objectives?

14. What is the ratio of the organization's total liabilities to the organization's unrestricted net assets?
    - How does the answer to this question compare with organization's objectives?

15. What is the balance of the organization's debt service reserves?
    - How many months of debt service for the organization's existing mortgage debt will this balance cover?
    - How does the answer to this question compare with organization's objectives?
    - Is there a plan in place to improve the debt service reserves balance? What is the plan? How are we doing with respect to implementing the plan?

16. Is there any information regarding the organization's overall liquidity or fiscal position not addressed by the above questions of which the organization's leadership should be aware? If yes, provide details.

17. Is the trending with respect to overall revenue favorable or declining?
    - If declining, what are the causes and what is the organization's leadership doing to address the matter?

18. Is per-capita giving trending favorably or unfavorably? Provide details.

19. What other information about the organization's revenues (especially revenues not related to contributions) is relevant to organization leadership?

20. With respect to expenditures, is the organization's staff leadership adhering to budget parameters? How do we know?

21. Are expenditures increasing or decreasing?

22. Are appropriate approval processes in place for all expenditures? Elaborate and succinctly describe the approval process for all areas of expenditure.

23. Is there any additional information about the organization's expenditures not covered by the questions above that would be relevant to the organization's leaders?

24. Is the organization generating a cash flow surplus from its operating activities? Why or why not?

25. How do the organization's fiscal operating results compare with expectations as set forth in the approved budget?
26. Are there any current vulnerabilities, specific risks, threats, or other similar matters that could adversely affect the organization's fiscal condition? If yes, elaborate.
27. On a scale of 1 to 10, where 1 is very weak and 10 is extraordinarily strong, how would the organization's staff leadership rate the organization's current fiscal condition? Explain the basis for the rating.

EXTERNAL REPORTING

An external financial report is written with the intention of circulating it among people outside the business while an internal fiscal report is written for managers and executives within the company. An external financial report has several purposes, including satisfying legal requirements and informing investors and shareholders of the fiscal status of the company. However, the company executives can use the information within the financial report for company planning and budget restructuring should it be needed.

The Securities and Exchange Commission (SEC) requires all publicly traded companies operating in the United States to submit an annual financial report and a Form 10K each fiscal year the corporation is operating. This is stated in the Act of 1934 issued by the SEC. The financial report informs the commission and potential investors of the company's financial standing.

Another reason an external financial report is provided is to inform existing shareholders and investors of the company's fiscal situation at the end of a given fiscal period. Investors and shareholders use the information to determine whether to continue investing in the company. Decisions are made based on how effectively the company administers its money, where the money is spent, and how much the company is earning each fiscal period.

A public company with a class of securities either registered under Section 12 or which is subject to Section 15(d) of the Securities Exchange Act of 1934 as amended ("Exchange Act") must file reports with the SEC ("Reporting Requirements").The underlying basis of the Reporting Requirements is to keep shareholders and the markets informed on a regular basis in a transparent manner. Reports filed with the SEC can be viewed by the public on the SEC's EDGAR website. The required reports include an annual Form 10K, quarterly Form 10Qs, and current periodic Form 8K as well as proxy reports and certain shareholder and affiliate reporting requirements.

A company becomes subject to the reporting requirements by filing an Exchange Act Section 12 registration statement on either Form 10 or Form 8A. A Section 12 registration statement may be filed voluntarily or per statutory requirement if the issuer's securities are held by either 2,000 persons or 500 persons who are not accredited investors and where the issuer's total assets exceed $10 million. In addition, companies that file a Form S1 registration statement under the Securities Act of 1933 as amended ("Securities Act") become subject to Reporting Requirement; however, such obligation becomes voluntary in any fiscal year at the beginning of which the company has fewer 300 shareholders.

A reporting company also has recordkeeping requirements, must implement internal accounting controls, and is subject to the Sarbanes Oxley Act of 2002, including the CEO/CFO certifications requirements, prohibition on officer and director loans, and independent auditor requirements. Under the CEO/CFO certification requirement, the CEO and CFO must personally certify the content of the reports filed with the SEC and the procedures established by the issuer to report disclosures and prepare financial statements.

All reports filed with the SEC are subject to SEC review and comment, and in fact the Sarbanes Oxley Act requires the SEC to undertake some level of review of every reporting company at least once every three years.

Following are the reports that generally make up a public company's Reporting Requirements and that are applicable to smaller reporting companies. A "smaller reporting company" is an issuer that is not an investment company or asset-backed issuer or majority-owned subsidiary and that had a public float of less than $75 million as of the last business day of its most recently completed second fiscal quarter; or in the case of an initial registration statement, had a public float of less than $75 million as of a date within days of the filing of the registration statement; or in the case of an issuer whose public float as calculated or is zero, had annual revenues of less than $75 million during the most recently completed fiscal year for which audited financial statements are available.

Annual Reports on Form 10K

All reporting companies are required to file an annual report with the SEC on Form 10K within 90 days of end of its fiscal year. An extension of up to 15 calendar days is available for a Form 10K as long as the extension notice on Form 12b-25 is filed no later than the next business day after the original filing deadline.

A Form 10K includes the company's audited annual financial statements, a discussion of the company's business results, a summary of operations, a description of the overall business and its physical property, identification of any subsidiaries or affiliates, disclosure of the revenues contributed by major products or departments, and information on the number of shareholders, the management team and their salaries, and the interests of management and shareholders in certain transactions. A Form 10K is substantially similar to a Form 10 registration statement and updates shareholders and the market on information previously filed in a registration statement on an annual basis.

Quarterly Reports on Form 10Q

All reporting companies are required to file a quarterly report on Form 10Q within 45 days of the end of each of its fiscal quarters. An extension of up to five calendar days is available for a Form 10Q as long as the extension notice on Form 12b-25 is filed no later than the next business day after the original filing deadline.

The quarterly report includes unaudited financial statements and information about the company's business and results for the previous three months and for the year to date. The quarterly report compares the company's performance in the current quarter and year to date to the same periods in the previous year.

Current Reports on Form 8K

Subject to certain exceptions, a Form 8K must be filed within four business days after the occurrence of the event being disclosed. No extension is available for an 8K. Companies file this report with the SEC to announce major or extraordinary events that shareholders should know about, including entry into material agreements; mergers and acquisitions; change in control; changes in auditors; the issuance of unregistered securities; amendments in company articles or bylaws; company name changes; issues with reliance on previously issued financial statements; changes in officer or directors; bankruptcy proceedings; change in shell status regulation FD disclosures, and voluntary disclosures (voluntary disclosures have no filing deadline).

The Fair Disclosure Regulation, enacted in 2000 ("Regulation FD"), stipulates that publicly traded companies broadly and publicly disseminate information instead of distributing it selectively to certain analysts or investors only. Companies are encouraged to use several means of information dissemination, including Form 8K, news releases, websites or webcasts, and press releases. A Form 8K under Regulation FD must be filed simultaneously with the release of the material that is subject of the filing (generally a press release); or the next trading day. Other than when there has been a change of shell status, the financial statements of an acquired business must be filed no later than 71 calendar days after the date the initial Form 8K was filed reporting the closing of the business acquisition (which initial Form 8K is due within 4 days).

Consequences and Issues Related to Late Filing

Late filings carry severe consequences to small business issuers. Generally the shareholders of late filing issuers cannot rely on Rule 144 for the sale or transfer of securities while the issuer is delinquent in its filing requirements. Rule 144(c) requires that adequate current public information with respect to the company must be available. The current public information requirement is measured at the time of each sale of securities. That is, the issuer, whether reporting or non-reporting, must satisfy the current public information requirements as set forth in Rule 144(c) at the time that each resale of securities is made in reliance on Rule 144. For reporting issuers, adequate current public information is deemed available if the issuer is, and has been for a period of at least 90 days immediately before the sale, subject to the Exchange Act reporting requirements and has filed all required reports, other than Form 8K, and has submitted electronically and posted on its website, if any, all XBRL data require to be submitted and posted.

An issuer that is late or has failed to maintain its Reporting Requirements is disqualified from use of Form S3, which is needed to conduct at the market direct public offerings, shelf registrations, and types of registered securities. Likewise, a Form S8 cannot be filed while an issuer is either late or delinquent in its Reporting Requirements. Late or delinquent filings may also trigger a default in the terms of contracts, including corporate financing transactions. Finally, the SEC can bring enforcement proceedings against late filers, including actions to deregister the securities.

Proxy Statements

All companies with securities registered under the Exchange Act (i.e. through the filing of a Form 10 or Form 8A) are subject to the Exchange Act proxy requirements found in Section 14 and the rules promulgated thereunder.

Companies required to file reports as a result of an S1 registration statement that have not separately registered under the Exchange Act are not subject to the proxy filing requirements. The proxy rules govern the disclosure in materials used to solicit shareholders' votes in annual or special meetings held for the approval of any corporate action requiring shareholder approval. The information contained in proxy materials must be filed with the SEC in advance of any solicitation to ensure compliance with the disclosure rules.

Solicitations, whether by management or shareholder groups, must disclose all important facts concerning the issues on which shareholders are asked to vote. The disclosure information filed with the SEC and ultimately provided to the shareholders is enumerated in SEC Schedules 14A.

Where a shareholder vote is not being solicited, such as when a company has obtained shareholder approval through written consent in lieu of a meeting, a company may satisfy its Section 14 requirements by filing an information statement with the SEC and mailing such statement to its shareholders. In this case, the disclosure information filed with the SEC and mailed to shareholders is enumerated in SEC Schedule 14C. As with the proxy solicitation materials filed in Schedule 14A, a Schedule 14C Information Statement must be filed in advance of final mailing to the shareholder and is reviewed by the SEC to ensure that all important facts are disclosed. However, Schedule 14C does not solicit or request shareholder approval (or any other action, for that matter), but rather informs shareholders of an approval already obtained and corporate actions which are imminent.

In either case, a preliminary Schedule 14A or 14C is filed with the SEC, who then reviews and comments on the filing. Upon clearing comments, a definitive Schedule 14A or 14C is filed and mailed to the shareholders as of a certain record date.

Generally, the information requirements in Schedule 14C are less arduous than those in a Schedule 14A in that they do not include lengthy material regarding what a shareholder must do to vote or approve a matter. Moreover, the Schedule 14C process is much less time-consuming, as the shareholder approval has already been obtained. Accordingly, when possible, companies prefer to utilize the Schedule 14C Information Statement as opposed to the Schedule 14A Proxy Solicitation.

Reporting Requirements for Company Insiders

All executive officers and directors and 10%-or-more shareholders of a company with securities registered under the Exchange Act (i.e. through the filing of a Form 10 or Form 8A) are subject to the Exchange Act Reporting Requirements related to the reporting of certain transactions. The initial filing is on Form 3 and is due no later than 10 days of becoming an officer, director, or beneficial owner. Changes in ownership are reported on Form 4 and must be reported to the SEC within two business days. Insiders must file a Form 5 to report any transactions that should have been reported earlier on a Form 4 or were eligible for deferred reporting. If a form must be filed, it is due 45 days after the end of the company's fiscal year.

Additional Disclosures

Other federal securities laws and SEC rules require disclosures about a variety of events affecting the company. Under the Exchange Act, parties who will own more than 5% of a class of the company's securities after making a tender offer for securities registered under the Exchange Act must file a Schedule TO with the SEC. The SEC also requires any person acquiring more than 5% of a voting class of a company's Section 12 registered equity securities directly or by tender offer to file a Schedule 13D. Depending on the facts and circumstances, the person or group of persons may be eligible to file the more abbreviated Schedule 13G in lieu of Schedule 13D.

Termination of Reporting Requirements

To deregister and suspend Reporting Requirements, an eligible issuer can file a Form 15. To qualify to file a Form 15, an issuer must either have fewer than 300 shareholders; or fewer than 500 shareholders and the issuer's assets do not exceed $10 million.

Considerations for the financial reporting process include the roles of decision makers and the constraints of cost, benefit, and materiality with the objective of providing information that is understandable and useful.[i]

---

[i] L. G. Anthony, PLLC, "Public Company SEC Reporting Requirements." Accessed March 2, 2019. http://www.legalandcompliance.com/securities-resources/sec-requirements-for-public-companies/.

CHAPTER TWENTY NINE

Budgeting and Forecasting

I NTRODUCTION: ACCOUNTABILITY STEMS FROM a well-defined organizational structure and hierarchy. It also is driven by well-established roles and responsibilities for each step of the closing process and a well-documented closing schedule and checklist.

Budgeting is a key responsibility for controllers and their staff and should be linked to the strategic planning process and results.

The controller's organization "controls" access to corporate funds. In many situations, professionals in the controller's organization must approve expenditures according to the organization's delegation of authority policy. Controllers typically are part of the organization led by an organization-wide or divisional chief fiscal officer (CFO). In smaller companies and organizations, the roles of controller and CFO may be combined into one position.

In most companies controllers and their staffs develop reports and analyses that are crucial to the management of the business. In addition to the measurement and analysis of corporate profitability, controllers work closely with people in the marketing function in setting prices for the company's products and services.

A large corporation will have multiple layers of controllers, depending on how its hierarchy of departments and divisions is organized. Working in a controllership function can be an excellent way to get a good overview of the entire company.

ABOUT THE BUDGET PROCESS

According to Price waterhouse Coopers (PwC), company and business unit budgets give fiscal expression to strategy, motivate managers to achieve commonly understood targets, and provide a coherent framework for the analysis of results. Historically, spreadsheets have been used as the main budgeting tool. However, they have a number of weaknesses when used for budgeting, including reconciliation problems arising from complex links across many sheets and workbooks and inflexibility of reporting structures. Many organizations of all sizes have moved toward automating their budget processes.

In order to make effective decisions and coordinate the decisions and actions of the various departments, a business needs to have a plan for its operations. Planning the fiscal operations of a business is called budgeting. A budget is a written fiscal plan of a business for a specific period of time, expressed in dollars. Each area of a business's operations typically has a separate budget.

For example, a business might have an advertising budget, a capital budget, a purchasing budget, a sales budget, a manufacturing budget, a research and development budget, and a cash budget. New and ongoing projects would each have a detailed budget. Each budget would then be compiled into a master budget for the operations of the entire company.

A business that does not have a budget or a plan will make decisions that do not contribute to the profitability of the business because managers lack a clear idea of goals of the business. A budget serves five main purposes:

1. Communication
2. Coordination
3. Planning
4. Control
5. Evaluation

The budget process is usually initiated after the completion and approval of the organization's strategic planning process.

 ## TYPES OF BUDGET PROCESSES

An organization cannot use only one type of budget to accommodate all its operations. Therefore, it chooses from among the following six budget types.

1. The Fixed Budget

The fixed budget, often called a static budget, is not subject to change or alteration during the budget period. A company "fixes" budgets in at least two circumstances:

1. The cost of a budgeted activity shows little or no change when the volume of production fluctuates within an expected range of values. For example, within a manufacturing company, a 10% increase in production has little or no impact on administrative expenses.
2. The volume of production remains steady or follows a tight, preset schedule during the budget period. A company may fix its production volume in response to an all-inclusive contract, or it may produce stock goods.

2. The Variable or Flexible Budget

The *variable* or *flexible budget* is called a *dynamic* budget. It is an effective evaluative tool for a company that frequently experiences variations in sales volume which strongly affect the level of production. In these circumstances a company initially constructs a series of budgets for a range of production volumes which it can reasonably and profitably meet.

3. The Continuous Budget

The continuous budget adds a new period (month) to the budget as the current period comes to a close. Under the fiscal year approach, the budget year becomes shorter as the year progresses. However, the continuous method forces managers to review and assess the budget estimates for a never-ending 12-month cycle.

4. The Operating Budget

The operating budget gathers the projected results of the operating decisions made by a company to exploit available business opportunities. In the final analysis, the operating budget presents a projected (pro forma) income statement which displays how much money the company expects to make. This net income demonstrates the degree to which management is able to respond to the market in supplying the right product at an attractive price, with a profit to the company.

The operating budget consists of a number of parts which detail the company's plans on how to capture revenues, provide adequate supply, control costs, and organize the labor force. These parts are: sales budget, production budget, direct materials budget, direct labor budget, factory overhead budget, selling and administrative expense budget, and pro forma income statement.

5. The Financial Budget

The operating budget and the fiscal budget are the two main components of a company's master budget. The fiscal budget consists of the capital expenditure budget, the cash budget, and the budgeted balance sheet. Much of the information in the fiscal budget is drawn from the operating budget, and then all of the information is consolidated into the master budget.

6. The Consolidated Budget

The consolidated budget aggregates all business activities into one comprehensive plan. It is not a single document, but the compilation of many interrelated budgets which together summarize an organization's business activities for the coming year. Standardization of the process facilitates comparison and aggregation even of mixed products and industries.

Preparation of the consolidated budget is a sequential process that starts with the sales budget. The sales budget predicts the number of units a company expects to sell. From this information, a company determines how many units it must produce. Subsequently, it calculates how much it will spend to produce the required number of units. Finally, it aggregates the foregoing to estimate its profitability.

BEST PRACTICE 20: CONSIDER FIVE STEPS FOR A SUCCESSFUL BUDGET PROCESS

The fiscal year also serves as a basis for budgeting and planning. Most firms also plan budgets using fiscal year calendars and cutoffs. These firms plan spending and revenue intake to cover the time between FY start and end and base budgets and forecasts on actual financial results.

The corporate budgeting, forecasting, and planning process presents a challenge to most companies, regardless of size or industry. Budgeting is often seen as burdensome and time consuming. Yet budgeting is also a crucial element of financial management, which in turn is a huge contributor to a company's overall success or failure. Some companies include the budget, forecasting, and planning process and results in their internal reporting processes.

There are several approaches and methodologies for developing the organization's budget. The approach will depend on the size and complexity of the organization. The budgeting process applies to organizations of all types and industries of all types. Many organizations have developed a standard budget process and template that fits the needs of their company.

Step 1: Determining the Flow of Information

A company gathers the data necessary to compile a budget in one of two ways as listed below.

1. It centralizes the process and has senior management establish the company's priorities and projections.
2. It directs individual work units and departments to assemble that information on their own. The former is referred to as top-down budgeting and the latter as bottom-up.

In general, budgets that are constructed from the bottom up are preferable, if only for the reason that individual workers and units know more about their departments than central management.

On the other hand, bottom-up budgeting requires more time to execute and is difficult to manage since all departments and divisions need to complete their budgets for approval and consolidation at the corporate level. There may be several iterations of the budget using this approach since changes may be needed after the consolidated budgets are reviewed and the results are either too high or too low.

Step 2: Organizing Your Budget Process

The budget process is driven by the way your organization is organized. The budget process can be organized by functions, product divisions, projects, facilities, regions, countries, and divisions.

Key Point: Budget processes can be driven by an organization's organizational or fiscal hierarchy as established within their Enterprise Resource Planning (ERP) system.

Step 3: Gathering Historic Data

After a company decides how it will organize the budget process, it turns its attention to gathering historic performance information. The first place to look for historic performance data is the company's financial statements: its balance sheet, income statement, and cash flow statement. Another source is the company's fiscal ratios.

Finally, the managerial reports supplied to company executives throughout the year serve as useful tools in gathering more specific data, such as sales trends for individual products, cost trends for those products, and divisional performance.

Key Point: Many organizations start with the actual results from prior years to establish a *run rate* for the budget process.

1. Gathering Sales Information

When it comes to gathering historic sales data, your company ought to know its past performance based on:

- Product lines
- Regions
- Customers

2. Gathering Expense Information

When it comes to gathering historic expense data, your organization should know its past performance based on actual spending based on the following criteria and report results in internal reporting processes.

- **Direct costs:** This includes raw materials, labor, and inventory costs.
- **Indirect costs:** This includes selling, research and development, and general and administrative expenses.
- **Fixed costs:** This includes many of the indirect costs of doing business, such as rent and depreciation, which are part of G&A expenses.
- **Variable costs:** This includes many of the direct costs of doing business, such as raw materials, energy, and labor costs as well as taxes, which are also considered a variable expense.

Step 4: Making Projections

The fourth step in the budgeting process is for the company to project its performance for the coming year. Establishing budget projections can be as simple or complicated a task as your company makes it.

Some companies rely on "incremental budgeting," in which forecasts are directly tied to past performance and are therefore easy to prepare. Others rely on "zero-based budgeting," in which forecasts have nothing to do with past performance and are therefore more difficult to prepare. And still others rely on a "hybrid approach."

Incremental Budgeting

- Incremental budget projections are the easiest to prepare. All you need to know is what the company spent or made in the previous year. Then you tack on whatever percentage increase or decrease you think is appropriate. This approach can also be described as adding a percentage to the organization's current run rate.
- The incremental approach is the least precise method for preparing a budget. Often, companies that rely on incremental budgets repeat past mistakes such as continuing to overspend.

Zero-Based Budgeting

Zero-based budgeting is the antithesis of the incremental approach. Made popular in the 1970s, zero-based budgets operate on the premise that the amount a company budgeted for a line item in one year has little to do with what it should be budgeting in future years. While more accurate than incremental budgets, zero-based budgets require tremendous amounts of information. As a result, this process is time-consuming and expensive.

The Hybrid Method

Many organizations rely on a hybrid approach to budgeting, in which projections are based in part on past performance. However, current industry trends and macroeconomic forces are also considered in part of the equation.

Step 5: Determining the Breakeven Point

The breakeven point is the level of sales where the organization neither makes money nor loses money. It is the level of sales where the gross profit is the same as the fixed costs. Using correct data and account financial reports is critical to determining a company's breakeven point.

TEN CONSIDERATIONS FOR A SUCCESSFUL BUDGET PROCESS

1. The Budget Process Should Be Part of the Corporate Culture

Excellent business management requires excellent financial management, which in turn requires a company-wide commitment to excellence in budgeting, forecasting, and reporting. Most companies acknowledge the importance of corporate planning and claim to be actively participating in ongoing planning. But in reality senior management may be engaged in strategic planning with finance running the budgeting show and department managers viewing the annual planning process as an unwelcome chore.

2. Align the Strategic and Operating Plans

Finance and accounting executives can help translate strategic goals into specific departmental plans and related expense drivers, such as headcount and equipment. By translating their strategic goals into operational plans, and by tracking and measuring performance against plan, leading companies are able to make meaningful progress in achieving their objectives.

3. Start the Budget Process at the Top and Bottom

An important ingredient in successful budgeting and forecasting lies in an organization's ability to plan from the bottom up and to meet top-down strategic objectives. Some companies establish top-down targets and then turn the annual budget process over to finance with a mandate to meet the numbers.

Other companies require detailed bottom-up planning, and then plug in the total company numbers at the top so that the plan meets strategic targets. Neither of these approaches reflects a commitment to planning excellence. Instead, leading companies provide initial guidance from senior management, a top-down perspective on strategic goals, objectives, and expectations. Next, department managers build a plan from the bottom up, showing how they intend to meet those goals. This process will often require frequent iterations for the top-down and bottom-up approaches to meet.

The result is a plan that:

- Is supported by department managers, because they helped create it and will be rewarded for meeting it. There is a greater sense of ownership and commitment to the budget process and its results.

- Is supported by senior management, because operational goals are aligned with the strategic goals.
- Is supported by finance, because they added value to a productive, collaborative effort rather than demanding participation in an exercise with little added value.

4. Drive Collaboration Between Functions

Not only should strategic and operating plans be aligned, but plans between functional areas should also be linked and ensure that all business partnerships are identified. Best practices include direct involvement from line-of-business managers and a collaborative approach to budgeting and forecasting. In addition to understanding strategic goals, department managers also need to know what other functions are planning. For example, in a company that is planning a new product rollout, manufacturing needs to ramp up production, marketing needs to produce new collateral, and sales needs to add new headcount. But the marketing plan should also include programs timed to support the new sales representatives. The facilities department needs to plan for new headcount, equipment, and product storage.

This collaborative planning can be accomplished through an iterative process that provides managers with the opportunity to forecast and share different scenarios with each other. Controllers can play a key role in facilitating the coordination of plans across the company.

5. Adapt to Changing Business Conditions

The next important steps are evaluating actual progress against budget and re-forecasting in response to changing business conditions. All businesses, particularly those in flux, are better served by a planning process that can quickly adapt to change in the company or in the market.

The key elements of such a process include:

- **Frequent Re-forecasting:** Especially in fast-moving, quickly growing businesses with multiple market pressures, forecasting may be needed on a monthly or even biweekly basis. Ongoing re-forecasting will help managers to continually answer critical questions such as "What did we expect?" "How are we doing against our plan?" and even more importantly, "How should we adapt our plans as a result?"
- **Rolling forecasts:** A company engaged in ongoing rolling forecasts is always looking forward to the immediate or near-term future. The forecast time frame should extend out two to eight quarters, depending on the

volatility of the business. Planning should be an ongoing process with frequent opportunities for managers to view the latest internal and external data on how the organization is doing. They should be able to make alterations to their plans based on new information, which can come.

6. Model Business Drivers

An important feature of a best-practice budget or forecast is that it is based on a model with formulas that are tied to fundamental business drivers. Simply importing and manipulating actual results does not reflect the underlying cause-and-effect relationships in a business. Building modeling into plans provides a way to ensure appropriate consistency across functions. It also provides a way to promote planning coordination between functions. For example, future sales forecasts can be tied to the marketing expenditure needed to generate the necessary number of leads.

The finance and accounting staff can provide business managers with a useful model that includes information about actual results and current headcount, as well as formulas that are driven by assumptions. This does not violate the best practice of requiring department managers to be responsible for creating their own budgets. Instead, it saves them time by providing a solid framework to flesh out—a starting point that contains important information about their organization's relationships to other functions. It also harmonizes with the best practice of collaboration across functions.

7. Manage Content That Is Material to the Organization

A focus on material content in budgeting will free managers from unnecessary detail, enabling them to produce better plans. While supporting detail can provide audit trail and insight into managers' thinking, more detail does not necessarily make for a better plan. According to a Hackett Group study of planning best practices, the fewer the number of line items, the better the planning practices. Hackett found that world-class companies average 15 to 40 line items in their budgets, compared to highly inefficient companies that averaged 2,000 line items.

Managing material content means that a company pays attention to whatever has a real and significant impact on expenses, revenues, capital, or cash flow. This company will:

- **Avoid false precision:** A complex model might not have any more precision than a simpler model. More detail and intricate calculations can lure managers into the trap of thinking their plan is therefore more accurate.

- **Monitor volatile—not stable—accounts:** Efforts are best spent on fluid expenses such as headcount and compensation.
- **Aggregate accounts:** The budget does not need to reflect the same level of detail that is in the general ledger (GL). Even if the GL has 15 different travel accounts, managers can provide a total travel budget.

8. Focus on a Timely and Accurate Budget Process

Many organizations have an inefficient and inflexible planning process, at the center of which is the annual budget. These companies' time-consuming distribution and consolidation processes practically guarantee that the plan data is irrelevant before it is even shared. And plans based on stale data and assumptions are of no value. According to the Hackett Group, the average annual planning and budgeting process is three to five months long. A plan that takes this long to prepare is out of date by the time it is completed. The Hackett Group reports that world-class organizations, on the other hand, spend less than two months preparing the annual plan.

9. Budget for Major Projects

Even though IT includes technology projects in their budget, it's important to consider the impact on other departments that may be required to support the project effort. It's also critical to ensure that the funding is agreed upon before the project is initiated and that the stakeholder is defined.

10. Establish a Budget Owner and Tracking Process

Lastly, a budget owner needs to be assigned to implement the process and track actual results on a monthly and quarterly process. Many organizations not only tie the budget process to strategic planning, but they operationalize the process by including a budget review with the monthly fiscal closing process. These organizations track the components listed below and are required to include explanations for established dollar or percentage variances.

- Actuals
- Forecast
- Budget

 VARIANCE ANALYSIS

Once a budget is established, one of the main fiscal tasks for the operations or support manager is to explain variances between actual performance and the budget. All types of companies, and most others, will require managers to review and explain any variances on the budget variance report.

Format for the Budget Variance Report

The variance is referred to as a positive or *favorable* variance, since it is better that actual be lower than budget for expenses. When expenses are greater than the budget, it is known as a negative or unfavorable variance. Report formats and terminology vary by company, so consult your finance department for specifics.

Explaining the Variances

It is generally a requirement that managers prepare an explanation for variances to finance and administration. Thresholds for reporting vary by company, but they usually consist of a combination of variance and percent.

A typical threshold is 10% *and* $5,000, although this may differ substantially for larger departments. Using this as an example, the supply expense above would not require an explanation.

The percent variance is 10%, but the dollar variance is only $1,000. This eliminates the need for unnecessary work in researching and identifying small variances. Similarly, if an item was off budget by $10,000, but was off a small percent, there would be no need for explanation. Some companies only require an explanation if there is a negative variance.

 ## OTHER FACTORS TO CONSIDER

Industry Trends

Industry trends can be an important company of your budget process. Organizations turn to a variety of sources to gather this information, including:

- **Trade associations and toolkits:** Most trade associations publish industry-wide sales and expense information based on figures provided by their members. In addition, companies like Dun & Bradstreet publish key fiscal ratios that can help businesses assess the health of their industries.
- **Available financial statements:** Publicly traded companies are required by the SEC to submit quarterly 10Q reports, annual 10K reports, and comprehensive annual reports that include financial statements. This

information is primarily useful for investors, but competitors can also use it to discover broad trends in the industry.

- **Available government data:** Various agencies, such as the Commerce Department, the Agriculture Department, and the Labor Department, put out regular reports on industry trends.
- **Internal experts:** Companies should also rely on their own officers who are intimately familiar with broad industry trends to contribute to this analysis.

Economic Data

The health of the economy can play a dramatic role in the health of your business, too. In fact, a number of outside influences will throw off your company's budget projections. Those include:

- **Economic downturns:** Sales projections are often predicated on a certain degree of overall economic health. A sudden recession, for instance, could reduce overall consumer demand for goods and services.
- **Inflation:** Even a slight increase in inflation can increase a company's expenses, from energy to raw materials to labor.
- **Interest rates:** If the Federal Reserve raises rates, it would increase the cost of borrowing money, which would increase a company's expenses. So interest rate fluctuations should be factored into budget projections.
- **Consumer confidence:** A slight decrease in consumer confidence could hurt consumer demand, which could alter your company's sales projections.
- **Currency trends:** A sudden change in exchange rates could wipe out potential profits for multinationals, exporters, and importers.
- **Politics:** When making budget projections, your company ought to keep similar political issues in mind such as health care reform. The world of health care was complex enough when everyone understood the rules. Now the old rules are gone, some new ones are here, and others are still a work in progress. Politics and legislation will continue to shape specific elements and timing, but the trajectory of health reform is unlikely to change and the momentum is not likely to disappear.
- **Natural disasters:** Insurers and companies that do business in disaster-prone regions must consider the potential effect of natural disasters—both positive and negative. If your company is a retailer or manufacturer, for instance, a single hurricane can wipe out a major portion of its business.

If your company is a contractor, natural disasters can actually boost sales, since communities must rebuild following disasters. These days, many companies consult with independent weather services before forecasting sales and inventory trends.

- **Technology:** New technological developments can often boost or reduce demand for your products. They can also impact your costs if your organization is implementing a new ERP system or automation project.
- **Regulatory trends:** Businesses must also assess potential changes in the regulatory environment.

CORPORATE PERFORMANCE MANAGEMENT (CPM)

As controllers are well aware, budgeting and forecasting are undergoing profound change. Responding to "new normal" business volatility, the revered annual budget exercise is steadily giving way to more dynamic forecasting and planning, sometimes powered by corporate performance management (CPM) solutions or online multiuser "spreadsheet" approaches.

Finance and accounting executives who think CPM is only for Fortune 1000-level organizations need to take another look. Not only are CPM providers aggressively marketing to midsize companies today, but the technology is also evolving rapidly. For example, Prophix offers a non-Enterprise CPM solution configured to a specific company's needs that can be up and running in a short time at a far lower cost than Enterprise solutions.

According to the Prophix whitepaper, "Budgeting for Mid-Market Companies," such a solution can enable "rolling forecast" and modeling capabilities along with variance and cost analysis, monthly reporting, midyear forecasting, fiscal consolidation, scorecards, and operational planning tools.

A MOVING TARGET

So many factors can require even the best-planned budget to need frequent midyear course corrections that some finance executives have begun to question the validity of the entire exercise. For example, the Beyond Budgeting Roundtable lists no fewer than 10 reasons "why budgeting causes significant problems today and needs to be replaced":

1. Prevents rapid response
2. Too detailed and expensive (absorbing around 20 percent of management time)

3. Out-of-date within a few months
4. Out-of-kilter with the competitive environment
5. Divorced from strategy
6. Stifles initiative and innovation
7. Protects non-value-adding costs
8. Reinforces command and control
9. Demotivates people
10. Encourages unethical behavior and increases reputational risk (aggressive targets and incentives drive people to meet the numbers at almost any cost)

Depending on the size of the organization, the controller may be assigned the role of the primary contact that is responsible for assembling and maintaining the plan and developing the fiscal schedules and statements to support the strategic plan. Here are eight additional key tasks:

1. Verify the sales and production plans.
2. Validate that expense levels are in proportion to other activities.
3. Ensure there is sufficient funding for the projected activity or program.
4. Determine if the plan meets the organization's requirement for return on investment.
5. Determine that other fiscal ratios and metrics are reasonable.
6. Ensure that the strategic, development, and operational plans link together.
7. Ensure that organizational changes are documented and well communicated.
8. Drive the budget process considering the following types of budgets depending on the type of organization:
   - Sales
   - Production
   - Purchases
   - Labor
   - Manufacturing expense budget
   - Inventory budget
   - Selling, general, and administrative budget
   - Research and development budget
   - Capital budget
   - IT budget
   - Cost of goods sold budget
   - Cash budget

Reduce Fiscal Close Cycle Times by Moving Your Finance Function to "Dynamic" Budgeting and Planning

NTRODUCTION: TO BE COMPETITIVE in today's volatile business conditions, controllers must help lead their companies beyond the traditional budgeting and planning cycles. In a recent Accenture study, two-thirds of respondents reported that their planning accuracy had decreased due to economic volatility. Just 10% said they were "fully satisfied" with their current planning capabilities.

DYNAMIC BUDGETING AND PLANNING

Clearly, alternatives are needed to the traditional time-consuming and poorly performing budget ritual. Budgeting and planning must evolve from a once-a-year exercise into a dynamic and continuously adjustable process.

This can be achieved by utilizing analytics-based modeling capabilities. Such technology enables "scenario planning"—posing "what-if" events that could significantly alter budget assumptions and then testing practical solutions. Such a dynamic model features "input dials" that are adjusted as needed, providing a built-in capability for rapid response and adjustment.

In contrast, traditional planning and budgeting tend to rely heavily on historical data that's unlikely to be relevant to future developments. To meet this challenge, more companies are moving toward a "rolling-quarters planning process" to replace the year-to-year model.

CHAPTER THIRTY ONE

Fixed Assets and the Capital Budget

NTRODUCTION: THE EFFICIENT ALLOCATION of capital resources is a most crucial function of financial management. This function involves organization's decision to invest its resources in long-term assets like land, building facilities, equipment, vehicles, and so forth.

The future development of a firm can hinge on the capital investment projects, the replacement of existing capital assets, and/or the decision to abandon previously accepted undertakings that turn out to be less attractive to the organization than was originally thought, and directing the resources to the contemplation of new ideas and planning.

BEST PRACTICE 21: ESTABLISH A CAPITAL BUDGET PROCESS

Introduction: All assets are extremely important to the firm because, in general, all the organizational profits are derived from the use of its capital in investment in assets that represent a very large commitment of fiscal resources, and these funds usually remain invested over a long period of time.

- Establish a procedure for the planning and control of fixed assets.
- Establish the criteria for the approval process.

- Review approval limits to ensure that the company's delegation of authority policy is followed.
- Establish a review and approval process.
- Review projected return rates.
- Ensure that capital expenditures reflect the organization's strategic plan and that the funds are available to pay for the expenditures.
- Review economic alternatives to asset purchases such as leasing, renting, or buying the item from another supplier.
- Establish a reporting system that informs managers about the cost of maintenance, idle time, productivity, and actual costs versus budget.
- Implement a depreciation policy for all types of equipment for book and tax purposes.
- Maintain property records that identify all assets, describe their locations, track transfers, and account for depreciation.
- Ensure that proper insurance coverage is maintained for the fixed assets.
- Develop internal controls to ensure that fixed assets are physically counted on a regular basis.

DEVELOPING THE CAPITAL BUDGET

Capital budgeting has many aspects. It includes new and more profitable investment proposals, investigating, engineering, and marketing considerations to predict the consequences of accepting the investment, and performing economic analysis to determine the profit potential of investment proposals. The three basic features of capital budgeting decisions are:

1. Current funds are exchanged for future benefits.
2. There is an investment in long-term activities.
3. The future benefits will accrue to the firm over a series of years.

Some organizations may have a capital planning committee that reviews and approves all requests for capital. The committee always meets on an annual basis to coincide with the budgeting process. The committee will also meet throughout the fiscal year on a quarterly basis to review the results of capital expenditures. The capital planning process begins with two primary questions:

1. What do we need?
2. Why do we need it?

BEST PRACTICE 22: IMPLEMENT THE CAPITAL REVIEW AND APPROVAL BOARD (CARB) PROCESS

Introduction: The controller has an active role within the Capital Budget and Fixed Assets Budget Process. The controller is usually responsible for driving the capital approval and review process and may establish a review board as described below.

To formalize the capital review and approval process, private and public companies utilize the review board approach to ensure that all capital requests are consolidated and reviewed within the same venue. The process provided below is an example of a Capital Approval and Review Board.

The Capital Approval and Review Board (CARB) is the formal approval and review committee for all worldwide capital expenditure programs greater than $1 million or the limits established by the approval limit.

Capital expenditures are defined as investments to acquire fixed or long-lived assets from which a stream of benefits is expected. A capital expenditure program is defined as all the capital required to complete a project; the total capital required from the first commitment through the completion of the project must be comprehended by the CARB at the time of program approval.

No capital expenditure programs over $1 million or the established approval limit can be funded until the approval of the CARB has been obtained. For those capital expenditure programs where CFO, CEO, and/or board of directors' approval is required, the CARB will review and approve these programs prior to their submission to the CFO, CEO, and/or board of directors. The CARB will also perform periodic reviews of previously approved capital expenditure programs.

Objectives of the CARB

The CARB's objectives are as follows:

- Determine if a particular capital-spending program is justified in terms of the expected benefits.
- Determine if there are alternative proposals that should be considered.
- Optimally allocate and ration capital to those programs that meet the company's operational and fiscal goals and objectives.
- Foster process improvement through post-program completion evaluation on a selective basis.

CARB Participants/Membership

1. Chair: Vice President, Corporate Controller
2. Approvers: Vice President, Corporate Controller, Vice President, Treasurer
3. Participants:
   - Program Sponsor (Presenter)
   - V.P. of Finance or Controller of the unit requesting capital (Presenter)
   - Legal (Review commentary and meeting minutes)

Specific Duties of the CARB

The CARB has responsibility for the following five tasks:

1. Review all capital expenditure budgets (both new and revised) for consistency of approach.
2. Recommend approval, amendment, or rejection of capital budgets.
3. Review all capital expenditure programs greater than $1 million or the established approval limit.
4. Periodically review the results of previous approved capital expenditure programs to ascertain if the project goals and objectives were attained.
5. Document all capital expenditure programs brought before the CARB and their disposition by the CARB.

Types of Programs for CARB Approval and Review

The CARB will approve and review all programs greater than $1 million of the following types:

- Land transactions
- Building purchase or lease transactions
- Purchase or lease of machinery, equipment, or furniture with a useful life greater than one year.
- All other leases of one year or more or that meet the requirements of a capital lease
- Capitalized improvements to owned land and buildings
- All other additions to tangible fixed assets
- All acquisitions of intangible fixed assets (patents and trademarks, etc.)
- All contingent expenditures or guarantees
- All third-party investments in equity shares, loans, etc.
- All other assets

In cases where several assets may be linked together as a single program, authorization should be obtained for the program as a whole and not for each asset individually. No transfer of authorized capital expenditure from one organization to another or from one program to another is allowed without the approval of the CARB.

The CARB will approve all requests for additional funding when original estimates used for existing approvals have been exceeded by the items of 10% or an established dollar limit. The revised approval will include all prior expended funds as well as the additional funding required.

The CARB will also re-approve any major changes in the scope of previously approved capital expenditure programs. A major change in scope is defined as: (1) a change in intended use or purpose, (2) an addition or deletion of a major program feature, or (3) plus or minus an established percent shift in the economics of the program.

The CARB will also approve all requests to retire assets with a book value (or salvage value) greater than $1 million that are no longer needed to support the organization's business.

Program Appraisal Post-Completion

Capital expenditure programs, on a selective basis, will undergo post-completion review under the auspices of the CARB. These reviews will focus on comparing the objectives and program costs articulated at the time the program was approved with the results actually achieved. Any unforeseen benefits and costs will also be identified during this process.

The goals of the post-completion exercise are to understand if the program has performed as expected and to provide meaningful feedback that can be used to improve the quality of the organization's capital expenditure programs on a go-forward basis.

Other Considerations

Other considerations during the capital budgeting process include the following questions.

- How long will our equipment and facilities last?
- What upgrades will be needed and when will they be needed?
- Where will we find the money?
- Which need is most important to the community and why is it important?
- How can we best schedule specific projects?

The Capital Budget

The capital budget is the result of the capital planning process. The capital budget includes planned outlays for long-lived assets that are expected to generate income or support business operations over a number of years.

The following table is an example of items that are usually included in the capital budget process. A description of the item is provided along with the proposed life of the asset.

Description	Suggested Life	Capital Examples
LAND, IMPROVEMENTS	20 Years	Landscaping, trees, grass, shrubbery, canals, waterways, drainage facilities, parking lots, roadways, bridges, fences, walls, sidewalks
LAND	N/A	The cost of land includes all expenditures made to acquire it and place it in condition for the purpose for which it was intended. This may include original contract price, broker's-finders-attorneys fees, surveys, special assessments, razing of old buildings
BUILDINGS	10 Years	Build-out architecture and material
	30 Years	Building shell architecture and material
BUILDINGS, EQUIPMENT	5 Years	Security, mini-blinds, carpeting, interior landscaping
	10 Years	HVAC
	20 Years	Cross-site utilities
EQUIPMENT, LEASED, FASB 13	5 Years or L.O.L.	Leased equipment classified as a capital lease
EQUIPMENT, DURABLE TOOLS	3 Years or L.O.P.	Dies, molds, patterns, punches, machining fixtures, jigs
EQUIPMENT, FACT & WAREHOUSE	3 Years	Carts & lifts
	5 Years	Factory & warehouse equipment
EQUIPMENT, TEST	5 Years	Scopes, meters, ovens, shakers, scales, shears
SOFTWARE	3 Years	Software with installed cost less than $1,000,000
	5 Years	Software with installed cost more than $1,000,000
	7 Years	Enterprise Resource Planning (ERP) system
COMP EQUIP, NON-CPQ, UNITS & OPTIONS	3 Years	All computer & office equipment

Description	Suggested Life	Capital Examples
COMP EQUIP, CPQ, DEMO/SEED	1 Year	Units & options utilized in special programs
EQUIPMENT, TELEPHONE	5 Years	Telecommunications equipment; includes channel banks, terminals, switches, satellite equipment, automated call distributors, data switches. PBXs
EQUIPMENT, VEHICLES	5 Years	Autos, trucks
	10 Years	Aircraft
FURNITURE & FIXTURES	7 Years	Desks, chairs, tables, conference and break room furniture, cabinetry, conventions, & exhibits
LEASEHOLD IMPROVEMENTS	5 Years or L.O.L.	Significant new structural changes, alterations or improvements to property leased by the organization, which increases durability or efficiency, or otherwise adds value
COMP EQUIP, CPQ, UNITS & OPTIONS	2 Years	Portable computers and devices

L.O.L. = Life of Lease; L.O.P. = Life of Product

Capital Budget Decision Making

There is a wide array of criteria for selecting capital investment projects. In a public company, some shareholders may want the firm to select projects that will show immediate surges in cash inflow; others may want to emphasize long-term growth with little importance given to short-term performance.

The goal of the public firm is to maximize present shareholder value. This goal implies that projects should be undertaken that result in a positive net present value, that is, the present value of the expected cash inflow less the present value of the required capital expenditures.

For both private and public firms, it is important to ensure that all investments maximize net present value.

Alternative Methods for Capital Budgeting

While net present value is usually the metric used in the decision-making process, some organizations use other criteria for their capital budgeting decisions. Each method is explained below:

- **Internal rate of return (IRR)** is the discount rate at which net present value of the project becomes zero. Higher IRR should be preferred.

- **Profitability index (PI)** is the ratio of present value of future cash flows of a project to initial investment required for the project.
- **Payback period** measures the time in which the initial cash flow is returned by the project. Cash flows are not discounted. Lower payback period is preferred.
- **Net present value (NPV)** is equal to initial cash outflow less sum of discounted cash inflows. Higher NPV is preferred and an investment is only viable if its NPV is positive. Using net present value (NPV) as a measure, capital budgeting involves selecting those projects that increase the value of the organization because they have a positive NPV.

   The timing and growth rate of the incoming cash flow is important only to the extent of its impact on NPV. Using NPV as the criterion by which to select projects assumes efficient capital markets so that the firm has access to whatever capital is needed to pursue the positive NPV projects. In situations where this is not the case, there may be capital rationing and the capital budgeting process becomes more complex.
- **Accounting rate of return (ARR)** is the profitability of the project calculated as projected total net income divided by initial or average investment. Net income is not discounted.
- **Real options** analysis has become important as option pricing models have gotten more sophisticated. The discounted cash flow methods essentially value projects as if they were risky bonds, with the promised cash flows known. But managers will have many choices of how to increase future cash inflows or decrease future cash outflows. In other words, managers get to manage the projects—not simply accept or reject them. Real options analysis tries to value the choices—the option value—that the managers will have in the future and adds these values to the NPV.
- **Ranked projects:** The real value of capital budgeting is to rank projects. Most organizations have many projects that could potentially be fiscally rewarding. Once it has been determined that a particular project has exceeded its hurdle, then it should be ranked against peer projects (e.g. highest Profitability index to lowest Profitability index). The highest ranking projects should be implemented until the budgeted capital has been expended.
- **Funding sources:** When a corporation determines its capital budget, it must acquire said funds. Three methods are generally available to publicly traded corporations: corporate bonds, preferred stock, and common stock. The ideal mix of those funding sources is determined by the fiscal managers of the firm and is related to the amount of fiscal risk that corporation

is willing to undertake. Corporate bonds entail the lowest fiscal risk and therefore generally have the lowest interest rate. Preferred stocks have no fiscal risk but dividends, including all in arrears, must be paid to the preferred stockholders before any cash disbursements can be made to common stockholders; they generally have interest rates higher than those of corporate bonds.

CONSTRUCTION IN PROCESS ACCOUNTING

Introduction: Fixed assets pass a few stages in their life at any enterprise. First, assets are acquired or constructed. Second, the assets are put in use and serve the company. During this time, the assets are depreciated. Finally, when the assets are utilized to their full extent, they are written off and potentially replaced with new assets.

The first stage—assets are acquired or constructed—may be quick or may take an extended period of time. There are computers, vehicles, or similar fixed assets which don't require much additional preparation work after they are purchased before they can be used by the company. But there are assets that may take weeks, months, or even years before they are fully functional and ready for use. Such assets may be production lines, buildings, and warehouses.

Fixed assets under construction represent Construction in Progress (CIP) and are recorded in a similarly named general ledger account. They remain in such an account until the assets are put in service, at which time the costs of the assets are transferred into respective property, plant and equipment accounts.

The CIP account accumulates costs for a fixed asset until it is ready for use. The costs can be accumulated from vendor invoices (for items purchased), use of company's inventory items in the fixed asset construction, transportation, and other expenses to make the asset ready for use.

The CIP account usually contains information for multiple fixed assets under construction. To differentiate costs in the account, they may be categorized by project. A project usually represents a single fixed asset.

FIXED ASSET MANAGEMENT

Introduction: Responsible asset management is fundamental to creating value for the organization as well as shareholder value for public companies. This requires that assets be planned and developed in a disciplined manner, efficiently operated and maintained, thoughtfully safeguarded, and accurately and completely reported. Fixed asset management should consider the following seven business rules.

1. All assets are operated, maintained, and protected in a manner that realizes their full potential.
2. Capital investments are managed using well-defined processes that cover budgeting, approval, appropriation, execution, and subsequent stewardship of such investments.
3. New or modified technology is adopted with limited risk of patent infringement.
4. All fixed asset transactions, including additions, movements, and disposals, are accurately and completely recorded in a timely manner.
5. Approved capital budgets that define how the full potential of the associated assets is to be realized must be established for each business unit and the results regularly stewarded.
   - Capital budgets are developed and implemented consistent with the company's annual business planning process.
   - Each business unit's capital budget must be reviewed and approved in accordance with the Delegation of Authority.
   - Financial and operating performance must be monitored and compared against original plan. Updated outlooks must be prepared at appropriate intervals.
   - Asset maintenance programs must comply with site approved standards.
6. All intellectual property—such as patents, copyrights, trademarks, and all aspects of the corporate identity—must be managed consistent with corporate standards and procedures. Furthermore, any agreements to sell an asset that involves such property must make adequate provision for protection of the intellectual property.
7. Each business unit must have an approved security program covering property, plant and equipment and any movement thereof, commensurate with the value of and risk associated with the assets involved.

DEPRECIATION METHODS

There are several depreciation methods to consider

Straight-Line Method of Depreciation

In the straight-line depreciation method, depreciation is charged uniformly over the life of an asset. In this method, residual value of the asset is subtracted from its cost to get the depreciable amount. The depreciable amount is then divided by the useful life of the asset in number of periods to get the depreciation expense per period. Due to the simplicity of the straight-line method of depreciation, it is the most commonly used depreciation method.

The formula to calculate the straight-line depreciation of an asset for a period is:

$$\text{Depreciation} = \frac{\text{Cost} - \text{Salvage Value}}{\text{Life in Number of Periods}}$$

Declining Balance Method of Depreciation

Declining balance method of depreciation is a type of accelerated depreciation in which the amount of depreciation that is charged to an asset declines over time. In other words, more depreciation is charged in the beginning of the lifetime and less is charged during the end.

Why is more depreciation charged in the beginning? The reason is that assets are usually more productive when they are new and their productivity declines continuously. This means that in the early years of their lifetime, they will be generating more revenue as compared to revenue generated in later years of their life. Now, according to the matching principle of accounting, we should depreciate more of the asset's cost in early years so as to match the depreciation expense with the revenue earned by the use of the asset.

Declining balance depreciation is calculated by the following formula:

$$\text{Depreciation} = \text{Depreciation Rate} \times \text{Book Value of Asset}$$

Depreciation rate is given by following formula:

$$\text{Depreciation Rate} = \text{Accelerator} \times \text{Straight Line Rate}$$

In the above formula, accelerator is the factor by which the depreciation rate is multiplied. The book value is the difference between cost of an asset and its accumulated depreciation. During the first period the accumulated depreciation is zero so book value is equal to cost. The book value decreases after each depreciation charge; therefore, depreciation amount declines in successive charges.

Depreciation is charged according to the above method as long as book value is less than salvage value of the asset. No more depreciation is provided when book value equals salvage value.

Double Declining Balance Depreciation Method

Double declining balance depreciation method is a type of declining balance depreciation method in which depreciation rate is double the straight-line depreciation rate. Thus, when straight-line depreciation rate is 8%, double declining balance rate will be $2 \times 8\% = 16\%$.

Sum of the Years' Digits (SYD) Method of Depreciation

Sum of the years' digits method of depreciation is one of the accelerated depreciation techniques which are based on the assumption that assets are generally more productive when they are new and their productivity decreases as they become old. The formula to calculate depreciation under SYD method is:

$$\text{SYD Depreciation} = \text{Depreciable Base} \times \frac{\text{Remaining Useful Life}}{\text{Sum of the Years' Digits}}$$

In the above formula, depreciable base is the difference between cost and salvage value of the asset and sum of the years' digits is the sum of the series: $1, 2, 3, \dots , n$; where n is the useful life of the asset in years.

Sum of the years' digits can be calculated more conveniently using the following formula:

$$\text{Sum of the Years' Digits} = \frac{n(n + 1)}{2}$$

Sum of the years' digits method can also be applied on monthly basis, in which case the above formula to calculate the sum of the years' digits becomes much useful.

Units of Production Method of Depreciation

In units of production method of depreciation, depreciation is charged according to the actual usage of the asset. Higher depreciation is charged when there is higher activity and less is charged when there is low level of operation. Zero depreciation is charged when the asset is idle for the whole period. This method is similar to straight-line method except that the life of the asset is estimated in terms of number of operations or number of machine hours, and so on. Such a method is useful where a company has many fixed assets with varying usage.

The following formula is used to calculate depreciation under this method:

$$\text{Depreciation} = \frac{\text{Number of Units Produced}}{\text{Life in Number of Units}} \times (\text{Cost} - \text{Salvage Value})$$

INTANGIBLE ASSETS

Identifiable long-term assets of a company having no physical existence are called intangible assets. They include goodwill, patents, copyrights, and so forth.

Intangible assets are either acquired in a business combination or developed internally. In case of acquisition in a business combination such assets are recorded at their fair value, whereas in case of internally generated intangible assets the assets are recognized at the cost incurred in development phase.

In relation to the development of internally generated intangible assets there are two phases: research phase and development phase. The research phase includes all activities and costs incurred before the intangible asset is commercially feasible, whereas the development phase includes all activities and costs incurred after the asset is established to be commercially feasible. All costs in research phase are expensed in the period incurred while costs incurred in development phase are capitalized.

Following are examples of common intangible assets:

Goodwill

Goodwill is an intangible that is recognized when a business acquires another business. It represents the excess of cost paid by the purchasing business to the purchased business over the fair value of purchased business identifiable assets.

Example: Tennis Ltd. acquired Racket Ltd. for $10 million. The fair value of Racket's net assets (assets minus liabilities) equaled $8 million at the time of purchase. The difference between the cost of $10 million paid by Tennis and $8 million fair value of the assets of Racket is goodwill, which amounts to $2 million. Goodwill is an intangible asset and represents Racket's business reputation, and so on.

Copyrights

Copyrights grant a business sole authority to reproduce and sell a software, book, magazine, journal, and so on.

Patents

Patents grant a manufacturing and research company control over the use and sale of a specific design in manufacturing process, and so on.

Amortization of Intangible Assets

Amortization is the process of expensing out intangible assets over their useful life. It is in effect the depreciation of intangible assets.

Some intangible assets have indefinite or unlimited useful life, such as goodwill. Such assets are not amortized. Others have a definite useful life and are amortized over their useful life. Most of intangible assets are amortized using the straight-line method. Useful life is the shorter of legal life and economic life.

In accounting, amortization refers to expensing the acquisition cost minus the residual value of intangible assets (often intellectual property such as patents and trademarks or copyrights) in a systematic manner over their estimated useful economic lives so as to reflect their consumption, expiry, obsolescence, or other decline in value as a result of use or the passage of time.

Amortization is recorded in the financial statements of an entity as a reduction in the carrying value of the intangible asset in the balance sheet and as an expense in the income statement.

While theoretically amortization is used to account for the decreasing value of an intangible asset over its useful life, in practice many companies will "amortize" what would otherwise be onetime expenses by listing them as a capital expense on the cash flow statement and paying off the cost through amortization, thereby improving the company's net income in the fiscal year or quarter of the expense.

There are considerable difficulties in assessing the increase in value of any particular asset. This is principally because of the variety of interpretations that can be attached to the concept of value itself, as well as the various instruments and methods used in the valuation process.

 ASSET APPRECIATION AND ASSET IMPAIRMENT

Asset Appreciation

Appreciation of an asset is an increase in its value. In this sense, it is the reverse of depreciation, which measures the fall in value of assets over their normal lifetime. Generally, the term is reserved for property or, more specifically, land and buildings. Applied to a currency, appreciation is a rise of its value in a floating exchange rate.

In times of high inflation, appreciation of assets will be common to all balance sheet assets. In any viable modern economy, such property tends to increase in value over the years, if only because the scarcity of usable land forces its price in a competitive situation. However, this belief has often caused speculative bubbles to arise.

Asset Impairment

Impairment of a fixed asset is an abrupt decrease of its fair value due to damage or obsolescence. When impairment of a fixed asset occurs, the business has to decrease its value in the balance sheet and recognize a loss in the income statement.

Recoverable Amount

Recoverable amount is the value of the benefits we can obtain from a fixed asset. Economic benefits are obtained either by selling the asset or by using the asset. Recoverable amount equals the higher of fair value less costs to sell and value in use.

Fair Value Less Costs to Sell

Fair value less costs to sell is the current market value minus the costs that would be incurred in selling the assets, such as commission, registration, and so on.

Value in Use

Value in use is the present value of the future net cash flows expected to be derived from the continuing use of the asset.

Recognition of Impairment Loss

If the carrying amount exceeds the recoverable amount, an impairment expense amounting to the difference is recognized in the period. If the carrying amount is less than the recoverable amount, no impairment is recognized.

DISPOSAL OF FIXED ASSETS

Disposal of a fixed asset is the withdrawal of a fixed asset from use based on the completion of its useful life or due to diminishing value.

Disposal of an Asset with No Salvage Value

In a rare situation where the salvage value of the fixed asset is zero, there will be no terminal cash flow and the journal entry will be as follows:

Accumulated Depreciation	100,000	
Cost		100,000

Gain on Disposal

However, if an asset has a salvage value, it is likely that the disposal will cause gain or loss.

When a fixed asset is sold at a price higher than its carrying amount at the date of disposal, the excess of sale proceeds over the carrying amount is recognized as gain.

Example: On January 1, 2006, Company A purchased equipment worth of $2 million. The company estimated the salvage value to be $0.2 million at the end of its useful life of 5 years.

The company charges depreciation expense of (2,000,000 − 200,000) ÷ 5 or $360,000 each year. Carrying amount at the end of its useful life (i.e. December 31, 2010) is $0.2 million. The company succeeded in selling the asset for $0.5 million on that date. The sale proceeds exceed the carrying amount by $0.3 million so a gain is recognized using the following journal entry:

Accumulated Depreciation	1,800,000	
Cash	500,000	
Equipment		2,000,000
Gain on Disposal		300,000

The equipment account and the related accumulated depreciation account are written off in the process of disposal and the gain is reported in the income statement.

Loss on Disposal

If a fixed asset is sold at a price lower than its carrying amount at the date of disposal, a loss is recognized equal to the excess of carrying amount over the sale proceeds.

Example: Assume that in the above example the sale proceeds were only $100,000. The carrying amount at the date of disposal was $200,000 so there is a loss of $100,000 since carrying amount exceeds sale proceeds.

The following journal entry is to record loss on disposal:

Accumulated Depreciation	1,800,000	
Cash	100,000	
Loss of Disposal	100,000	
Equipment		2,000,000

The loss is reported in the income statement.

No Gain/Loss on Disposal

If the carrying amount of a fixed asset at the date of disposal is equal to the sale proceeds, there is neither gain nor loss.

Example: Assume further that at the date of purchase Kingston Inc. entered into an agreement with USB Ltd. according to which USB had to purchase the asset at the end of its useful life of 5 years at a price of $0.2 million.

On December 31, 2006, Kingston delivered the derecognized asset to USB for $0.2 million. Carrying amount is equal to sale proceeds so no gain or loss is to be recognized. The journal entry would be:

Accumulated Depreciation	1,800,000	
Cash	200,000	
Equipment		2,000,000

Revaluation of Fixed Assets

Revaluation of fixed assets is the process of increasing or decreasing their carrying value in case of major changes in fair market value of the fixed asset. International Financial Reporting Standards (IFRS) require fixed assets to be initially recorded at cost but they allow two models for subsequent accounting for fixed assets, namely the cost model and the revaluation model.

Cost Model

In the cost model, fixed assets are carried at their historical cost less accumulated depreciation and accumulated impairment losses. There is no upward adjustment to value due to changing circumstances.

Example: Axe Ltd. purchased a building worth $200,000 on January 1, 2008. It records the building using the following journal entry:

Equipment	200,000	
Cash		200,000

The building has a useful life of 20 years and the company uses *straight-line depreciation*. Yearly depreciation is hence $200,000/20 or $10,000. Accumulated depreciation as at December 31, 2010, is $10,000*3 or $30,000 and the carrying amount is $200,000 minus $30,000, which equals $170,000.

We see that the building remains at its historical cost and is periodically depreciated with no other upward adjustment to value.

Revaluation Model

In the revaluation model, an asset is initially recorded at cost but subsequently its carrying amount is increased to account for any appreciation in value. The difference between the cost model and the revaluation model is that the revaluation model allows both downward and upward adjustment in value of an asset while the cost model allows only downward adjustment due to impairment loss.

Example: Consider the example of Axe Ltd. as quoted in case of cost model. Assume on December 31, 2010, the company intends to switch to revaluation model and carries out a revaluation exercise which estimates the fair value of the building to be $190,000 as at December 31, 2010. The carrying amount at the date is $170,000 and revalued amount is $190,000 so an upward adjustment of $20,000 is required to building account. It is recorded through the following journal entry:

Building	20,000	
Revaluation Surplus		20,000

Revaluation Surplus

Upward revaluation is not considered a normal gain and is not recorded in the income statement; rather it is directly credited to an equity account called revaluation surplus. Revaluation surplus holds all the upward revaluations of a company's assets until those assets are disposed of.

Depreciation after Revaluation

The depreciation in periods after revaluation is based on the revalued amount. In case of Axe Ltd. depreciation for 2011 shall be the new carrying amount divided by the remaining useful life or $190,000/17, which equals $11,176.

Reversal of Revaluation

If a revalued asset is subsequently valued down due to impairment, the loss is first written off against any balance available in the revaluation surplus, and if the loss exceeds the revaluation surplus balance of the same asset, the difference is charged to income statement as impairment loss.

Example: Suppose on December 31, 2012, Axe Ltd. revalues the building again to find out that the fair value should be $160,000. Carrying amount as at December 31, 2012, is $190,000 minus 2 years' depreciation of $22,352, which amounts to $167,648.

The carrying amount exceeds the fair value by $7,648 so the account balance should be reduced by that amount. We already have a balance of $20,000 in the revaluation surplus account related to the same building, so no impairment loss shall go to the income statement. The journal entry would be:

Revaluation Surplus	7,648	
Building Account		7,648

Had the fair value been $140,000, the excess of carrying amount over fair value would have been $27,648. In that situation the following journal entry would have been required:

Revaluation Surplus	20,000	
Impairment Losses	7,648	
Building		20,000
Accumulated Impairment Losses		7,648

THE CAPITAL BUDGET AND FIXED ASSETS BUSINESS PROCESS RISKS AND CHALLENGES

Within the Capital and Fixed Assets Business process, there are several risks and challenges that should be considered when determining the key controls and standards. Controllers for public and private companies should consider:

1. **Theft:** *Theft* is defined as the physical movement of the asset from the company to the employee's control. Employees may remove the asset:

- In the normal course of their duties
- During normal work hours
- In an off-hour scheme

2. **Theft point:** Assets may be diverted before or after the company takes possession. If the asset is diverted before possession, it usually is indicative of weaknesses in the receiving function. Diversion after possession is indicative of weaknesses in physical security controls.

3. **Parties to theft:** The theft may occur through employees, an accomplice, or a fictitious vendor or customer.

4. **Concealment:** This stage refers to how employees conceal the theft or misuse of the asset. The schemes range from nothing to creating internal documents to reflect a sale, transfer, or obsolescence of an asset.

5. **Time:** The amount of time between the theft and identification of the loss is a subset of the concealment phase.

6. **Conversion:** In this phase, employees convert the asset to economic gain. In misuse cases, the conversion is the use of the asset. In theft, the conversion is the personal use or resale of the asset.

7. **Likelihood:** The controller need to assess whether an employee or group of employees could divert the company's fixed assets for personal gain.

8. **Opportunity:** The type, nature, and extent of the asset conversion will impact this phase. In the simplest form, the employee walks out of the company with the asset.

9. **Misuse:** *Misuse* refers to business assets that are used for personal use or to bribe customers or government officials. In government contracts, the asset is purchased for a specific purpose but is used for nongovernmental contract purposes. These areas are typical for misuse fraud cases:
   - Real estate, such as apartments and storage facilities
   - Transportation assets, such as vehicles, air transportation, or boat transportation
   - Office equipment
   - Equipment and tools
   - Assets used in other businesses

10. **No business use of the asset:** In this scheme, the asset does not have a legitimate business purpose. The asset may be a disguised compensation scheme for a senior executive or an asset used to bribe customers or politicians.

11. **Excessive expenditure scheme:** In this fraud scheme, the asset is acquired for a valid business purposes, but its cost exceeds the utility requirement of the organization. The New York City apartment in the

Tyco case illustrates this fraud scheme. In terms of executive management, the Tyco scheme is a form of disguised compensation. The audit procedure is to determine by whom and how the asset is being used, understand the comparable costs, and ensure there is a reporting mechanism for the use of the asset.

12. **Asset purchase scheme:** In the asset purchase scheme, the asset is acquired from a related party without disclosure at an inflated price. Real estate flips are often associated with this scheme. The property changes hands several times to artificially increase the perception of the market value. This scheme is associated with kickback schemes. The audit procedure is to focus on the sales history of the asset and to what parties.

13. **Asset retirement scheme:** In an asset retirement scheme, the asset is intentionally sold below fair market value. The purchaser then either retains it for personal use or resells it at fair market value. Company automobiles are often associated with this fraud scheme. In one instance, a company-leased vehicle had zero miles usage for the two-year lease. The manager responsible for the lease purchased the car from the vendor at the end of the lease period. In essence, he purchased a new car at the price of a two-year-old car.

CHAPTER THIRTY TWO

The Forecast Process

NTRODUCTION: A FORECAST LOOKS the same as a plan or budget. The mechanics of putting a forecast together are the same as for a strategic plan or budget. However, a forecast is really quite different from a budget, principally because of the way it is used and the data it contains. If you use them wisely, forecasts will be the major tool that can be used for the management of your organization.

Budgeting refers to preparing a list of guidelines for expenditures for one year and it is usually done a year in advance. It is used as a benchmark in analyzing the fiscal health of a business. Forecasting refers to taking the fiscal information for a time in the past and trying to compare it to how the same numbers would look in the future taking the additional circumstances into consideration.

A budget for the upcoming year includes all the expenses and income that the company anticipates and must link to the organization's strategic plan.

The budget also sets targets for the company to meet such as staying within a certain amount of money for expenses and showing a high percentage of profit at the end of the year. Forecasting is similar, but it is a prediction of what could happen based on a previous set of numbers. It does not set any targets to meet or exceed.

In a budget, specific funds are allotted and the information in the budget explains how that money will be spent. There are also contingency plans included just in case an unexpected expense arises that could result in less income than anticipated.

ABOUT THE FORECAST PROCESS

A forecast may or may not be accurate because it makes a prediction about the coming year based on the performance of the company in the past. Forecasting is predicting, but budgeting is planning. You can prepare a budget by using forecasting techniques. A company rarely makes a big expenditure without studying the impact it will have on the budget and the business activities.

Many organizations define their budget process as an annual event and forecast actual results on a monthly or quarterly basis. Some smaller firms may forecast revenue and expenses on a weekly basis to determine if the company needs to borrow funds to sustain the operation. In summary,

1. Budgeting refers to planning for the future, but forecasting uses the past to predict the future.
2. Budgeting is based on certainties, but forecasting is based on uncertainties.
3. Budgeting is done for a year at a time.
4. For companies that do not do budgeting, there should be some form of forecasting.

 TYPES OF FORECASTING MODELS

Introduction: There are several types of fiscal forecasting models that finance and accounting executives should be aware when developing a forecasting process for their organizations and to support the internal reporting process. A consistent and well-managed forecasting process will help drive a faster close and allow additional analysis to determine spending and revenue trends.

Macroeconomic Financial Models

The models are usually econometric analysis–based, built by government departments, universities, or economic consulting firms, and used to forecast the economy of a country. Macroeconomic models are used to analyze the like effect of government policy decisions on variables such as foreign exchange rates, interest rates, disposable income, and the gross national product (GNP).

Industry Financial Models

Industry models are usually econometric-based models of specific industries or economic sectors. Industry models are often similar to macroeconomic models and typically used by industry associations or industry research analysts to forecast key performance indicators within the industry in question.

Corporate Financial Models

Corporate fiscal models are built to model the total operations of a company, and often perceived to be critical in the strategic planning of business operations in large corporations and startup companies alike. Almost all corporate fiscal models are built in Excel, although specialized fiscal modeling software is increasingly being used, especially in large corporations, to ensure standardization and accuracy of multiple fiscal models or to comply with spreadsheet management requirements imposed by the Sarbanes Oxley Act of 2002 (SOX) financial reporting act.

Deterministic Financial Models

In a deterministic model, a fiscal analyst enters a set of input data into a spreadsheet, programs the spreadsheet to perform a series of mathematical calculations, and displays an output result. Most deterministic fiscal models are built by performing an analysis on historical data to derive the relationship between key forecast variables. In a corporate context, historical accounting relationships are often used to forecast key revenue and cost variables. Most deterministic models use one- or two-dimensional sensitivity analysis tables built into the model to analyze the question of risk and uncertainty in the model's output results. Each sensitivity analysis table allows a fiscal analyst to perform a "what-if" analysis on one or two variables at a time. The advantages of sensitivity tables are its simplicity and ease of integration into existing deterministic fiscal models that have already been built.

Multiple sensitivity analysis tables can be combined in a scenario manager. The scenario manager is useful when there are interdependencies between the changing variables, as fiscal analysts can configure and change multiple variables in each scenario.

In certain scenarios, multiple regression analysis is used to determine the mathematical relationship between multiple variables in a deterministic fiscal model, and such analysis is termed *econometric analysis.*

The deterministic model is probably the most common type of fiscal model used in business and finance today. Most fiscal forecasting models used for revenue management, cost management, and project financing are primarily deterministic fiscal models.

Simulation-Based Financial Models

While a deterministic fiscal model is normally structured in such a way that a single-point estimate is used for each input variable, simulation-based fiscal models work by entering the likely distribution of key inputs defined by the mean, variance, and type of distribution.

Simulation models use these ranges of inputs to recalculate the defined mathematical equation in the fiscal model through a few hundred iterations, normally 500 or more. The results of the analysis will produce the likely distribution of the result, thereby providing an indication of the expected range of results instead of a single-point estimate.

Where risk is a dominant factor in the fiscal modeling scenario being analyzed, a reliable estimation of the likely range of results is often more useful than a single-point estimate. Simulation-based fiscal models therefore allow a fiscal analyst to model the question of risk and uncertainty using a higher level of granularity.

Specialized Financial Models

Specialized fiscal models are narrower in scope and essentially sophisticated calculators built to address a specific business problem or fiscal computation. Cost management models, marginal contribution analysis models, and option pricing models are examples of specialized fiscal models.

THE FORECASTING PROCESS FOR SMALL BUSINESSES

According to Osmond Vitez of Demand Media, in the article "Financial Forecasting Tools,"

> Small businesses often use a variety of tools and techniques for measuring performance and forecasting future fiscal returns. Financial forecasting is the business function responsible for analyzing current internal business information, external economic information and processing these items through a fiscal calculation. Financial calculations determine the profitability of business expansion or new business opportunities. Smaller or home-based businesses may not use fiscal forecasting tools as frequently as larger business organizations.[i]

---

[i] Osmond Vitez, "Financial Forecasting Tools," Chron.com. Accessed on May 9, 2019, https://smallbusiness.chron.com/financial-forecasting-tools-4583.html.

Vitez lists the types of fiscal forecasting tools utilized by small businesses below.

Forecasting Tools

Net Present Value

The net present value calculation estimates future cash inflows from expanded business or new business opportunities and discounts these dollar amounts back to today's dollar value. The discount rate is usually a predetermined rate of return percentage companies want to achieve on new business opportunities. A baseline percentage is usually 10% or 12%, which is commonly seen as the rate of return earned by investing money in the stock market. The sum of discounted cash inflows is compared with the initial cash outflow used to expand operations or begin new business opportunities. If the future cash inflows are higher than the initial cash outflow, the opportunity is usually seen as a good investment.

Cost of Capital

A cost of capital fiscal forecast usually compares the interest rates companies must pay on debt or equity financing to current or future business operations. The weighted average cost of capital and capital asset pricing model are two basic forecasting tools used to compare financing interest rates. These fiscal forecasting tools usually rely on the market cost of debt or equity—prime interest rate or similar interest rates—to determine if a company should use external financing when accepting new business opportunities.

Financial Statement Analysis

Financial statement analysis is a basic form of fiscal forecasting. Companies often compare several financial statements during a specific time period to determine if any trends exist relating to the company's fiscal information. Trends may include increases or decreases in revenue sales, cost of goods sold, or business expenses listed on the company's income statement. Companies can also use fiscal ratios to break down their balance sheet and determine how well they are generating economic value through the use of assets. Ratios indicate how well the company can meet short-term fiscal obligations, generate profit from the sale of individual goods or services, and generate capital from assets and other specific information.

Decision Forecasting

Small businesses may use fiscal forecasting models to make business decisions. Financial models include decision trees, game theory, or supply-and-demand analyses. These decision forecasting models usually require business owners or managers to lay out the type or number of decisions that can be made regarding business operations. The future fiscal impact of each decision will also be outlined in these forecast models. Companies often attach a percentage relating to the likelihood of each forecast generating the expected profits. Business owners usually select the opportunity that will lead to the highest fiscal returns for their business.

CHAPTER THIRTY THREE

The Fiscal Close and Strategic Planning

NTRODUCTION: THE STRATEGY OF an organization is formalized by the development of the strategic plan. The purpose of strategic planning is to set the company guidelines and policies that serve as the foundation for all other planning activities within the organization. The strategic plan focuses on the needs, goals, opportunities, and risks facing the company and the strategic plan identifies the key decisions that are needed to achieve the company's goals.

The strategic plan establishes the strategy for the organization for one to five years and is supported by divisional or budget unit plans which span one to three years. The annual budget process should be linked to the strategic planning process.

 ## EXPECTED OUTCOMES OF THE STRATEGIC PLAN

The strategic plan has four basic outcomes and benefits to the organization:

1. Helps management or an entrepreneur to clarify, focus, and research their businesses or project's development and prospects
2. Provides a considered and logical framework within which a business can develop and pursue business strategies over the next three to five years

3. Serves as a basis for discussion with third parties such as shareholders, agencies, banks, investors, and so on
4. Offers a benchmark against which actual performance can be measured and reviewed

The strategic plan is the foundation of all other planning processes for the organizations. Controllers and CFOs have a significant level of involvement in both private and public organizations and should be comfortable with strategic planning methodologies, components, roles and responsibilities, risks, challenges, and controls. Because mergers and acquisitions could be part of the strategic plan, this section also includes the due diligence process required when considering a merger-and-acquisition activity.

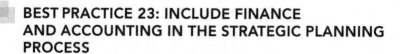

BEST PRACTICE 23: INCLUDE FINANCE AND ACCOUNTING IN THE STRATEGIC PLANNING PROCESS

Introduction: Depending on the size of the organization, the controller may be assigned the role of the primary contact that is responsible for assembling and maintaining the plan and developing the fiscal schedules and statements to support the strategic plan. Here are eight additional key tasks.

1. Verify the sales and production plans.
2. Validate that expense levels are in proportion to other activities.
3. Ensure there is sufficient funding for the projected activity or program.
4. Determine if the plan meets the organization's requirement for return on investment.
5. Determine that other fiscal ratios and metrics are reasonable.
6. Ensure that the strategic, development, and operational plans link together.
7. Ensure that organizational changes are documented and well communicated.
8. Drive the budget process considering the following types of budgets depending on the type of organization:
   - Sales
   - Production
   - Purchases
   - Labor
   - Manufacturing expense budget

- Inventory budget
- Selling, general, and administrative budget
- Research and development budget
- Capital budget
- IT budget
- Cost of goods sold budget
- Cash budget

BEST PRACTICE 24: USE A STRATEGIC PLANNING READINESS CHECKLIST

Sample Strategic Planning Readiness Checklist

Overall Corporate Strategy

- What is the future direction of the organization in terms of developing new product, entering a new market, increasing current market share, developing corporate competence, and capacity?
- Is everyone in the organization aware of the company's direction?
- What support is needed by the employees of the organization to implement the strategy?
- Do employees understand the organization's vision, mission, values, and industry direction?
- How much emphasis should be placed on innovation within the organization?
- Has the organization identified potential partners and competitors?
- Has the organization identified a company to acquire or merge with?

Business Unit Strategy

- Is the strategic plan developed at the headquarters level or at the business unit level?
- Does the business unit have its own vision, mission, and plan? If so, are the business unit's visions, missions, and plans aligned with the strategic plan developed by headquarters?
- What resources should be invested in innovation?
- What types of innovation should the organization focus on?
- How will this innovation align with the organization's strategy?

Risk Management (Refer to Chapter 4)

- Is risk addressed within the strategic plan?
- Does the strategic plan create any new risks for the organization?
- Are there new compliance issues that need to be considered?

Human Resources Management

- Does the strategic plan require additional resources or new levels of competencies within the organization?
- Does the organization need to hire new talent or should the organization implement a training and development plan?
- Are employees compensated according to professional and industry markets?

Sample Strategic Planning Readiness Checklist

Management and Performance

- Does management establish performance requirements for employees?
- Do performance requirements align with the organization's strategic plans?
- Is the management team of the organization held accountable for meeting the goals and objectives defined in the strategic plan?

 ## BEST PRACTICE 25: FOLLOW THESE SEVEN STEPS FOR YOUR STRATEGIC PLANNING PROCESS

Introduction: According to the Small Business Administration (www.sba .gov), a strategic plan is an essential roadmap for the business success. "This living, breathing document generally projects 3–5 years ahead and outlines the route a company intends to take to reach, maintain, and grow revenues."

This definition can be applied to organizations of all sizes. Here is a suggested strategic process methodology from the book *Corporate Strategic and Operational Controls* by John Kyriazoglou and Frank Nasuti (Institute for Internal Controls, 2012). The seven steps of this methodology are included here.

Seven Steps for the Strategic Planning Process

---

1. Preparing for Strategy
2. Articulating the Mission and Vision
3. Assessing the Situation
4. Developing Strategies, Goals, and Objectives
5. Writing the Strategic Plan
6. Strategy Implementation
7. Strategy Evaluation

 ## BEST PRACTICE 26: IMPLEMENT SIX KEY ELEMENTS FOR YOUR STRATEGIC PLAN

Introduction: According the Stephen M. Bragg in the book, *The Controller's Function: The Work of the Managerial Accountant* (John Wiley & Sons, 2011), the strategic plan of an organization must contain the following six elements as summarized here.

Six Key Elements for Your Strategic Plan

---

1. A statement of purpose for the strategic plan.
2. Actions: Specific actions should be defined in this section of the plan. The actions should be specific enough to be defined to resources.
3. Resources: This section defines the resources needed to complete the actions defined within the plan.
4. Goals: The goals define the level of accomplishment expected from the actions required.
5. Time schedules or the project plan to follow.
6. Assumptions: The assumptions establish the scenario and conditions that the strategic plan is based on.

BEST PRACTICE 27: USE A STANDARDIZED TABLE OF CONTENTS FOR YOUR STRATEGIC PLAN

Introduction: The table of contents below provides an outline for the contents that should be included in the strategic plan for your company. As you can see, the budget is usually included with the strategic plan since it is based on the strategies defined during the planning process.

Strategic Plan Table of Contents

---

1. Executive Summary: This is written to the scope and level of content that an "outsider" can read the summary and grasp the mission of the organization, its overall major issues and goals, and key strategies to reach the goals.
2. Authorization: This section includes all of the necessary signatures from the board of directors (if applicable) and other top management designating that they approve the contents of, and support implementation of, the plan. This section may also include the members of the strategic planning committee.
3. Organizational Description: This section describes, for example, the beginnings and history of the organization, its major products and services, highlights and accomplishments during the history of organization, etc.
4. Mission, Vision and Values Statements: These statements describe the strategic foundation of the organization. After approval, these statements are typically placed on the company's website.
5. Goals and Strategies: Lists all of the major strategic goals and associated strategies identified during the strategic planning process.
6. Assumptions: Lists all the assumptions that were made in developing the plan.
7. Risks Analysis: Includes the organizational risks and how they will be addressed.
8. Budget: The budget is included in the strategic plan. This section should contain pertinent analysis that compares the current year's budget to the previous year's budget. Significant increases should be explained and tied to goals and strategies. The budget section of the strategic plan may include staffing plans.

Strategic Plan Table of Contents

9. Major Company Initiatives: This section provides a listing of all major company projects to be implemented during the life of the strategic plan (1–5 years). The listing may contain IT projects, outsourcing or offshoring plans, or merger-and-acquisition activities plans.
10. Supporting Organizational Plans: This section includes the plans for business development and operations.
11. Supporting Exhibits: This optional section should include the results of SWOT or PERT analysis, project plans for major company initiatives, and communication plans.

STRATEGIC PLANNING METHODOLOGIES

Introduction: Several methodologies can be used to ensure that the organization's strengths, weaknesses, opportunities, threats, and environmental influences are identified. These three tools will help identify the critical issues and challenges that the organization should address when developing the strategic plan. The SWOT, PEST analysis, and balanced scorecard methodologies are described in this section.

Tool 1: SWOT Analysis

The SWOT tool was developed at Stanford University in the late 1960s. It is used by most Fortune 500 companies and several private companies in the strategic planning process. The SWOT matrix involves a frank evaluation of a business's strengths, weaknesses, opportunities, and threats as detailed below.

A successful business is founded on a series of sound decisions, so the way you analyze situations and choose to react is essential. When trying to assess the lay of the land, few tools are more useful than the SWOT analysis. The SWOT analysis is a planning process that allows your company to overcome challenges and determine what new leads to pursue.[i]

> **Strengths:** Attributes of the organization that can positively impact achieving objectives. These are the company's core competencies, and include proprietary technology, skills, resources, market position, patents, and others.

---

[i] Nick Fallon, "SWOT Analysis: What It Is and When to Use It," *Business News Daily*. Last modified March 2, 2018. Accessed April 4, 2019. https://www.businessnewsdaily.com/4245-swot-analysis.html.

Weaknesses: Attributes of the organization that can prevent the organization from achieving its objectives. Weaknesses are conditions within the company that can lead to poor performance, and can include obsolete equipment, no clear strategy, heavy debt burden, poor product or market image, long product development cycle, weak management, and others.

Opportunities: External conditions that can help achieve the objective. Opportunities are conditions or circumstances that the company could turn to its advantage, and could include a specialty niche skill or technology that suddenly realizes a growth in broad market interest.

Threats: External conditions that can negatively impact achieving the objective of the organizations. Threats are current or future conditions in the outside environment that may harm the company, and might include population shifts, changes in purchasing, serious competitive barriers, changes in governmental or environmental regulations, and others.

Tool 2: PEST Analysis

PEST analysis is different from the SWOT analysis mainly because the PEST deals with external factors only. PEST analysis is a simple but important and widely used tool that helps you understand the big picture of the political, economic, sociocultural, and technological impacts on your organization.

PEST is used by business leaders of all types of organizations to build their vision of the future. By making effective use of PEST analysis, the organization considers all external risks during the planning process.

A PEST analysis is a strategic business tool used by organizations to discover, evaluate, organize, and track macroeconomic factors that can impact their business now and in the future. The framework examines opportunities and threats due to political, economic, social, and technological forces.[ii]

Tool 3: The Balanced Scorecard

Introduction: The balanced scorecard is a strategic planning and management system that is used extensively in business and industry, government, and nonprofit organizations worldwide to align business activities to the vision and strategy of the organization, improve internal and external communications, and monitor organization performance against strategic goals.

[ii] Group Map, "What Is PEST Analysis?" Accessed April 4, 2019. https://www.groupmap.com/map-templates/pest-analysis/.

It was originated by Drs. Robert Kaplan (Harvard Business School) and David Norton as a performance measurement framework that added strategic non-fiscal performance measures to traditional fiscal metrics to give managers and executives a more balanced view of organizational performance.

The balanced scorecard is a management system (not only a measurement system) that enables organizations to clarify their vision and strategy and translate them into action. It provides feedback around both the internal business processes and external outcomes in order to continuously improve strategic performance and results. When fully deployed, the balanced scorecard transforms strategic planning from an academic exercise into the nerve center of an enterprise.

The balanced scorecard is a strategic planning and management system that organizations use to:

- Communicate what they are trying to accomplish.
- Align the day-to-day work that everyone is doing with strategy.
- Prioritize projects, products, and services.
- Measure and monitor progress toward strategic targets.[iii]

Steps for Implementing the Balanced Scorecard

1. **Assessment:** Step 1 of the BCS scorecard building process starts with an assessment of the organization's mission and vision, challenges or pain points, enablers, and values. Step 1 also includes preparing a change management plan for the organization, and conducting a focused communications workshop to identify key messages, media outlets, timing, and messengers.
2. **Strategy:** The most important element of this step is to ensure that you have defined what your customers are looking for from your organization in terms of function, relationship, and image.
3. **Objectives:** This step validates that your organization's objectives and continuous improvement activities are linked to the strategic plan.
4. **Strategy maps:** The theme strategy maps are merged into an overall corporate strategy map that shows how the organization creates value for its customers and stakeholders.
5. **Performance measures:** The performance measures are developed for strategic objectives. Performance measures should be defined clearly,

---

[iii] Balanced Scorecard Institute (BSI), "Balanced Scorecard Basics." Accessed April 4, 2019. https://www.balancedscorecard.org/BSC-Basics/About-the-Balanced-Scorecard.

differentiating the outcome and output measures as well as the leading measures (future expected performance) and lagging measures (past performance history).

6. **Strategic initiatives:** The strategic initiatives are developed that support the strategic objectives. This is where the projects that have to be undertaken to ensure the success of the organization (the extent to which the organization fulfills its mandate or vision) are drafted and assigned. To build accountability throughout the organization, performance measures and strategic initiatives are assigned to owners and documented in data definition tables.

7. **Software and automation:** Automation is purposely put as Step 7 in the 9-step framework to make sure that the proper emphasis is placed on strategic thinking and strategy development.

8. **Cascading:** Cascading is the key to organization alignment around strategy. Objectives for customer-facing processes can be integrated into the alignment process to produce linked outcomes and responsibilities throughout the organization.

    Performance measures are developed for all objectives at all organization levels. As the scorecard management system is cascaded down through the organization, objectives become more operational and tactical, as do the performance measures.

    Accountability will follow objectives and measures, as ownership is defined at each level. An emphasis on results and the strategies needed to produce results is communicated throughout the organization. Many companies base employee performance on the results of the balanced scorecard and focus on the achievement of performance measures when determining salary increases and bonuses. The results of the balanced scorecard are often reported through monthly internal reporting processes.

9. **Evaluation:** This step involves evaluating the success of chosen business strategies. The evaluation step includes the following:

    - Ensuring that organizational learning and knowledge building are incorporated into planning
    - Making adjustments to existing service programs
    - Adding new programs if they are more cost effective
    - Eliminating programs that are not delivering cost-effective services or meeting customer needs
    - Linking planning to budget

BEST PRACTICE 28: ESTABLISH PERFORMANCE METRICS TO DETERMINE THE EFFECTIVENESS OF YOUR STRATEGIC PLAN

Introduction: The effectiveness of the strategic plan must be monitored to determine if revisions must be made. The steps for monitoring the strategic plan are included below.

Steps for Monitoring the Strategic Plan
1. Define parameters to be measured.
2. Define target values for those parameters.
3. Perform measurements.
4. Compare measured results to the predefined standard.
5. Make necessary changes.

When evaluating the effectiveness of the strategic plan, the organization should determine the performance metrics that will validate the effectiveness of the plan. These metrics are usually reported in an organizational scorecard such as the balanced scorecard methodology already described. Examples of performance metrics are included below.

Strategic Planning Performance Metrics
1. Number of improvements after budget and performance reviews
2. Well-defined business objectives for all departments
3. Number of hours spent on strategic reviews
4. Percent of investments that have exceeded targets
5. Changes in stock price
6. Situations where the corporate strategy was not followed
7. Cash flow improvements
8. Profit/revenue by function
9. Profit by new products and services
10. Total profits/revenues/ROI
11. Market share increase
12. Changes to customer base
13. Customer satisfaction

CHAPTER THIRTY FOUR

Analytics to Detect Financial Statement Fraud

NTRODUCTION: FINANCIAL STATEMENT FRAUD, commonly referred to as "cooking the books," involves deliberately overstating assets, revenues, and profits and/or understating liabilities, expenses, and losses. A business that engages in such a practice stands to lose a tremendous amount of money when penalties and fines, legal costs, the loss of investor confidence, and reputational damage are taken into account.

Red flags are events, conditions, situational pressures, opportunities, or personal characteristics that may cause management to commit fraud on behalf of the company or for personal gain. They can be used as an early warning system by both auditors and other stakeholders to assess the risk of fiscal statement fraud. Although red flags may not necessarily indicate the presence of fraud, they are conditions believed to be commonly present in the event of fraudulent activities and may therefore warrant concern and additional investigation.

In the past red flags were addressed from the perspective of the auditors. The problem is that the red flags identified by auditors are not necessarily relevant to lenders and investors. Lenders and investors require red flags that are appropriate to their particular interests and their access to information on the company and its management. It is also lenders and investors who may take legal action against auditors and management based on their perception of negligence in respect of fiscal statement fraud.

BEST PRACTICE 29: USE RED FLAGS TO DETECT FINANCIAL STATEMENT FRAUD

Introduction: Finance and accounting managers know that red flags can signal events, conditions, situational pressures, opportunities, or personal characteristics that may be of concern about a possible fraudulent activity. They can be used as an early warning system by controllers, their staffs, auditors, and internal control experts to assess the risk of fiscal statement fraud.

When an auditor, internal controls expert, fraud investigator, or forensic accountant investigates fiscal statement fraud, he or she looks for red flags or accounting warning signs. A good controller should also be aware of these flags.

Key Point: Of the general indicators, top management personality and character are by far the most compelling with regard to fiscal statement fraud. Typically, a senior executive who is inclined to cook the books possesses low ethical standards, though this trait may often be difficult to detect prior to the commission of a crime. However, most executives with ethical weaknesses also exhibit very noticeable signs of aggressiveness in almost everything they do—including making critical fiscal decisions. General red flags for the record to report (R2R) process are included in the table below.

General Record to Report (R2R) Red Flags
1. Secretive or distinctly evasive attitude regarding critical financial information.
2. Overly domineering, disrespectful, or abusive management style vis-à-vis subordinates.
3. Actively "steering" internal and external auditors away from financial reports that could reveal the fraud.
4. Aggressive revenue recognition practices, such as recognizing revenue in earlier periods than when the product was sold or the service was delivered. This practice may be evidenced by product left on the shipping dock or in trailers after fiscal revenue cutoff periods.
5. Unusually high revenues and low expenses at period-end that cannot be attributed to seasonality trends.
6. Significant growth in inventory that does not correlate with the company's growth in sales.
7. Improper capitalization or accounting treatment of expenses in excess of industry norms and standards.
8. Reported earnings that are positive and growing when operating cash flow is declining.
9. Growth in revenues that is far greater than growth in other companies in the same industry or peer group.
10. Gross margin or operating margins out of line with peer companies.

General Record to Report (R2R) Red Flags

11. Extensive use of off-balance-sheet entities that are not considered standard in the industry.
12. Sudden increases in gross margin or cash flow as compared with the company's prior performance and with industry averages.
13. Unusual increases in the book value of assets such as inventory and receivables.
14. Disclosure notes so complex that it is impossible to determine the actual nature of the transaction.
15. Accounts payable invoices that go unrecorded in the company's fiscal books and accruals that are not properly booked.
16. Loans to executives or other related parties that are written off.
17. Pressure is exerted on accounting personnel to complete financial statements in an unusually short time period as reflected by approval date of financial statements.
18. Unusually long business cycles to complete the fiscal close compared to previous periods.
19. Several "post-close" journal entries approved outside of normal closing cycle time.
20. Rapid expansion into new product lines that may not fit the company's business model.
21. Extensive borrowing with limited collateral available.
22. The company has a significant investment in an industry or product line noted for rapid change.
23. Poor interpersonal relationships among executives, the controller, and CFO.
24. The entity is heavily dependent on one or a few products, customers, or suppliers.
25. Declining demand for products.
26. Key executives are feeling undue family, peer, or community pressure to succeed.
27. The company is facing adverse political, social, or environmental impact.
28. The company has had extreme turnover at the controller and CFO levels.
29. Complex or unstable organizational structure.
30. Unusually intricate or confusing fiscal transactions with third-party entities.
31. Sudden or gradual increase in gross margin compared with the company's prior performance and with industry averages.
32. Cash flows that are negative for the first three quarters and suddenly positive for the fourth quarter—not by just a little, but by more than all losses to date.

Key Point: This scenario is exactly what happened at Enron. It is why Sherron Watkins said, after the company's demise, that if anyone had been paying attention to the cash flows they would have known that Enron's statements were suspicious and/or fraudulent.

33. Significant sales to companies or individuals whose identity and business track record are questionable.
34. Sudden above-average profits for specific quarters.
35. Executives or board members have direct personal dependence on the company's performance or conspicuously lax board oversight of top management.

THE NATIONAL COMMISSION ON FRAUDULENT FINANCIAL REPORTING (THE TREADWAY COMMISSION)

Introduction: COSO's research project analyzes 347 fraudulent financial reporting cases among U.S. public companies for the 10-year period 1998–2007. This study updates the 1999 monograph and expands previous research by comparing fraud firms with similar no-fraud firms. The study finds that fraudulent financial reporting cases are becoming larger, are more likely to involve larger companies, are more likely to involve the CEO and/or CFO, and are more likely to involve the misstatement of revenues.

Observable board governance characteristics do not differ meaningfully between fraud and no-fraud firms, suggesting the need for research on governance processes and interactions of governance characteristics. Fraud firms are more likely to change audit firms, and the consequences of fraud continue to be severe, with significant stock price declines and frequent bankruptcies, stock exchange de-listings, and asset sales for fraud firms.

Public Company Summary Recommendations

According to COSO's Report of the National Commission on Fraudulent Financial Reporting, prevention and earlier detection of fraudulent financial reporting must start with the entity that prepares financial reports. These recommendations, taken together, will improve a company's overall financial reporting process and increase the likelihood of preventing fraudulent financial reporting and detecting it earlier when it occurs.

The report states, for some companies, implementing these recommendations will require little or even no change from current practices; for other companies, it will mean adding or improving a recommended practice. Whether it means adding or improving a practice, the benefits justify the costs.

The commission's recommendations for the public company deal with (1) the tone set by top management, (2) the internal accounting and audit functions, (3) the audit committee, (4) management and audit committee reports, (5) the practice of seeking second opinions from independent public accountants, and (6) quarterly reporting.

Recommendations for the Independent Public Accountant

Recommendations from the COSO report stress the independent public accountant's role, while secondary to that of management and the board of directors, is crucial in detecting and deterring fraudulent financial reporting. To ensure and improve the effectiveness of the independent public accountant, the commission recommends changes in auditing standards, in procedures that enhance audit quality, in the independent public accountant's communications about his role, and in the process of setting auditing standards.

Recommendations for the SEC and Others to Improve the Regulatory and Legal Environment

The COSO report recommends strong and effective deterrence is essential in reducing the incidence of fraudulent financial reporting. While acknowledging the SEC's significant efforts and achievements in deterring such fraud, the Commission concludes that the public- and private-sector bodies whose activities shape the regulatory and law enforcement environment can and should provide stronger deterrence.

The commission's recommendations for increased deterrence involve new SEC sanctions, greater criminal prosecution, and improved regulation of the public accounting profession, adequate SEC resources, improved federal regulation of financial institutions, and improved oversight by state boards of accountancy. In addition, the commission makes two final recommendations in connection with the perceived insurance and liability crises, which are: (1) New SEC Sanctions and Greater Criminal Prosecution and (2) Improved Regulation of the Public Accounting Profession.

Recommendations for Education

The final set of recommendations provided in the report stress the importance of education. The report communicates that education can influence present or future participants in the financial reporting system by providing knowledge, skills, and ethical values that potentially may help prevent, detect, and deter fraudulent financial reporting. To encourage educational initiatives toward this end, the commission recommends changes in the business and accounting curricula as well as in professional certification examinations and continuing professional education.

The commission outlines several opportunities for public companies to educate their directors, management, and employees about the problem of fraudulent financial reporting. The tools provided in this toolkit can greatly assist with educating companies on the best practices, checklists, policies, process narratives, and standards of internal control that can help ensure a faster and accurate fiscal close.

COSO recommends and provides the following additional tools:

- Interactive Scorecards
- Anti-Fraud Data Analytics Tests
- Risk Assessment and Follow-Up Action Templates
- Points-of-Discussion Templates

Five Categories of Financial Statement Fraud

Financial statement fraud has five distinct categories as reported below. Each fraud category has its unique red flags and detection methods.

1. **Revenue recognition or timing schemes (also known as improper treatment of sales):** This fraud category is possibly the most common form of fiscal statement fraud, usually employed when management seeks to conceal the real numbers for a weak quarter or two. If a sale is legitimate, but is posted prematurely, the fraud flag would be a GAAP violation by early recording of the sale. Similarly, channel stuffing, where sales are recorded before they've actually been made, would be indicated by an excessive number of subsequent period returns of merchandise, accompanied by an unusual jump in credits.

2. **Fictitious revenue:** This is one of the oldest fiscal statement schemes around and involves posting sales that simply never occurred. Fraud flags include:
   - Unusual increase in assets—the other side of the entry to mask fictitious revenues.
   - "Customer" records are missing key data such as physical address and phone number.
   - Unusual changes in ratio patterns—such as a spike in revenues with no commensurate increase in accounts receivable.

3. **Concealed liabilities (improper or underreporting of expenses and other liabilities):** By shifting expenses from one entity to another or reclassifying liabilities as assets, which is what got WorldCom into trouble when it improperly reported $3.8 billion in expenses as capital expenditures, management can make the company's fiscal condition appear much rosier than it is. Fraud flags include:
   - Use of different audit firms for different subsidiaries or business entities
   - Recurring negative cash flows from operations or an inability to generate cash flows from operations while reporting earnings growth

- Invoices and other liabilities go unrecorded in the company's fiscal records
- Writing off loans to executives or other parties
- Failure to record warranty-related liabilities

4. **Inadequate disclosures:** This tactic is used after a fiscal statement fraud has occurred as indicated by the following fraud flags:
   - Disclosure notes are so complex that it is impossible to determine the actual nature of the event or transaction.
   - Discovery of undisclosed legal contingencies.

5. **Improper asset valuation:** Fraudulently inflating asset valuations is a common form of profit manipulation as described by the following fraud flags:
   - Unusual or unexplained increases in the book value of assets such as inventory, receivables, long-term assets, and so on
   - Odd patterns in relationships of assets to other components of the fiscal report, such as sudden changes in the ratio of receivables to revenues
   - GAAP violations in recording expenses as assets

USE DETECTION METHODS FOR GENERAL FINANCIAL STATEMENT FRAUD

The following items are suggested methods used to detect general fiscal statement fraud.

1. Internal audit is consistently engaged in substantive antifraud activities.
2. Auditors aggressively apply standards of SAS No. 99.
3. Frequent and thorough fraud-oriented ratio analysis—focusing in particular on long-term trends and on comparisons between business units.
4. Surprise audits and account reconciliations.
5. Implementation of an anonymous, user-friendly tip hotline for use by employees, vendors, and customers.
6. Data mining using one of the common auditing software applications.
7. Horizontally and vertically analyzing all financial reports using the methodologies proposed in this toolkit, which includes conducting frequent ratio analysis, including assessment of trends over periods of several years.
8. Using the Beneish model, which pinpoints anomalies in year-to-year measures of gross margins, sales growth, receivables levels, and other key accounting ratios. The model is explained in the following table.

Definition of Beneish Model

A mathematical model that uses fiscal ratios and eight variables to identify whether a company has manipulated its earnings. The variables are constructed from the data in the company's financial statements and, once calculated, create an M-Score to describe the degree to which the earnings have been manipulated.[i]
　The eight variables are:

1. DSRI—Days' sales in receivable index
2. GMI—Gross margin index
3. AQI—Asset quality index
4. SGI—Sales growth index
5. DEPI—Depreciation index
6. SGAI—Sales and general and administrative expenses index
7. LVGI—Leverage index
8. TATA—Total accruals to total assets

Once calculated, the eight variables are combined together to achieve an M-Score for the company. An M-Score of less than –2.22 suggests that the company will not be a manipulator. An M-Score of greater than –2.22 signals that the company is likely to be a manipulator.

9. Rigorously applying the guidance of SAS 99 to all audit exercises. SAS 99 requires auditors to look for fraud throughout the entire audit process. The standard defines fraud as an intentional act resulting in a material misstatement in the financial statements. Fraud consists of two major types: (1) misstatements resulting from fraudulent financial reporting and (2) misstatements resulting from the misappropriation of assets (often referred to as theft or defalcation).

SAS 99 describes three conditions typically present when fraud is committed: incentives/pressures, opportunities, and attitudes/rationalizations. Specifically, the perpetrator of the fraud likely is under pressure or has an incentive to commit the fraudulent act. Second, opportunities probably exist for the perpetrator to commit the fraud. Finally, the perpetrator likely is able to rationalize his or her fraudulent act or possesses an attitude that the act was acceptable.

---

[i] GMT Research, "Beneish's M-Score." Accessed April 4, 2019. https://www.gmtresearch.com/beneishs-m-score/.

There is a direct relationship between the existence of the three conditions and the likelihood of the occurrence of fraud. However, SAS 99 emphasizes that all three conditions do not need to be present for fraud to occur. (The appendix to SAS 99 provides examples of each of the three conditions. Exhibit 1 on page 42 shows a sampling of some of the fraudulent financial reporting examples.)

SAS 99 reiterates the importance of exercising professional skepticism throughout the audit. The auditor must maintain a questioning mind and critically assess the responses from the reporting entity's management and other evidence examined to determine the risk or existence of fraudulent misstatements. The auditor should never accept less-than-persuasive evidence based on the assumption that management is honest.

CHAPTER THIRTY FIVE

Checklists for the Analysis and Reporting Process

CHECKLIST 11: QUARTER-END FISCAL CLOSE (10Q)

Introduction: This checklist provides the tasks for the external (10Q) reporting processes required for each quarterly close.

Quarter-End Fiscal Close
Period Ending _____

EXTERNAL REPORTING

Steps:	Description	Applicable Business Unit	Responsible Party	Initial & Date Completed	Comments
1.0	Create and enter prior-period information in Form 10Q draft	Corporate	CFO		
2.0	Request update of "New Accounting Pronounce-ments" section from SEC expert	Corporate	CFO		

Steps:	Description	Applicable Business Unit	Responsible Party	Initial & Date Completed	Comments
3.0	Update "New Accounting Pronouncements" section in Form 10Q draft	Corporate	CFO		
4.0	Enter Financial Statements in the Form 10Q draft	Corporate	FRM		
5.0	Update Footnotes, excluding the Debt, Stock-Based Compensation, Acquisition, Income Taxes footnotes	Corporate	FRM		
6.0	Update the Debt, Stock-Based Compensation, Acquisition and Income Taxes footnotes	Corporate	CFO		
7.0	Draft Item 2—MD&A section of Form 10Q	Corporate	CFO		
8.0	Draft Item 3—Market Risk section of Form 10Q	Corporate	CFO		
9.0	Draft Item 4—Controls section of Form 10Q	Corporate	CFO		
10.0	Draft Part II—Other Information	Corporate	CFO		
11.0	Draft Signature section	Corporate	CFO		
12.0	Draft Certification section	Corporate	CFO		
13.0	Review Form 10Q draft prior to circulation	Corporate	CFO		

Steps:	Description	Applicable Business Unit	Responsible Party	Initial & Date Completed	Comments
14.0	Distribute initial draft of Form 10Q to CEO, Audit Committee Chairman, Executive Management, Disclosure Committee, SEC legal counsel, SEC expert and outside auditors for comments.	Corporate	CFO		
15.0	Incorporate necessary revisions from CEO, Audit Committee Chairman, Executive Management, Disclosure Committee, SEC legal counsel, SEC expert and outside auditors in draft of Form 10Q	Corporate	CFO		
16.0	Distribute Form 10Q draft to Audit Committee of the board of directors for final comments	Corporate	CFO		
17.0	Provide Disclosure Committee with completed Disclosure questionnaires	Corporate	CFO		
18.0	Send draft of Form 10Q to R.R. Donnelley to prepare for filing with the SEC	Corporate	CFO		

Steps:	Description	Applicable Business Unit	Responsible Party	Initial & Date Completed	Comments
19.0	Obtain Form 10Q filing approval from Audit Committee of the board of directors	Corporate	CFO		
20.0	Send signed Management Letter to outside auditors	Corporate	CFO		
21.0	Obtain Form 10Q filing approval from outside auditors	Corporate	CFO		
22.0	Verify all attachments have been included in complete document fling with the SEC	Corporate	CFO		
23.0	Verify all properly signed documents have been received from Form 10Q signees	Corporate	CFO		
24.0	Notify to authorize filing with the SEC on EDGAR	Corporate	CFO		
25.0	Verify filing by listing of Form 10Q on SEC's EDGAR	Corporate	CFO		
26.0	Verify filing on Edgar agrees to authorized final document filing	Corporate	FRM		

CHECKLIST 12: YEAR-END FISCAL CLOSE (10K)

Introduction: This checklist provides the tasks for the external (10K) reporting processes required at fiscal year-end.

Year-End Closing Checklist

Period Ending _____

EXTERNAL REPORTING

Steps:	Description	Applicable Business Unit	Responsible Party	Initial & Date Completed	Comments
Prior to Year-End:					
1.0	Create and enter prior period information in Form 10K draft.	Corporate	CFO		
2.0	Inform the company's actuarial consulting firm with the discount rate to use for the pension and medical plans.	Corporate	CFO		
3.0	Order the company's stock 5-year comparison chart for "Performance Graph" section of Form 10K.	Corporate	CFO		
4.0	Request update of "New Accounting Pronouncements" section from SEC expert.	Corporate	CFO		

Steps:	Description	Applicable Business Unit	Responsible Party	Initial & Date Completed	Comments
Draft Form 10K:					
Front Section					
5.0	Draft Items 1–15 and Signatures	Corporate	CFO		
Financial State-ments Section					
6.0	External Audi-tor Letter	Corporate	CFO		
7.0	Financial State-ments:				
	Consolidated balance sheets	Corporate		FRM	
	Consolidated Statements of Operations	Corporate		FRM	
	Consolidated Statements of Share-holders' Equity	Corporate		FRM	
	Accumulated Other Com-prehensive Loss	Corporate		FRM	
	Consolidated Statements of Cash Flows	Corporate		FRM	
	Supplemental Disclosures of Cash Flow Information	Corporate		FRM	

Steps:		Description	Applicable Business Unit	Responsible Party	Initial & Date Completed	Comments
8.0		Footnotes:				
	1	Nature of Business and Significant Accounting Policies	Corporate	FRM		
	2	Financial Instruments	Corporate	FRM		
	3	Accounts Receivable	Corporate	FRM		
	4	Cost and Estimated Earnings on Uncompleted Contracts	Corporate	FRM		
	5	Inventories	Corporate	FRM		
	6	Property and Equipment	Corporate	FRM		
	7	Goodwill and Intangible Assets	Corporate	FRM		
	8	Accounts Payable and Accrued Expenses	Corporate	FRM		
	9	Debt	Corporate	CFO		
	10	Subordinated Notes	Corporate	CFO		
	11	Shareholders' Equity	Corporate	CFO		
	12	Pension and Employee Benefit Plans	Corporate	FRM		
	13	Commitments and Contingencies	Corporate	CFO		
	14	Income Taxes	Corporate	CFO		
	15	Related-Party Transactions	Corporate	FRM		

Steps:		Description	Applicable Business Unit	Responsible Party	Initial & Date Completed	Comments
	16	Backlog of Uncom-pleted Contracts from Continuing Operations (unaudited)	Corporate	FRM		
	17	Acquisitions	Corporate	CFO		
	18	Subsequent Event	Corporate	CFO		
	19	Major Customers	Corporate	FRM		
	20	Quarterly Financial Data (unaudited)	Corporate	FRM		

Other Form 10K Steps

9.0		Draft Signature section.	Corporate	CFO		
10.0		Draft Certification section.	Corporate	CFO		
11.0		Review Form 10K draft prior to circulation.	Corporate	CFO		
12.0		Distribute initial draft of Form 10K to CEO, Audit Committee Chairman, Executive Manage-ment, Disclosure Committee, SEC legal counsel, SEC expert and outside auditors for comments.	Corporate	CFO		

Steps:	Description	Applicable Business Unit	Responsible Party	Initial & Date Completed	Comments
13.0	Incorporate necessary revisions from CEO, Audit Committee Chairman, Executive Management, Disclosure Committee, SEC legal counsel, SEC expert and outside auditors in draft of Form 10K.	Corporate	CFO		
14.0	Distribute Form 10K draft to Audit Committee of the board of directors for comments.	Corporate	CFO		
15.0	Send Director & Officers questionnaires.	Corporate	CFO		
16.0	Send Disclosure memo & questionnaires.	Corporate	CFO		
17.0	Send Director & Officers questionnaires.	Corporate	CFO		

Steps:	Description	Applicable Business Unit	Responsible Party	Initial & Date Completed	Comments
18.0	Send Disclosure memo & question-naires.	Corporate	CFO		
19.0	Provide Legal with completed question-naires.	Corporate	CFO		
20.0	Provide Disclosure Committee with completed Disclosure question-naires.	Corporate	CFO		
21.0	Send draft of Form 10K to R.R. Donnelley to prepare for filing with the SEC.	Corporate	CFO		
22.0	Obtain Form 10K filing approval from Audit Committee of the Board of Directors.	Corporate	CFO		
23.0	Send signed Manage-ment Letter to outside auditors.	Corporate	CFO		
24.0	Obtain Form 10K filing approval from outside auditors.	Corporate	CFO		

Steps:	Description	Applicable Business Unit	Responsible Party	Initial & Date Completed	Comments
25.0	Verify all attachments have been included in complete document fling with the SEC.	Corporate	CFO		
26.0	Verify all properly signed documents have been received from Form 10K signees.	Corporate	CFO		

SEC Filing Steps					
26.0	Authorize filing with the SEC on EDGAR.	Corporate	CFO		
27.0	Verify filing by listing of Form 10K on SEC's EDGAR.	Corporate	CFO		
28.0	Verify filing on Edgar agrees to authorized final document filing.	Corporate	FRM		

CHECKLIST 13: PERFORMING FINANCIAL STATEMENT ANALYSIS

Introduction: One of the ways in which financial statements can be put to work is through ratio analysis. Ratios are simply one number divided by another; as such they may or may not be meaningful. This checklist provides ratios and recommended methodologies for performing financial statement analysis.

In financial statement analysis, ratios are usually two fiscal statement items that may be related to one another and may provide the prudent user a good deal of information.

Generally, ratios are divided into four areas of classification that provide different kinds of information: liquidity, turnover, profitability, and debt.

1. Liquidity ratios indicate a firm's ability to meet its maturing short-term obligations.
2. Turnover indicates how effectively a firm manages resources at its disposal to generate sales.
3. Profitability indicates the efficiency with which a firm manages resources.
4. Debt indicates the extent to which a firm is financed by debt.

Ratio analysis using financial statements includes accounting, stock market, and management-related limitations. First, ratio analysis is hampered by potential limitations with accounting and the data in the financial statements themselves. This can include errors as well as accounting mismanagement, which involves distorting the raw data used to derive financial ratios.

In another view on stock markets, technical analysts argue that sentiment is as much if not more of a driver of stock prices as is the fundamental data on a company like its fiscals. Behavioral economists attribute the imperfections in fiscal markets to a combination of cognitive biases such as overconfidence, over-reaction, representative bias, information bias, and various other predictable human errors in reasoning and information processing. These audiences also see limits to ratio analysis as a predictor of stock market returns.

At the management and investor level, ratio analysis using financial statements can also leave out a number of important aspects of a firm's success, such as key intangibles, like brand, relationships, skills, and culture. These are primary drivers of success over the longer term even though they are absent from conventional financial statements.

Once ratios are calculated, a fiscal analyst should utilize benchmarks to find out where the company stands at that particular point. Useful benchmarks are industry comparisons and company trends include:

- **Commercial sources:** A number of companies publish information on industry comparisons. Among these sources are private credit reporting agencies such as Dun & Bradstreet.

- **RMA:** The Risk Management Association. Rating agencies such as Moody's and Standard & Poor's also provide industry information.
- **Government sources:** There are a number of government sources of helpful industry information, such as the U.S. Industrial Outlook and Quarterly Financial Reports.
- **Trade associations:** Many industries have trade associations or industry groups that regularly publish information for and about members.

Examples of Financial Statement Ratios

Here are some examples of fiscal statement ratios, how to perform the calculation, and what the ratio tells you. The examples are grouped into the following categories:

1. Balance Sheet Ratios
2. Accounts Receivable Ratios
3. Inventory Ratios
4. Debt-to-Equity Ratio
5. Ratios Based on the Income Statement
6. Free Cash Flow Ratio

Balance Sheet Ratios

Financial Ratio	How to Calculate It	What It Tells You
Working Capital =	Current Assets – Current Liabilities	An indicator of whether the company will be able to meet its current obligations (pay its bills, meet its payroll, make a loan payment, etc.). If a company has current assets exactly equal to current liabilities, it has no working capital. The greater the amount of working capital, the more likely it will be able to make its payments on time.
=	$89,000 – $61,000	
=	$28,000	

Financial Ratio		How to Calculate It	What It Tells You
Current Ratio	=	Current Assets ÷ Current Liabilities	This tells you the relationship of current assets to current liabilities. A ratio of 3:1 is better than 2:1. A 1:1 ratio means there is no working capital.
	=	$89,000 ÷ $61,000	
	=	1.46	
Quick Ratio (Acid Test Ratio)	=	[(Cash + Temp. Investments + Accounts Receivable) ÷ Current Liabilities] : 1	This ratio is similar to the current ratio except that Inventory, Supplies, and Prepaid Expenses are excluded. This indicates the relationship between the amount of assets that can quickly be turned into cash versus the amount of current liabilities.
	=	[($2,100 + $100 + $10,000 + $40,500) ÷ $61,000] : 1	
	=	[$52,700 ÷ $61,000] : 1	
	=	0.86 : 1	

Accounts Receivable Ratios

Financial Ratio		How to Calculate It	What It Tells You
Accounts Receivable Turnover	=	Net Credit Sales for the Year ÷ *Average Accounts Receivable* for the Year	The number of times per year that the accounts receivables turn over. Keep in mind that the result is an average, since credit sales and accounts receivable are likely to fluctuate during the year. It is important to use the average balance of accounts receivable during the year.
	=	$500,000 ÷ $42,000 (a computed average)	
	=	11.90	

Financial Ratio	How to Calculate It	What It Tells You
Days Sales Outstanding	= 365 days in Year ÷ Accounts Receivable Turnover in Year	The average number of days that it took to collect the average amount of accounts receivable during the year. This statistic is only as good as the Accounts Receivable Turnover figure.
	= 365 days ÷ 11.90	
	= 30.67 days	

Inventory Ratios

Financial Ratio	How to Calculate It	What It Tells You
Inventory Turnover	= Cost of Goods Sold for the Year ÷ *Average* Inventory for the Year	The number of times per year that inventory turns over. Keep in mind that the result is an average, since sales and inventory levels are likely to fluctuate during the year. Since inventory is at cost (not sales value), it is important to use the Cost of Goods Sold. Also be sure to use the average balance of inventory during the year.
	= $380,000 ÷ $30,000 (a computed average) 12.67	
	=	
Day's Sales in Inventory	= 365 days in Year ÷ Inventory Turnover in Year	The average number of days that it took to sell the average inventory during the year. This statistic is only as good as the Inventory Turnover figure.
	= 365 days ÷ 12.67 28.81	
	=	

Debt-to-Equity Ratio

Financial Ratio	How to Calculate It	What It Tells You
Debt to Equity	= (Total liabilities ÷ Total Stockholders' Equity) : 1	The proportion of a company's assets supplied by the company's creditors versus the amount supplied the owner or stockholders. In this example the creditors have supplied $1.66 for each $1.00 supplied by the stockholders.
	= ($481,000 ÷ $289,000) : 1	
	= 1.66 : 1	

Ratios Based on the Income Statement

Financial Ratio	How to Calculate It	What It Tells You
Gross Margin	= Gross Profit ÷ Net Sales	Indicates the percentage of sales dollars available for expenses and profit after the cost of merchandise is deducted from sales. The gross margin varies between industries and often varies between companies within the same industry.
	= $120,000 ÷ $500,000	
	= 24.0%	
Profit Margin (after tax)	= Net Income after Tax ÷ Net Sales	Tells you the profit per sales dollar after all expenses are deducted from sales. This margin will vary between industries as well as between companies in the same industry.
	= $23,000 ÷ $500,000	
	= 4.6%	

Earnings Per Share (EPS)	=	Net Income after Tax ÷ *Weighted Average* Number of Common Shares Outstanding	Expresses the corporation's net income after taxes on a per-share of common stock basis. The computation requires the deduction of preferred dividends from the net income if a corporation has preferred stock. Also requires the weighted average number of shares of common stock during the period of the net income.
	=	$23,000 ÷ 100,000	
	=	$0.23	

Times Interest Earned	=	Earnings for the Year before Interest and Income Tax Expense ÷ Interest Expense for the Year	Indicates a company's ability to meet the interest payments on its debt. In the example the company is earning 3.3 times the amount it is required to pay its lenders for interest.
	=	$40,000 ÷ $12,000	
	=	3.3	
Return on Stockholders' Equity (after tax)	=	Net Income for the Year Taxes ÷ *Average* Stockholders' Equity during the Year	Reveals the percentage of profit after income taxes that the corporation earned on its *average common* stockholders' balances during the year. If a corporation has preferred stock, the preferred dividends must be deducted from the net income.
	=	$23,000 ÷ $278,000 (a computed average)	
	=	8.3%	

Free Cash Flow Ratio

Financial Ratio	How to Calculate It	What It Tells You
Free Cash Flow =	Cash Flow Provided by Operating Activities – Capital Expenditures	This statistic tells you how much cash is left over from operations after a company pays for its capital expenditures (additions to property, plant and equipment). There can be variations of this calculation. For example, some would only deduct capital expenditures to keep the present level of capacity. Others would also deduct dividends that are paid to stockholders, since they are assumed to be a requirement.
=	$25,000 – $28,000	
=	($3,000)	

CHECKLIST 14: TREND ANALYSIS

Introduction: In addition to using fiscal ratio analysis to compare one company with others in its peer group, ratio analysis is often used to compare the company's performance on certain measures over time. Trend analysis is the practice of collecting information and attempting to spot a pattern, or trend, in the information. This often involves comparing the same metric historically, by examining it either in tables or charts.

Trend analysis can be performed in different ways in finance. For example, in technical analysis the direction of prices of a particular company's public stock is calculated through the study of past market data, primarily price and volume. Fundamental analysis, on the other hand, relies not on sentiment measures (like technical analysis) but on fiscal statement analysis, often in the form of ratio analysis. Creditors and company managers also use ratio analysis as a form of trend analysis. For example, they may examine trends in liquidity or profitability over time.

What Is Trend Analysis?

Trend analysis is one of the tools for the analysis of the company's monetary statements for the investment purposes. Investors use this analysis tool a lot in order to determine the fiscal position of the business. In a trend analysis, the financial statements of the company are compared with each other for the several years after converting them in the percentage. In the trend analysis, the sales of each year from 2008 to 2011 will be converted into percentage form in order to compare them with each other.

Other Techniques

Apart from trend analysis, the investors also use other techniques for analysis purposes, and this helps them in achieving complete data and updated view on the company's current fiscal position.

Formula of Calculating Trends

In order to convert the fiscal results into percentages for comparison purposes, the percentages are calculated in the following way:

Trend analysis percentage

= (figure of the previous period – figure of the current period)

/total of both figures

The percentage can be found this way and if the current-year percentages were greater than previous year percentage, this would mean that current-year result is better than the prior-year result.

Trend analysis has the great advantage that it can also be used to predict the future events. This is possible by forecasting the future cash flow based on the data available of the past. With the help of trend analysis, you can predict the future and track the variances to add performance.

However, in management accountancy, the calculation of trends is based on the data of the past. This is favorable in deducing the current situation of the company and the increase in the fiscal position of the company and growth over the past years.

Apart from investments and fiscal data of the company, trend analysis can also be used effectively for projections. This allows a company to conduct market research and draw trends to forecast the demand of different products. This helps in marketing purposes, and a company can deduce results to select the right marketing approach to address various issues. Trend analysis can pretty much apply to all the techniques which require forecasting; therefore, it is a very useful tool in business.

Trend Analysis Example

If I want to see the trend of a company's revenues, net income, and number of clients during the years 2006 through 2013, trend analysis will present 2006 as the base year and the 2006 amounts will be restated to be 100. The amounts for the years 2007 through 2012 will be presented as the percentages of the 2006 amounts. In other words, each year's amounts will be divided by the 2006 amounts and the resulting percentage will be presented. For example, revenues for the years 2006 through 2012 might have been $31,691,000; $40,930,000; $50,704,000; $63,891,000; $79,341,000; $101,154,000; $120,200,000. These revenue amounts will be restated to be 100, 129, 160, 202, 250, 319, and 379.

Let's assume that the net income amounts divided by the 2006 amount ended up as 100, 147, 206, 253, 343, 467, and 423. The number of clients when divided by the base year amount is 100, 122, 149, 184, 229, 277, and 317.

From this trend analysis we can see that revenues in 2012 were 379% of the 2006 revenues, net income in 2012 was 467% of the 2006 net income, and the number of clients in 2012 was 317% of the number in 2006. Using the restated amounts from trend analysis makes it much easier to see how effective and efficient the company has been during the recent years. Trend analysis can also include the monitoring of a company's fiscal ratios over a period of many years.

Other disadvantages of this type of analysis are that if used alone it can present an overly simplistic view of the company by distilling a great deal of information into a single number or series of numbers. Also, changes in the information underlying ratios can hamper comparisons across time and inconsistencies within and across the industry can also complicate comparisons.

Horizontal Analysis

Horizontal analysis is a fiscal statement analysis technique that shows changes in the amounts of corresponding fiscal statement items over a period of time. It is a useful tool to evaluate trend situations.

Statements for two or more periods are used in horizontal analysis. The earliest period is usually used as the base period and the items on the statements for all later periods are compared with items on the statements of the base period. The changes are generally shown both in dollars and percentage.

Dollar and percentage changes are computed by using the following formulas:

1. Dollar change = Amount of the item in comparison year

   − Amount of the item in base year

2. Percentage change = $\dfrac{\text{Dollar change}}{\text{Amount of the item in base year}} \times 100$

Horizontal analysis may be conducted for balance sheet, income statement, schedules of current and fixed assets, and statement of retained earnings. In a horizontal analysis the changes in income statement and balance sheet items are computed (in dollars and percentage) and compared with the expected changes. For example, you start an advertising campaign and expect a 25% increase in sales. But if sales revenue increases by only 5%, then it needs to be investigated. Or if you find an unexpected increase in cost of goods sold or any operating expense, you can investigate and find the reason.

Trend Analysis Using Financial Ratios

One popular way of doing trend analysis is by using fiscal ratio analysis. If you calculate fiscal ratios for a business, you have to calculate at least two years of ratios in order for them to mean anything. Ratios are meaningless unless you have something to compare them to, in this case the previous year's data. For example, an important ratio is the Current Ratio, which is the ratio of current, or short-term, assets to current liabilities on your fiscal statement. Ideally, your ratio is higher than 1.0, which would mean that for every dollar of short-term liability you have a dollar of short-term assets. Short-term assets are cash, accounts receivable, inventory, and other highly liquid accounts. Short-term liabilities are those that are due in one year or less, such as accounts payable, and so on.

Trend analysis using fiscal ratios can be complicated by the fact that companies and accounting can change over time. For example, a company may change its business model so that it begins to operate in a new industry or it may change the end of its fiscal year or the way it accounts for inventories. When examining historical trends in ratios, analysts will often make adjustments to the ratios for these reasons, perhaps performing some ratio analysis in which they separate out business segments that are not consistent over time or they separate recurring from nonrecurring items.

Ratio analysis can be hampered by potential limitations with accounting and the data in the financial statements themselves. This can include errors as well as accounting mismanagement, which involves distorting the raw data used to derive fiscal ratios.

- Proponents of the stronger forms of the efficient-market hypothesis, technical analysts, and behavioral economists argue that fundamental analysis is limited as a stock valuation tool, all for their own distinct reasons.
- Ratio analysis can also omit important aspects of a firm's success, such as key intangibles like brand, relationships, skills, and culture. These are primary drivers of success over the longer term even though they are absent from conventional financial statements.
- Another disadvantage of this type of analysis is that if used alone, it can present an overly simplistic view of the company by distilling a great deal of information into a single number or series of numbers that may not provide adequate context or be comparable across time or industry.

Common Size Financial Statement Analysis

Common size fiscal statement analysis is analyzing the balance sheet and income statement using percentages. All income statement line items are stated as a percentage of sales. All balance sheet line items are stated as a percentage of total assets. For example, on the income statement, every line item is divided by sales and on the balance sheet every line item is divided by total assets. This type of analysis enables you to view the income statement and balance sheet in a percentage format which is easy to interpret.

If you look at the income statement, for example, you can develop a common size income statement. If you calculate the percentage that net income is of total sales, the formula is \$64,000/\$1,000,000 = 6.4%. You can apply that formula to every line item on the income statement to develop your common size income statement. As with fiscal ratio analysis, you can compare the common size income statement from one year to other years of data to see how your firm is doing. It is generally easier to make that comparison using percentages rather than absolute numbers.

Percentage Change Financial Statement Analysis

Percentage change fiscal statement analysis gets a little more complicated. When you use this form of analysis, you calculate growth rates for all income statement items and balance sheet accounts relative to a base year. This is a very powerful form of fiscal statement analysis. You can actually see how different income statement items and balance sheet accounts grew or declined relative to growth or declines in sales and total assets.

Here is an example of percentage change analysis. Let's say that XYZ Inc. has $500 in inventory on its balance sheet in 2011 and $700 in inventory on its balance sheet in 2013. How much has inventory grown in 2013? The formula to calculate the growth rate in inventory is the following: Change in inventory/Beginning inventory Balance = $200/$500 = 0.40 = 40%. The change in inventory for XYZ Inc. in 2012 is 40%.

Benchmarking

Benchmarking is also called industry analysis. Benchmarking involves comparing a company to other companies in the same industry in order to see how one company is doing fiscally compared to the industry. This type of analysis is very helpful to the fiscal manager as it helps to see if any fiscal adjustments need to be made.

Compiling, analyzing, and understanding financial statements provides business owners one of the most important tools for reducing the considerable risk involved in starting and growing a business. The comparison of fiscal ratios to industry standards is, perhaps, one of the best uses of fiscal information, as it allows the business owner to compare the performance of his or her business with other like businesses.

CHAPTER THIRTY SIX

Sample Policies for the Analysis and Reporting Process

 POLICY 5: BASIC POLICIES ON FINANCIAL REPORTING

<u>Introduction:</u> Financial reporting by the company provides information that is highly important for the company's shareholders and other stakeholders to verify the company's activities.

Ensuring of the reliability of the company's financial reporting is therefore conducive to the sustainment and enhancement of both shareholder and society's confidence in the company. Conversely, incorrect financial reporting may cause not only unexpected loss to a number of stakeholders, but also significant damage to confidence to the company's reputation. In order for the company, its parent, and subsidiaries to sustain and enhance both shareholder and society's confidence, the Basic Policies on Financial Reporting are required as follows.

Purpose of Financial Reporting

The purpose of financial reporting is to report the company's financial position and its results of operations on a consolidated basis to shareholders and other stakeholders in a timely and appropriate manner. A financial report refers to consolidated financial statements in principle. These basic policies must be observed not only by the company that is primarily responsible for the

271

preparation and submission of consolidated financial statements, but also by each of the company's consolidated subsidiaries and affiliates.

Confirmation by the Management

The company's management confirms his or her responsibility to report the accurate and timely financial position and its results of operations to shareholders and other stakeholders.

Ensuring Proper Financial Reporting

The company ensures that its financial statements are prepared in compliance with generally accepted accounting principles (GAAP) and the applicable international financial reporting standards (IFRS), and properly indicate the conditions of the company's financial position, results of operations, and cash flow to ensure proper financial reporting. Applicable project accounting and sound account settlement are crucial for ensuring reliable financial reporting.

Establishment and Assessment of Internal Control over Financial Reporting

With the aim of achieving proper financial reporting, the company establishes the internal control system according to internal control standards and Sarbanes Oxley requirements. To ensure that the status of the design and operations of internal control can be properly assessed, separate evaluations are conducted by an auditing division independent from the performance of business activities.

CHAPTER THIRTY SEVEN

Process Narratives for the Analysis and Reporting Process

 PROCESS NARRATIVE 7: DISCLOSURE CHECKLIST

Introduction: This process narrative defines some of the key process steps within the final phase of the record to report (R2R) process. Roles and responsibilities to ensure good segregation-of-duties controls are identified throughout this process narrative for the Disclosure Checklist.

Process Activity Description

1. **Disclosure Checklist:** The external report department completes the quarterly SEC filings and General Accounting provides certain information to external reporting to contribute to the finished product. On a quarterly basis, the external reporting department provides general accounting with a disclosure checklist for items or transactions that may require disclosure. Once the checklist is completed, the director of general accounting reviews the checklist and forwards to the VP of general accounting.
2. **Disclosure Templates:** External reporting also provides general accounting with various disclosure templates that include specific schedules that must be completed for inclusion in SEC filings. The schedules are completed by the relevant subject matter expert based on the information required by the template. The processes and controls around the completion of these templates are addressed in the package relevant to the specific template (debt, equity, cash flow, etc.).

Process Activity Description
3. **Quarterly Process:** On a quarterly basis, external reporting provides the VP of general accounting with a blank accounting disclosure checklist (the "Checklist") for the relevant quarter. The checklist identifies key types of transactions or other situations that may require disclosure in the 10K or 10Q reports.
4. **Answering Questions:** The VP of general accounting forwards the checklist to the directors of general accounting, who coordinate with general accounting managers to answer all questions required of the VP general accounting.
5. **Review:** The VP of general accounting performs a review of the checklist. If additional explanation or supporting documentation, such as a technical whitepaper, is required, such information is provided by the director of general accounting. If no additional information is necessary, then the VP of general accounting returns the completed checklist to external financial reporting.

PROCESS NARRATIVE 8: FLUCTUATION ANALYSIS

Introduction: This process narrative defines some of the key process steps in the final phase of the record to report (R2R) process. Roles and responsibilities to ensure good segregation-of-duties controls are identified throughout this process narrative for Fluctuation Analysis. The fluctuation amounts included are examples and should be defined by your company.

Process Activity Description
1. **Analysis Process:** The general accounting group performs a fluctuation analysis within one day of the GL close for the purpose of detecting unusual or significant fluctuations. Any unusual or significant fluctuations are researched and presented to upper management prior to the controller's review meeting. Management is responsible for determining whether the issue warrants an adjustment in the period under review. Significant fluctuations are defined as variances in excess of 10% over the prior period balance and over $500,000 in value.
2. **Focus of Analysis:** A designated accountant generates an account listing with month-over-month and quarter-over-quarter activity in the following subcategories listed in the Current Assets and Other Long-Term Assets section of the balance sheet, Other Current Assets, Marketable Securities Deposits, Investments, Notes Receivable, Deferred Customer Credits, Asset Disposal, and Other Long-Term Assets.
3. **Identification of Unusual Activity:** The accountant examines the report to ensure that all unusual and significant fluctuations in activity are identified and to ensure all accounts in the Current Assets and Other Long-Term Assets section of the balance sheet have been included in the report. Significant fluctuations are defined as variances in excess of 10% over the prior period balance and over $500,000 in value.

Process Activity Description

---

4. **Research:** If an account indicates an unusual or significant fluctuation, the accountant drills down to detailed activity and identifies the major component comprising the fluctuation. Significant fluctuations are defined as variances in excess of 10% over the prior-period balance and over $500,000 in value. The accountant researches the cause of the fluctuation with the reconciler of the account or other appropriate party.

5. **Documentation of Explanations:** The accountant documents the explanation for each significant account fluctuation and submits to the manager for review. Significant fluctuations are defined as variances in excess of 10% over the prior-period balance and over $500,000 in value.

6. **Manager Review:** The manager reviews the documentation to verify the accuracy and completeness of the fluctuation explanation and supporting documentation. If appropriate, the manager suggests corrective action. Management decides if it requires corrections to report. If the manager notes any issues with the documentation, the accountant addresses accordingly and resubmits for manager review and approval

If the manager approves the documentation, the documentation, along with any suggested adjusting entries, is submitted to the director prior to the controller's review meeting.

7. **Director Review:** The director reviews the fluctuation analysis. Director determines whether any issue should be addressed in the controller's review meeting and submits a summary variance analysis to the controller's close meeting.

8. **Post-Close Adjustment:** If there is a proposed post-close adjustment and the adjustment is significant, submit to the appropriate director for review and approval. For quarter-end or year-end close, a significant post-close adjustment is defined as an adjustment in excess of $500,000. If not a quarter-end or year-end close, only proposed post-close adjustments in excess of $5 million are presented at the controller's close meeting.

9. **Significant Post-Close Adjustments:** Proposed post-close adjustments which are significant are reviewed and approved by the director. The approval for posting to the closed period is determined at the controllers' close meeting by the corporate controller. For quarter-end or year-end close, a significant post-close adjustment is defined as an adjustment in excess of $500,000. If not a quarter-end or year-end close, only proposed post-close adjustments in excess of $5 million are presented at the controller's close meeting.

10. **Not Significant Post-Close Adjustments:** Proposed post-close adjustments that are not significant are posted in the subsequent period. For quarter-end or year-end close, a significant post-close adjustment is defined as an adjustment in excess of $500,000. If not a quarter-end or year-end close, only proposed post-close adjustments in excess of $5 million are presented at the controller's close meeting.

PROCESS NARRATIVE 9: CASH FLOW STATEMENT RECONCILIATION

<u>Introduction:</u> This process narrative defines some of the key process steps in the final phase of the record to report (R2R) process. Roles and responsibilities to ensure good segregation-of-duties controls are identified throughout this process narrative for Cash Flow Statement Reconciliation.

Process Activity Description

1. **Cash Flow Model:** The model starts with the balance sheet for the current period and the prior fiscal year-end. The model calculates a variance from the prior fiscal year-end. This variance is then investigated in order to put the current period activity in the appropriate section (operating, investing, or financing) of the cash flow statement. Once all balance sheet line items have been completed, the model has a check total to ensure that the activity captured equals the variance calculated. If the check total is not zero, the model is not complete and therefore the cash flow statement does not balance. The model also considers non-cash items. Once the model is complete, all the information is available in the model to prepare the statement of cash flows.

2. **Gathering Data:** Gather data from debt, investment, intangibles, capital leases, discontinued operations, equity, and PP&E templates provided by respective groups, along with income statements and balance sheets. IT controls that ensure that all information is properly captured by these systems are covered in the IT Controls package documentation to ensure that systems access controls are in place.

3. **Updating Data:** The balance sheets and P&L are updated into the cash flow statement model using formulas, and a variance over the prior period is calculated. IT controls that ensure that all information is properly captured by these systems are covered in the IT Controls package documentation to ensure that systems access controls are in place.

4. **Populating the Model:** After the model is populated, totals are reconciled to inputs provided.

5. **Activity and Variances:** The activity/variance for each balance sheet line item is determined using the templates provided. For line items where no template is provided, judgment is used to determine if the activity is:
   - Cash vs. non cash or;
   - A change in assets or liabilities and belongs in the operating section or;
   - An investing or financing activity.

6. **Non-Cash Transactions:** Analysis of the templates and financial statements is completed to determine if the activity initiating a change in the balance sheet is a non-cash transaction. If it is determined that the activity is a non-cash transaction, ascertain if the change in balance sheet is also a reconciling item to net income (depreciation and amortization, bad debt expense, realized gain/loss on sale of investment and property, etc.). If it is determined that the non-cash transaction is a reconciling item to net income, the amount is placed in the reconciliation to net income portion of the operating section of the model. If the activity is non-cash and not a reconciling item to net income, the journal entry is obtained and both sides of the transaction are placed in the non-cash portion of the operating section of the model.

Process Activity Description

7. **Completion of the Financing Section:** In completing the financing section, the equity template is used to determine the cash sources and uses for the period. This includes items such as proceeds from stock options exercised, or new issuance or redemption of securities. This activity is then placed in the appropriate section in the model. In completing the financing section, the debt and capital lease templates are also used to determine the cash sources and uses for the period. This includes items such as debt borrowing and repayments. This activity is then placed in the appropriate section in the model.

8. **Completion of the Investing Section:** In the investing section, the investment template is used to determine the cash sources and uses for the period. This includes items such as sale and purchases of investments. This activity is then placed in the appropriate section in the model. In the investing section, the PP&E template is also used to determine the cash sources and uses for the period. This includes items such as capital expenditures and disposition of assets. This activity is then placed in the appropriate section in the model. All gains and losses are tied out to the P&L.

9. **Analysis:** Analyze the model outcome to determine if the balance sheet line items reconcile for activities not included in the financing or investing sections. If there are reconciling items, research the model and template data and contact appropriate functional VPs and/or their staff to identify existence and justification for year-to-date changes in balance sheet accounts that are not related to financing or investing activities.

10. **Completing a Draft Cash Flow Statement:** Once data is accumulated, a draft cash flow statement is completed. Evaluate statement against FAS95 and other authoritative guidance to ensure that the statement draft meets disclosure requirements. Determine if all disclosure requirements have been met based on information that is currently available. If the statement does not meet disclosure requirements, or reasonableness, discuss discrepancies with management to resolve the discrepancy.

11. **Review Process:** General accounting and the director of general accounting review a draft cash flow statement and model for completeness and accuracy to determine if any changes required to model or statement. General accounting makes changes to model or statement and resubmits to the director for approval. The templates are pre-populated with prior period cash flow activity. The templates request current period cash flow activity. The director of general accounting reviews Cash Flow & Enhanced Cash Flow templates for completeness and accuracy.

PROCESS NARRATIVE 10: REPORTING DEBT

Introduction: This process narrative defines some of the key process steps in the final phase of the record to report (R2R) process. Roles and responsibilities to ensure good segregation-of-duties controls are identified throughout this process narrative for reporting debt. Fluctuation amounts are recommendations and should be defined by your company.

Process Activity Description

1. **Reconciliation Process:** The accountant is responsible for preparing the reconciliation analysis, including reconciling opening and closing balances, identifying issues, providing status of items being resolved, and providing supporting documentation required for adjustments. Additionally, account balance variance analysis is performed for each account. The analysis is designed to assist in identification of unusual or unexpected balances and activity that may indicate a specific risk of material misstatement or deficiencies in controls.

General Accounting performs monthly, quarterly, and annual account balance variance analysis, identifying and investigating significant fluctuations, providing explanations for significant fluctuations, and submitting explanations for review and approval. General Accounting ensures that the review and approval of the reconciliation effort is performed independently of the preparation. The manager reviews monthly, quarterly, and annual account reconciliations to determine accuracy of account balances and whether the company's liabilities are reasonably stated in the financials and are in accordance with GAAP and IFRS requirements.

2. **Debt Accounts:** The company notes are currently held in the three Long-Term Debt accounts above and reconciled on a monthly basis. One monthly entry is required to record accrued interest on the notes. A separate binder is maintained for each reconciliation.

3. **New Debt:** Treasury notifies general accounting of any new debt-related transaction (new debt issues, retirements, credit facilities, etc.). When the debt transaction is complete, Treasury forwards the supporting documentation to the accountant stating all terms of the debt transaction. This paperwork could include an indenture, contract, prospectus, and so on. If a new debt is issued, the accountant performs a preliminary account review.

4. **Accounting:** The accountant reviews the paperwork and determines the short-term versus long-term portion of the new debt in accordance with GAAP. The accountant reviews the paperwork and determines if the debt was issued at par or at a premium or discount in accordance with GAAP. The accountant reviews the paperwork and determines whether any derivatives exist by completing the company's FAS 133 Contract Review Sheet and consulting with the general accounting technical group.

Any derivatives identified are properly accounted for in accordance with SFAS 133. The accountant reviews the supporting documentation and paperwork to determine the amount of the deferred issue costs and verify that the issue costs are subject to deferral.

5. **Understanding the Account:** Obtain an in-depth understanding of the nature of the account, including the type of transactions that post to the account and the sources of the entries, by reviewing the supporting documentation. Document this information in the reconciliation folder. This process also serves to verify the account has been properly classified. Determine how the account is supported by reviewing the accompanying supporting documentation (indenture, contract, prospectus, etc.). Determine the (debit, credit, zero) balances expected for the account.

Process Activity Description

6. **Reviewing Supporting Documentation:** Determine the type and frequency of activity that should post to the account by reviewing the supporting documentation.

7. **Company Codes and Profit Centers:** Determine which company codes and profit centers are normally used for the account by reviewing associated support.

8. **Contact Information:** Obtain contact information from the treasury department by company code for those who are responsible for providing explanations/supporting documentation or are otherwise knowledgeable regarding the account.

9. **Debt Retirement:** Determine if the debt-related transactions under review represent a debt retirement. The accountant determines the amount of gain or loss on retirement.

10. **Accounting for New Debt:** The accountant reviews the paperwork and prepares amortization tables for new debt or revises the amortization table if necessary for other debt transactions (i.e. retirements). The amortization tables are used throughout the life of the debt to verify interest and debt entries. The accountant emails the amortization table to the treasury department for their review in order to verify the accuracy of the table (i.e. rates, dates, etc.). If no revisions are necessary, then the preliminary debt transaction review is complete.

11. **Preliminary Debt Review:** The accountant accumulates all documentation from the Preliminary Debt Transaction Review and forwards to management for review.

12. **Management Approval:** If management notes any issues or has questions with the documentation, the accountant addresses accordingly and resubmits for manager review and approval. Upon final approval by Management, all supporting documentation is filed in reconciliation binder.

13. **Additional Entries:** The accountant determines whether any additional entries are required for new debt issues or debt retirements based on Preliminary Debt Transaction Review above (i.e. record any premium/discount on new debt, record gain/loss on debt retirement).

14. **Journal Entries:** Upon approval, the accountant processes the journal entry or entries according to JE process. (See Process Narrative 1.)

15. **Debt Classification:** On a monthly basis, the accountant determines the portion of debt to be classified as short term versus long term in accordance with GAAP. Determination is made as to whether a reclassification entry is required. If necessary, a re-class entry is proposed to properly classify the debt balance as short term versus long term.

16. **Monthly Entries:** One entry is required each month to record accrued interest on the debt. The accountant prepares the monthly entry to record accrued interest on the debt using the amortization table previously prepared. While reconciling accrued interest account, the accountant verifies accrual calculation and reviews subsequent disbursements to true-up accrual to actual payment. After review by management, determine if corrections are necessary.

17. **Reconciliation:** The accountant compares the prior-period reconciliation's ending balances to current-period beginning balances to ensure there have been no changes since the last month's reconciliation process.

Process Activity Description

18. **Account Fluctuations:** To identify significant fluctuations early in the reconciliation process, the accountant performs month-over-month, quarter-over-quarter, and year-over-year account balance variance analysis. Significant fluctuations are defined as variances in excess of 10% over the prior-period balance and over $500,000 in value. Significant fluctuations are defined as variances in excess of 10% over the prior-period balance and over $500,000 in value. The accountant investigates significant fluctuations by obtaining supporting documentation from and/or the field contacts. The accountant prepares a report explaining the significant fluctuations and includes the report in the reconciliation binder for management review.

19. **Account Activity:** Determine if the monthly account activity posted to the account is inclusive of all account activity. This can be determined by comparing the account's prior months' activity run rates and verifying similar transactions previously recorded in the account continue to be recorded. This knowledge is acquired from reviewing prior reconciliations or other communications to the accountant. The accountant's review of account activity includes analysis of estimates of accruals, true-ups to actual payments, or any other dispositions of the accrual. If activity is missing, the accountant makes inquiries of the responsible parties to get an understanding of why the adjustments were not made and when the adjustments will be made.

20. **Reconciliation:** Reconciling items not requiring an adjusting entry (i.e. immaterial or timing differences) should be clearly identified. Supporting documents for all proposed adjustments and reconciling items should be placed in the reconciliation folder. The accountant prepares a reconciliation that shows line-item detail by transaction description. This reconciliation shows the beginning balance, the monthly activity, for all 12 months, classified by transaction description, vendor, etc., the resulting ending balance, reconciling Items, and the reconciled balance. Reconciling items are the transactions needed in the account to properly reflect the liabilities of the company.

21. **Account Information:** The accountant prepares a standardized Account Information/Reconciliation Form, which includes Account Description, Accounting Methodology, a listing of Account Contacts, a listing of Posting Sources and Reporting Information Sources, the Account's Normal Balance (Debit or Credit) and the Reconciliation Rating (Low, Medium, High) based on criteria by the company. The account rating is determined by the complexity of the account and the transaction level within the account.

22. **Account Adjustments:** If the general ledger is closed for the period being reconciled and the proposed adjustment is significant, submit to Director for review and approval. For quarter-end or year-end close, a significant post-close adjustment is defined as an adjustment in excess of $500,000. If not a quarter-end or year-end close, only proposed post-close adjustments in excess of $5 million are presented at the controller's close meeting.

Process Activity Description

23. **Post-Close Account Adjustments:** If the general ledger is closed for the period being reconciled, proposed adjustments that are significant are reviewed and approved by the director. The approval for posting to the closed period is determined at the controller's close meeting by the corporate controller and then the person authorized to initiate the journal entry process through the applicable ERP system is given special authorization to post such entries to the closed period.

For quarter-end or year-end close, a significant post-close adjustment is defined as an adjustment in excess of $500,000. If not a quarter-end or year-end close, only proposed post-close adjustments in excess of $5 million are presented at the controller's close meeting.

24. **Debt Roll-Forward Entry:** The accountant prepares a debt roll-forward report on a monthly basis. The monthly report is generated and lists debt by instrument, by account, and by company code. The accountant validates the accuracy of the debt roll-forward report balances by tracing the account balances back to the applicable ERP system.

25. **Debt Template:** The accountant prepares a debt template based on information from the debt roll-forward report. The template includes current versus long-term debt, letters of credit outstanding, significant issuances and retirements of debt, and discounts/premium amortization. General Accounting Liability Manager reviews the debt template for completeness and accuracy.

26. **Debt Covenant Actions:** General accounting is notified by the treasury debt management group of any debt covenant violations or other covenant-related transactions that could potentially impact the short- and long-term classification of debt. General accounting analyzes the information for proper classification and disclosure in accordance with GAAP.

27. **Review of Debt Roll-Forward:** The general accounting liability manager forwards debt roll-forward report, debt template, and covenant analysis to the director of general accounting. The manager approves the hardcopy to indicate approval and forwards soft copy to the director. The director of general accounting reviews and approves the debt roll-forward report, debt template, and covenant analysis. The director of general accounting forwards the completed debt template to the financial reporting group.

CHAPTER THIRTY EIGHT

Standards of Internal Control for the Analysis and Reporting Process

STANDARDS OF INTERNAL CONTROL 7: DISCLOSURE CHECKLIST

Introduction: These standards of internal controls define the control objectives, risks, control assertions, control activity title, and frequency to ensure that good controls are in place for the Disclosure Checklist process.

Control Objective	Risk	Control Assertion	Control Activity Title	Control Activity	Frequency
1. Ensure that external financial reporting is provided with accurate and complete data for purposes of disclosures in the 10Q or 10K submissions.	A material item or transaction requiring disclosure in the financial statements may be omitted.	Completeness valuation or allocation information and disclosure	VP Checklist Review	The VP of general accounting reviews accounting disclosure checklist and signs and dates the checklist denoting approval.	Quarterly

STANDARDS OF INTERNAL CONTROL 8: FLUCTUATION ANALYSIS

Introduction: These standards of internal controls define the control objectives, risks, control assertions, control activity title, and frequency to ensure that good controls are in place for the Fluctuation Analysis process.

Control Objective	Risk	Control Assertion	Control Activity Title	Control Activity	Frequency
1. Ensure that all unusual and material fluctuations are identified.	Unidentified material variances in account balances could represent errors or irregularities leading to misstatements if not adequately explained or supported.	Completeness Valuation or Allocation	Identify Material Fluctuations	The accountant examines the applicable reports to ensure that all unusual and significant fluctuations in activity are identified and to ensure all accounts in the Current Assets and Other Long-Term Assets section of the balance sheet have been included in the report.	Monthly
2. Review fluctuation report and supporting documentation to verify accuracy and completeness.	Fluctuation reports not adequately reviewed by management could result in misstatements.	Completeness Valuation or Allocation	Manager Review of Fluctuation Report	The manager reviews the documentation to verify the accuracy and completeness of the fluctuation explanation and supporting documentation. If the manager approves the report, it is submitted to the director for submission to the controller's close meeting.	Monthly
3. Review fluctuation report to verify accuracy and completeness and assess potential need for adjustment.	Unsupported variances that are not reviewed and could result in misstatements if potential adjustments are not considered.	Completeness Valuation or Allocation Presentation and Disclosure	Director Review of the Fluctuation Report	The director reviews the fluctuation analysis and determines whether any issue should be addressed in the controller's review meeting and submits a summary variance analysis to the controller's close meeting.	Monthly

Control Objective	Risk	Control Assertion	Control Activity Title	Control Activity	Frequency
4. Ensure significant proposed post-close entries are presented at controller's close meeting for posting in current period.	Significant adjustments will not be reflected in the proper period.	Completeness	Director Review of Significant Adjustments for Controller's Close Review and Meeting	If the general ledger is closed for the period being reconciled, proposed adjustments which are significant are reviewed and approved by the director. The approval for posting to the closed period is determined at the controller's close meeting by the corporate controller and then the person authorized to initiate the journal entry process through the applicable ERP system is given special authorization to post such entries to the closed period. For quarter-end or year-end close, a significant post-close adjustment is defined as an adjustment in excess of $500,000 or as defined. If not a quarter-end or year-end close, only proposed post-close adjustments in excess of $5 million are presented at the controller's close meeting.	Monthly

STANDARDS OF INTERNAL CONTROL 9: CASH FLOW STATEMENT RECONCILIATION

Introduction: These standards of internal controls define the control objectives, risks, control assertions, control activity title, and frequency to ensure that good controls are in place for the Cash Flow Statement Reconciliation process.

Control Objective	Risk	Control Assertion	Control Activity Title	Control Activity	Frequency
1. Ensure that figures manually entered into cash flow model reconcile to templates and financial statements.	The cash flow statement will not tie to other financial statements and/or classification of activity may not be correct.	Presentation and Disclosure	Cash Flow Report Preparation	Compare the cash flow model output to each of the inputs to ensure consistency and accuracy of manual inputs.	Quarterly
2. Validate that all cash activity has been included in the cash flow statement.	The statement will not reconcile to the ending cash balance.	Presentation and Disclosure	Cash Flow Report Preparation	The model used to create the cash flow statement has a check column that compares total change by line item to specific transactions accounted for. The check column is reviewed and any non-zero balances are investigated.	Quarterly
3. Ensure that cash flow statement meets relevant disclosure requirements in accordance with GAAP.	Disclosure requirements defined by GAAP and SEC regulations are not met.	Disclosure	Review Disclosure Checklist	Evaluate cash flow statement against disclosure checklist to make sure it is in accordance with reporting requirements.	Quarterly

Control Objective	Risk	Control Assertion	Control Activity Title	Control Activity	Frequency
4. Verify reasonableness of cash flow statement	The statement may contain errors.	Presentation and Disclosure	Analytical Review	Perform an analytical review of the statement to determine if the cash sources or uses make sense and fluctuations period over period are reasonable and agree to what was expected.	Quarterly
5. Ensure completeness and accuracy of the cash flow model and cash flow template.	The statement may contain errors.	Presentation and Disclosure	General Accounting Director Review	The cash flow statement is reviewed with the general accounting director for completeness and accuracy. Any adjustments to the presentation are discussed and implemented at this time.	Quarterly

STANDARDS OF INTERNAL CONTROL 10: REPORTING DEBT

<u>**Introduction:**</u> These standards of internal controls define the control objectives, risks, control assertions, control activity title, and frequency to ensure that good controls are in place for the Debt Reporting process.

Control Objective	Risk	Control Assertion	Control Activity Title	Control Activity	Frequency
1. Ensure all accounting and disclosure issues related to new debt issuances are identified.	Required disclosure items or accounting matters could be overlooked, resulting in inaccurate and/or incomplete quarterly and/or annual financial statements.	Existence or Occurrence Rights and Obligations Presentation and Disclosure Valuation or Allocation	Analysis of New Debt arrangements	Upon receipt of a new debt issuance from treasury, the accountant reviews the paperwork and supporting documentation to understand all terms and conditions of new or amended debt arrangements. Paperwork could include an indenture or loan agreement, contract, prospectus, etc. The accountant reviews to assess, among other things, the classification of the debt (current or non-current), whether the debt was issued at a premium or discount, whether there are derivatives embedded into the agreement, and whether there were debt issue costs included that need to be accounted for.	Transaction Based

Control Objective	Risk	Control Assertion	Control Activity Title	Control Activity	Frequency
2. Ensure that all account activity has been captured for analysis.	Inconsistent data reported by the different sources of data could result in errors requiring adjustment.	Completeness Valuation or Allocation	System Report Comparison	The account reviews the documentation and the applicable ERP system detail report for specific account and determines if all account activity has been captured in each report.	Monthly
3. Ensure all journal entries resulting from prior period reconciliation process were posted to correct account and no post-closing adjustments were made after completion of the prior-period reconciliation.	Incorrect posting of prior-period activity could result in unreconciled current-period beginning balances, resulting in errors requiring adjustment.	Completeness Valuation or Allocation	Prior Period Balance Confirmation	The accountant identifies the prior-period-ending account balance from the prior month's reconciliation binder and compares the amount to current-period beginning balance.	Monthly

Control Objective	Risk	Control Assertion	Control Activity Title	Control Activity	Frequency
4. Ensure significant fluctuations in account balances are identified and supported by relevant documentation.	Errors or irregularities resulting from large variances in account balances may not be detected or understood.	Valuation or Allocation Existence or Occurrence Rights and Obligations	Investigation of Significant Fluctuations	The accountant reviews account balance variance analysis for fluctuations exceeding established thresholds and obtains supporting documentation the applicable ERP system, and/or the field contacts related to such variances. The variance analysis along with the supporting documentation is filed in the standard reconciliation binder.	Monthly
5. Ensure that the recorded balance is complete and accurate and supported by appropriate documentation.	Inadequate supporting documentation for a transaction underlying an account balance could represent or result in an error or irregularity that goes undetected.	Existence or Occurrence Rights and Obligations Valuation or Allocation	Transaction Support Analysis	Accountant reviews supporting documentation, including schedules, invoices, agreements, etc. and verifies the information supports the journalized transaction amounts outlined in the activity query. Supporting documentation is referenced or placed in reconciliation binder.	Monthly

Control Objective	Risk	Control Assertion	Control Activity Title	Control Activity	Frequency
6. Ensure that the recorded balance is inclusive of all activity for the period.	Incomplete transactions may be recorded or transactions that have occurred during the period may not be recorded or may be recorded incorrectly.	Completeness	Transaction Analysis	Determine if the monthly account activity posted to the account is inclusive of all account activity. This can be determined by comparing the accounts prior months' activity run rates and verifying similar transactions previously recorded in the account continue to be recorded. This knowledge is acquired from reviewing prior reconciliations or other communications to the accountant. The accountant's review of account activity includes analysis of estimates of accruals, true-ups to actual payments, or any other dispositions of the accrual.	Monthly

Control Objective	Risk	Control Assertion	Control Activity Title	Control Activity	Frequency
7. Reconciliations are complete and accurate and prepared in a timely manner.	Errors or irregularities in an account balance may go undetected, unreconciled, or uncorrected, resulting in potential misstatements.	Completeness Existence or Occurrence Valuation or Allocation	Reconciliation Preparation	The accountant prepares a reconciliation which shows line item account detail by transaction description. This reconciliation includes the beginning account balance, the monthly activity, for all 12 months, classified by transaction description, vendor, etc., and the resulting ending balance. The schedule then discloses reconciling Items, which are the transactions needed to be recorded in the account to properly reflect the account balance at period end.	Monthly
8. Ensure that the recorded balance is complete and accurate and unusual trends are understood and addressed.	Errors or irregularities in an account balance may go undetected or unreconciled, resulting in potential misstatements.	Completeness/ Valuation or Allocation	Trend Analysis	The accountant reviews the reconciliation to identify long-term unusual trends, potentially missing transactions, or potentially undetected incorrect postings.	Monthly

Control Objective	Risk	Control Assertion	Control Activity Title	Control Activity	Frequency
9. Ensure significant proposed entries are presented to Controller's close for posting in current period.	Significant adjustments will not be reflected in the proper fiscal period.	Completeness	Director Review of Significant Adjustments for Controllers' Close	If the general ledger is closed for the period being reconciled, proposed adjustments which are significant are reviewed and approved by the director. The approval for posting to the closed period is determined at the controller's close meeting by the corporate controller and then the person authorized to initiate the journal entry process through the applicable ERP system is given special authorization to post such entries to the closed period. For quarter-end or year-end close, a significant post-close adjustment is defined as an adjustment in excess of $500,000 or as defined. If not a quarter-end or year-end close, only proposed post-close adjustments in excess of $5 million or as defined presented at the controller's close meeting. All limits are reviewed periodically by management.	Monthly

Control Objective	Risk	Control Assertion	Control Activity Title	Control Activity	Frequency
10. Management is provided with adequate timely and accurate information to enable them to discharge their responsibility.	Errors or irregularities in an account balance may go undetected, unreconciled, or uncorrected, which can result in potential misstatements.	Completeness Existence or Occurrence Rights and Obligations Valuation or Allocation Presentation and Disclosure	Manager Review and Approval of Reconciliation	Manager performs a review of the reconciliation folder. Review entails the following: 1. Verify accuracy of accruals, account trending. 2. Verify accurate classification (long term vs. current). 3. Review account reconciliation detail—do schedules foot and tie, are reconciling items disclosed and supported, are JEs proposed, are variances explained adequately? 4. Review and approve any journal entries. Completion of manager review is evidenced by comments provided of folder and if applicable, manager signoff on the account reconciliation.	Monthly

Control Objective	Risk	Control Assertion	Control Activity Title	Control Activity	Frequency
11. Reconciliations are complete and accurate and prepared in a timely manner.	Errors or irregularities in an account balance may go undetected, unreconciled, or uncorrected, which can result in potential misstatements.	Completeness Valuation or Allocation	Monitor/ update Resolution of Reconciling Items	Update as items are cleared to show that outstanding items have been resolved and sign off on the account reconciliation.	Non-Routine
12. Ensure that debt is properly presented and disclosed in financial statements.	New debt transactions are not properly recorded in the financial statements.	Presentation & Disclosure	Review and Approve Financial Statement Disclosures for Debt	The director of general accounting reviews and approves the debt roll-forward report, debt template, and covenant analysis.	Quarterly
13. Ensure that new debt transactions are properly recorded in financial statements.	Errors or irregularities in financial statements. Disclosures may go undetected, unreconciled, or uncorrected, which can result in potential misstatements.	Valuation or Allocation	Review and Approve Initial Evaluation and Accounting for New Debt Transactions	The director of general accounting reviews and approves the preliminary debt transaction review for new debt transactions.	Quarterly

CHAPTER THIRTY NINE

The Virtual Close: Myth or Reality?

NTRODUCTION: THE VIRTUAL CLOSE was once looked upon as the "holy grail" of finance efficiency. The expected benefits were substantial—faster results for decision makers and a less painful and cumbersome process for the finance and accounting staff.

Then along came SOX, IFRS, and XBRL. The new regulations added back some manual steps to the closing process. As a result, the virtual close became a low priority, and by the time the financial crisis hit in 2008, the virtual close was no longer on the corporate radar screen. Now that companies have embedded the new regulatory requirements into their corporate DNA, a tighter close process is getting more attention. Companies are now prioritizing the need for a faster, higher-quality close, with the goal of getting accurate, comprehensible information about the business to decision makers as quickly as possible.

WHAT IS THE VIRTUAL CLOSE?

A virtual close involves the use of fully integrated company-wide accounting systems to produce financial statements at any time, on demand. This approach requires not only enterprise resources planning (ERP) systems, but also a great deal of effort to ensure that the underlying information is correct. The required investment is so large that you rarely see a virtual close in smaller companies. The virtual close requires attention to the following areas:

- **Centralized accounting:** It is nearly impossible to achieve a virtual close without a great deal of accounting centralization combined with ERP software. Conversely, that means you cannot have accounting operations scattered throughout the business.
- **Standardized accounting:** Business transactions must be defined and treated the same way everywhere. Otherwise, the accounting staff must spend time investigating transaction irregularities throughout the business.
- **Error tracking:** Any errors found must be tracked down and their underlying causes eliminated. Otherwise, there are too many problems with the virtual close financial statements to place much reliance on them.

The results of a virtual close may not be completely accurate, since some expense accruals, cost allocations, and reserves are difficult to automate.

HOW IS THE VIRTUAL CLOSE DIFFERENT FROM THE SOFT CLOSE?

A virtual close differs from a soft close in that the soft close requires a limited number of closing steps; and because of those closing steps, the soft close is usually only used at month-end. Since a virtual close is essentially automated, there are no closing steps, which allows you to run financial statements for any time period at all; thus, daily financial statements are possible.

CASE STUDY: THE VIRTUAL CLOSE AT CISCO

In many companies, days, weeks, or even months can go by between the time a sale is made or an expense generated and the time the finance department provides an accurate report of these events to management. As a result, executives, salespeople, and production managers have to make important day-to-day decisions without an up-to-date, concrete understanding of the business's status. In effect, employees have to act in the dark.

Cisco set out to radically accelerate their financial reporting process. The lack of reliable and up-to-date fiscal information was a real hindrance. It took

14 days to close the books, and until then the company couldn't be sure exactly where operations stood or whether the organization was on track to hit revenue and profit goals. Cisco's decision makers needed more than quarterly reports; they needed daily fiscal insight.

So the finance group set some aggressive goals: Cisco would generate consolidated financial statements in one day, cut finance costs in half, and transform the way finance supported the company's decision makers. Cisco wanted to move from being a gatekeeper of information to being a catalyst for change throughout the organization.

After five years of refining the company's accounting processes, honing the quality of data collected, and dramatically increasing the speed of its distribution, the finance group was able to achieve the "virtual close." As a result, Cisco could literally close their books within hours, producing consolidated financial statements on the first workday following the end of any monthly, quarterly, or annual reporting period. More important, the decision makers who need to achieve sales targets, manage expenses, and make daily tactical operating decisions now have real-time access to detailed operating data.

While it's difficult to find a single, standard definition for "virtual close," it's generally described as an organization's ability to close its books and provide performance results in real-time, or at least near-real-time. Having this information should enable management to make more rapid yet informed decisions, providing a competitive advantage.

Certainly, the benefits of having real-time access to a company's performance results appear compelling. And to be sure, executives still strive to streamline their processes. Yet the desire over the past decade to close the company's books almost instantaneously, once a reporting period is over, appears to have virtually abated.

One reason is the implosion of Enron in late 2001, followed by the revelation of accounting debacles at WorldCom and Adelphi in 2002. These bankruptcies, all of which involved some sort of fiscal malfeasance, were catalysts in the creation of the Sarbanes Oxley Act of 2002.

In early 2001, Larry Carter, then CFO with Cisco Systems Inc., wrote in the *Harvard Business Review*[i] about the company's success achieving the so-called virtual close. "We can literally close our books within hours, producing consolidated financial statements on the first workday following the end of any monthly, quarterly, or annual reporting period. More important,

---

[i] Karen Kroll, "Why the 'Virtual Close' Virtually Died," CIO.com. Accessed on May 9, 2019. https://www.cio.com/article/2403445/why-the--virtual-close--virtually-died.html.

the decision makers who need to achieve sales targets, manage expenses, and make daily tactical operating decisions now have real-time access to detailed operating data."

But for companies in the new environment of external and internal scrutiny that resulted, "The focus became 'get the numbers right,'" says Beth Kaplan, director of finance transformation services with Deloitte & Touche LLP. That's not to suggest that supporters of the virtual close advocated speed at the expense of accuracy. However, Corporate America wasn't in a mood for taking chances. "No one wanted misstatements or jail time," Kaplan adds.[ii]

Achieving the virtual close was not just a matter of rolling out new technology. It required a sustained, companywide effort to redesign processes and align disparate parts of the business. Every month, finance meticulously reviewed the closing process to pinpoint opportunities for improvement. Cisco established quality standards—and metrics—for all data-collection activities. For example, the company standardized the definition of bookings and backlogs, thereby avoiding disputes among the sales, manufacturing, and accounting departments about order status. The company consolidated responsibilities for accounts payable and purchasing—most finance groups split these tasks—which boosted productivity and cut down on errors. Cisco eliminated practices that yielded little fiscal gain for the required effort, such as capitalizing assets valued at less than $5,000. Through such steps, the company reduced the number of transactions that their systems and employees had to monitor.

Finance also worked closely with all of Cisco's divisions to give employees real-time access to crucial business metrics such as orders, discounts, revenues, product margins, and staffing expenses. The company developed Internet applications and other mechanisms to ensure that all operating and fiscal data were reported consistently, avoiding the time-consuming task of reconciling the numbers. By 1998, the company had globally consistent information available online for Cisco's decision makers. Today, Cisco updates their bookings, revenues, and product margins by the minute.

These tools and data have been invaluable in helping Cisco manage its rapid growth. Executives can constantly analyze performance at all levels of the organization. Regional sales managers can compare their performance with forecasts. Business heads and hiring managers can evaluate whether their staffing budgets will allow them to accelerate or decelerate hiring during any given week.

[ii] Ibid.

Additionally, Cisco shares fiscal data with outside suppliers; daily information about our product backlog, product margins, and lead times triggers decisions throughout the supply chain. Suppliers use the information to order inventory, adjust manufacturing capacity, and anticipate shipment volumes. They can, for example, review sales forecasts for a particular product and plan their inventory accordingly.

 ## IMPLEMENTING A VIRTUAL CLOSE

When implementing a virtual close, consider eight implementation advisories that support the implementation of a virtual close.

Eight Implementation Advisories:

1. **Use integrated financial systems.** Integrated financial systems—ideally within a single ERP suite—are the groundwork for real-time posting of expenses, revenues, and cash. This will reduce the need to balance huge batch-interface files on a periodic basis.

2. **Minimize the number of financial ERP systems.** Fewer sets of books on fewer ERP systems will speed the closing processes. This will reduce the amount of information that accounting needs to be harmonized and consolidated during the fiscal close.

3. **Standardize on best practices and common charts of accounts (COAs).** Common business processes and COAs will help accounting consolidate information more easily. Maintain more detailed COAs at the business-unit level and simple COAs for consolidation at corporate. **Key Point:** Business units often have data in their COA that is important to their own operations but not germane to that of other business units.

4. **Close operational systems before month-end.** Closing operational systems in advance of month-end close will expedite accrual processes and enable accounting to focus on the fiscal ledgers.

5. **Deploy operational data stores.** On a frequent and regular basis, use a data warehouse approach or data stores approach to accumulate and book results from core operational systems into accounting systems.

6. **Minimize accounting data in the core general ledger.** Limit certain account code segments to sub-ledgers and management ledgers. *Advantage:* When account dimensions or account segments in the account code decrease, there are fewer code fields that departments need to validate. To eliminate detailed project-costing codes from the general ledger, deploy

project-accounting systems that accumulate and analyze project results outside the general ledger.

7. **Use cloud-based reporting.** With cloud-based systems, accounting can push results to the line managers. Such reporting can provide current results, including flash reporting, as well as data for balanced scorecards, through the Web.

8. **Leverage consolidation tools.** These (FRx, Hyperion, and so on) consolidate detailed ledgers from multiple ERP systems into a single, summary ledger. At the same time, they eliminate intercompany activity and create standard journal entries for statutory reporting. Many organizations still perform consolidations offline, adding days to the closing process.

According to E&Y, consolidation can make the reporting process more complicated and can introduce stringent timelines for many organizations. An effective and consistent reporting process requires a reliable database. This is often achieved by using dedicated consolidation and reporting software. This software allows for an automated process, a reliable audit trail, and a protected database. But it can be costly in terms of time and resources. Some smaller organizations may consolidate using spreadsheets. Examples of consolidation tools are: Oracle, NetSuite, Sage Intacct, Multiview, Adaptive, Insights, Budget Maestro, and the applicable ERP system ERP Core Finance.

CHAPTER FORTY

Roadmap: Benefits of the Fast Close

NTRODUCTION: THERE ARE NUMEROUS benefits to achieving a fast fiscal close, which will vary based on the perspective of the recipient. Those who will benefit from the results of a fast close include: company management, investors, auditors, and the accounting department. The benefits are significant, as listed below:

Benefits of the Fast Close

---

1. **Quicker access to fiscal information:** Company management generally feels that the primary benefit of the fast close is having access to fiscal information more quickly, allowing it to take rapid steps to improve a company's strategic and tactical position in the marketplace.
2. **Marketing tool:** A company's marketing staff can use the rapid issuance of fiscal information to "spin" the company's openness to the investing public. This does not necessarily mean that the company will issue sterling fiscal results, only that it will issue results faster. Still, it implies some level of expertise on the part of the accounting department in processing transactions and compiling them into reports, and so may impart some level of comfort to investors in that regard.
3. **More time for financial analysis:** Closing the books fast does not necessarily mean that one must issue financial statements sooner. An alternative is to spend additional time analyzing the preliminary financial statements in order to issue more complete notes alongside the fiscals at a later date.

Benefits of the Fast Close

---

4. **Improved processes and accurate results:** Because the fast close improvement process requires careful attention to process enhancement, there will inevitably be side benefit improvements to many accounting processes, leading to heightened efficiency and fewer errors. Within the accounting department, this may be seen as the top benefit of the fast close.

5. **Improved control systems:** Internal and external auditors appreciate the enhanced attention to control systems needed to ensure that information is compiled properly and fast.

6. **More time to analyze fiscal results and address any potential issues:** Although some aspects of the fast close simply push activities into the period either before or after the core closing period, some actions are completely eliminated or at least reduced in size.

 ## DIFFERENT TYPES OF FAST FISCAL CLOSING PROCESSES

Several variations on the fast close concept have appeared, causing some confusion about the nature of each one. The fast close is simply an acceleration of the standard closing process, resulting in approximately the same financial reporting package being issued (possibly somewhat stripped down).

The focus of this approach is a careful examination of the closing process to strip out wait times, consolidate tasks, eliminate unnecessary functions, add transaction best practices, and selectively apply automation where necessary.

 ## SOFT CLOSE

The "soft close" is less labor intensive than a regular close, because it does not generate as much information. It is designed solely for internal corporate use, so its end product is only those management reports needed to run operations. With this reduced reporting goal in mind, the accounting staff can eliminate the use of overhead allocations. It may also be possible to stop some accruals and ignore the elimination of intercompany transactions, depending on the level of reporting detail desired. The soft close is most commonly seen in companies that issue only quarterly or annual reports to outside entities, leaving all other months available for the soft close.

VIRTUAL CLOSE

The "virtual close" involves the use of a largely automated accounting system—one that can produce required fiscal information at any time, on demand. This approach is rarely used, and only in the largest companies that can afford to install an Enterprise Resources Planning (ERP) system. The underlying transactions that feed into the ERP system must be essentially error free, so an accurate virtual close is really the result of a hefty software investment as well as years of continual process improvements.

The financial reports resulting from a virtual close tend to be stripped-down versions of generally accepted accounting principles—GAAP-compliant reports—because this approach avoids the need for such manual tasks as overhead allocation, accrual transactions, and the establishment of various reserves. If achieved, a virtual close can be useful in fast-moving industries where fiscal results must be monitored frequently in order to make rapid-fire changes to a company's tactical or strategic direction, or at least to identify problem areas for fast management attention.

LEGAL ISSUES IMPACTING THE FAST FINANCIAL CLOSE

The Sarbanes Oxley Act has made it more difficult to achieve a fast close. The problem is Sections 302 and 404 of the Act, which require formal management certification of the accuracy of the financial statements. Section 302 requires that the financial statements of publicly held companies not contain any materially false statements or material omissions or be considered misleading. Understandably, those signing this certification want to spend more time ensuring that the financial statements are indeed correct.

Finally, the Securities and Exchange Commission (SEC) has accelerated its requirement for the timely filing of quarterly and annual reports by publicly held companies. The rule change calls for a three-year decline in the reporting period, to 60 days for annual reports and to 35 days for quarterly reports (down from 90 days and 45 days, respectively). This rule applies to domestic companies having a public float of at least $75 million and that have previously filed at least one annual report.

STEPS TO ACHIEVE A FASTER FINANCIAL CLOSE

Several steps are required to achieve a faster close, which are outlined below. They are listed in the following recommended order of implementation:

Step 1. Reviewing the Closing Process

The first step in achieving a fast close is to examine the current state of the closing process and determine the time required to complete each functional area (i.e. inventory, billing, payroll, payables, and cash processing, as well as final closing activities). It is useful to summarize the results of this investigation into a timeline that can be used to spot which segments of the closing process are particularly in need of improvement.

Step 2. Altering the Timing of Closing Activities

A set of changes that are easy to implement and yet have a startling positive impact on the duration of the close is to shift many of the closing activities either into the preceding month or into the period immediately following the issuance of financial statements.

Step 3. Revising the Contents of the Financial Statements

The close will take less time if there is less information to report. There are several variations on this concept, such as eliminating custom reports entirely, shifting to electronic modes of report delivery, and reporting some operating or metric information separately from the financial statements.

Step 4. Optimizing the Use of Journal Entries and Chart of Accounts

Journal entries require excessive amounts of time, may be entered incorrectly, and do not always contribute to the accuracy of the financial statements. Thus, standardizing journal entries, eliminating inconsequential ones, and automating them can be of considerable assistance. Also, using a common chart of accounts or at least the development of mapping tables will reduce the labor associated with consolidating results reported by subsidiaries.

Step 5. Standardization and Centralization

If a company has multiple locations, the closing process will be nearly impossible to improve unless the controller pays considerable attention to the standardization of accounting transactions so that they are completed in exactly the same way in all locations. Even greater closing improvements can be attained by centralizing accounting functions for the entire company in a single location or shared services organization.

Step 6. Closing the Inventory Function

The topic of inventory makes many controllers shudder, because a combination of poor controls and large investments in this area makes the cost of goods sold an extremely difficult area to calculate, leading to massive time requirements during the closing process. This problem can be reduced by implementing tight inventory tracking and cycle counting systems, as well as by adopting better materials management policies to reduce the overall level of inventory investment.

Step 7. Closing the Billing Function

Generating period-end invoices may be the bottleneck operation during the close. This problem can be reduced by shifting recurring invoices and the rebilling of expenses out of the closing period, electronically linking the shipping database to the accounting department and ensuring fast completion of billable hours reporting.

Step 8. Closing the Payroll Function

The payroll function principally interferes with the closing process because employees are often late in recording their billable hours. This issue can be resolved through the use of automated time clocks and web-based time recording systems. There are also several ways to streamline the commission calculation process so it takes much less time during the core closing period.

Step 9. Closing the Accounts Payable Function

Waiting for late supplier invoices to arrive, as well as pushing those invoices through a Byzantine approval process, can seriously interfere with the month-end close. There are several approaches for streamlining the basic approval process while the intelligent use of expense accruals, coupled with the purchase order database, can eliminate the wait for late invoices.

Step 10. Closing the Cash Processing Function

Some controllers like to wait until the bank statement arrives in the mail before issuing financial statements, so that they can first conduct bank reconciliation. The postal float on the bank statement can be two or three days, which directly delays the issuance of financial statements. This can be avoided through the use of online bank reconciliations while several techniques are available for improving the speed of processing incoming checks.

Step 11. Incorporating Automation into the Closing Process

There are several ways to use automation to improve the closing process, ranging from a series of small efficiency-related improvements to workflow management software, a data warehouse, consolidation software, and an ERP system.

Step 12. Ongoing Improvements in the Closing Process

Although the preceding action items may have achieved a considerable improvement in the speed of the close, there is always room for improvement. Consequently, constant attention to the process flow and measurement of key metrics and trends will ensure that the fast close remains fast and accurate.

 CONCLUSION

Although the soft close and virtual close are available as alternatives to the fast close, most companies need to issue a complete set of financial statements every month, which precludes the soft close. The virtual close requires considerable resources to achieve, and so is also not an option in most cases. Consequently, the focus is on the standard fast close, which presents considerable benefits to the implementing company.

Achieving a faster month-end closing is a process improvement project that requires the full attention of the accounting staff for a long period of time. Before committing to such a project, one should be clear about what type of fiscal close works best for a company's specific needs, what kinds of benefits will result, and the general steps required for completing the close.

CHAPTER FORTY ONE

Accelerating the Close with Automation

INTRODUCTION: NO MATTER THE size of your organization, the monthly fiscal close can be a daunting effort. It often requires hundreds or thousands of tasks executed by scores of people working across the enterprise. And it's inherently a fire drill and a new adventure every month.

Even if they automate some parts of the fiscal close process, organizations still must perform time-consuming double-checking and rework, with the potential for error growing each time someone touches the data. The fiscal close is a reality that all organizations must deal with. While automation has helped in parts of the process, modern solutions that enable end-to-end management can allow finance departments to make huge steps in accelerating the close.

KEY REQUIREMENTS FOR AUTOMATING THE FISCAL CLOSE

When automating your fiscal close process, determine if the alternative will achieve the following requirements when selecting a solution.

- Reduces the cycle times of individual close tasks
- Adds visibility and predictability to close processes

- Ensures trust and reliability that the numbers are complete and accurate
- Increases collaboration
- Improves the consistency and quality of the fiscal close
- Delivers modern best practice out-of-the-box
- Addresses the extended close process comprehensively
- Provides solutions that are integrated, connected, secure, and auditable

KEY QUESTIONS TO ASK DURING IMPLEMENTATION

- How valuable would it be to structure account numbers in your chart of accounts differently than your current system allows?
- Does your current system allow you to easily modify screens to fit your business needs?
- Does your current software allow you to quickly access information online, tracking, for example, a transaction back to the original source with easy-to-use audit trails?
- How easily will your system be able to expand to accommodate your company's future growth?
- Does your system's architecture allow you to integrate new technologies without changes to existing software?
- How easily does your current system allow you to access data from a diverse range of sources without sacrificing data integrity?
- Do you have business partners who need access to financial information, such as customer purchase histories, but lack access to the current systems?
- How concerned are you about the safety and security of your company's information?

SYSTEM EASE OF USE

- How much training time do employees require to learn to operate your current accounting and performance-measurement system?
- How often do your employees need to re-input or upload data when transferring accounting information from one application to another?

- How well does your current system allow you to prepare supplier invoices automatically and efficiently?
- How well does your current system allow you to manage inventory costs and data?
- How valuable would a company-wide automated purchase-order system be?
- How easily can you export information to provide reports, analytics, metrics, and dashboards?
- Does your software enable you to perform detailed project accounting analysis?

QUALITY OF FINANCIAL INFORMATION

- How would you rate the quality of the day-to-day operating information you receive from your current system? Is the data accurate? Are additional reconciliations needed to validate financial data?
- Does your current system provide instant access to sales information and trends?
- Does your current system permit easy development of customized reports for communicating with your business partners?
- How long after the close does it take to complete financial results and reports?
- How manageable do users find your chart of accounts?
- How manageable is your forecasting and budgeting processes?
- How easily are you able to compare your budgets to actual performance without re-keying budget and actual information? Are you using additional systems or spreadsheets to perform this comparison?
- How easily can you restrict access to certain accounts based on the user's role or position in your company to ensure system access and segregation of duties controls?
- How many hours per week do you spend searching for information about a transaction?
- How easily does your current system allow you to view the profitability of particular product or service?
- How well can your system track complex customer orders with line items details and status?

ACCOUNTS PAYABLE AND PURCHASING

- How well does your current system reduce the administrative work associated with managing intercompany payables and receivables?
- How efficiently does your current system allow you to process accounts payable payments and analyze supplier spending?
- How much would automatic three-way matching help with the accounts payable process?

 ## PROJECT ACCOUNTING

- How tightly is your project-tracking and management system integrated with your accounting system?
- Does your current software make it easy to track expenses related to time and materials invested in projects?
- How easy is it for employees to submit time and/or expense reports for services your company provides to clients?
- How closely is your customer billing system integrated with your project-tracking system?
- How effectively does your current software allow you to perform cost analysis of cross-departmental projects and complex deliverables?
- How effectively does your current software allow you to forecast and budget for projects and track results?

Addendum: Fast Close Tools and Additional Best Practices

CONTINGENCY PLANNING

Introduction: The concern of not being able to "close the books" and prepare fiscal results in the event of a disaster or system failure is a significant risk. Having a well-defined set of SOPs with clearly defined roles and responsibilities is a great starting point for a company's contingency planning process.

The business continuity plan is used by organizations of all sizes to detail how business will continue if a disaster or emergency occurs. The business continuity plan documents all business operational functions by department, company, employee, and supplier information, inventory, emergency procedures, and post-disaster plan.

The objective of disaster recovery and business continuity planning for computer systems and telecommunications is to ensure the continuance of the company's applications in the event of unanticipated computer processing disruptions such as operational failures or site disasters that destroy or prevent access to the computer or telecommunications equipment, data, and software.

When developing a business continuity plan for the fiscal close, the planning process should encompass the steps that are needed if a disruption in business or a disaster occurs. The plan should consider both the closing process and IT impacts.

The recovery plan is not intended to duplicate a normal business environment, but is intended to minimize the potential loss of assets, lessen the impact on customers, and keep the company in business. Through decisive action, which is based on advanced planning, business disruptions and losses can be minimized.

The only applications that management may choose to exempt from this standard are those that can be reproduced from other existing information, are not input to a critical application, or would incur more expense from following these standards than the application's worth to the company in the event of destruction by a disaster.

Additionally, applications that are critical to the successful operation of the company should be prioritized and acceptable downtime should be determined when establishing business continuity plans.

Business Continuity versus Disaster Recovery (Definitions)

Critical Application: A critical business application is one that the company must have to support major revenue activities, movement of goods to customers (particularly those that can spoil or that are time-critical for the customer), a strategic manufacturing process, or to fulfill contractual or regulatory obligations. In addition, the application's availability is deemed by management to be vital to the continued functioning of company business. Examples of critical applications are: customer service support, order entry, inventory control, manufacturing resource planning, purchasing, warehouse control, quality assurance, and fiscal systems.

Disaster: A loss of computing or telecommunications resources to the extent that routine recovery measures cannot restore normal service levels within 24 hours, which impacts the company's business significantly.

Disaster Recovery: The restoration of computing and telecommunication services following an outage resulting from a disaster. Disaster recovery is a small subset of business continuity. It is also sometimes confused with work area recovery (due to loss of the physical building in which the business is conducted), which is but a part of business continuity.

Vital Business Assessment: A process required to determine what business functions and supporting applications are critical for the company to continue to conduct business in the event of a disaster.

Business Continuity Plan: The prearranged plans and procedures that critical business functions will execute to ensure business continues relatively unscathed until computer and telecommunications facilities are reestablished following a disaster.

Business Continuity Checklists

Introduction: The business continuity planning process should encompass the steps that are needed if a disruption in business or a disaster occurs. The plan should consider the business process and IT impacts as well as the applications that are maintained in the cloud.

Business Continuity Process Checklist

1. **Document internal key personnel with backups.** These are key employees who are integral to the function of your business processes. A controller should identify the key employees by each business process. It's important to identify backups.
   - Consider which job functions are critically necessary every day. Think about who fills those positions when the primary job-holder is on vacation.
   - Make a list of all those individuals with all contact information, including business phone, home phone, cell phone, pager, business email, personal email, and any other possible way of contacting them in an emergency situation where normal communications might be unavailable.
2. **Identify who can telecommute.** Some people in your company might be perfectly capable of conducting business from a home office.
3. **Document external contacts.** If you have critical suppliers, contractors, or consultants, build a special contact list that includes a description of the company (or individual) and any other absolutely critical information about them, including key personnel contact information. Include in your list people like attorneys, bankers, IT consultants, and solution providers. This list should include anyone whom you might need to call to assist with various operational issues.
4. **Document critical equipment and access to ERP Systems.** Determine if a copy machine and FAX are necessary if ERP access is not possible. **Identify critical files and documents.** These include articles of incorporation, fiscal key supplier contracts, utility bills, banking information, critical HR documents, building lease papers, and tax returns.
5. **Identify your contingency location.** This is the place you will conduct business while your primary offices are unavailable. Depending on the situation it could be a hotel or telecommuting may be a viable option.
6. **Make a "how-to."** It should include step-by-step instructions on what to do, who should do it, and how. Your organization's policies and procedures are critical. Public companies can use Sarbanes Oxley documentation. Ensure that business processes are assigned to a "lead" person as suggested in step 1. Key processes should be prioritized.
7. **Put the information together.** A business continuity plan is useless if all the components are scattered all over the company. Each key business process should have an electronic folder (and backup) with all the key information. If necessary, the contents of the folder can be printed.
8. **Communicate.** Make sure everyone in your company is familiar with the business continuity plan. Hold mandatory training classes for each and every employee. Schedule refreshers periodically.
9. **Test the plan.** All business continuity plans should be tested to make sure all the key components have been identified and the plan can be executed. Schedule refreshers of tests of the plan periodically.
10. **Plan to update the plan.** No matter how good your plan is, and no matter how smoothly your test runs, it is likely there will be events outside your plan.
11. **Review and revise.** Every time something changes, update all copies of your business continuity plan and initiate the business continuity plan communication process again. With all the changes in technology, it's important to ensure that the plan is never outdated.
12. **Consider next steps.** Consider the next steps for recovery and identify what needs to happen to bring the organization, region, country, or division back online.

Information Technology (IT) Considerations

IT business continuity plans provide step-by-step procedures for recovering disrupted systems and networks. The goal of this process is to minimize any negative impacts to company operations. The IT business continuity process identifies critical IT systems and networks; prioritizes their recovery time objective; and delineates the steps needed to restart, reconfigure, and recover them. A comprehensive IT business continuity plan also includes all the relevant supplier contacts, sources of expertise for recovering disrupted systems, and a logical sequence of action steps to take for a smooth recovery.

According to National Institute for Standards and Technology (NIST) Special Toolkit 800-34, "Contingency Planning for Information Technology Systems" (accessed **April 1, 2019)**, the following summarizes the ideal structure for an IT disaster recovery plan:

Ideal Structure for an IT Disaster Recovery Plan

---

1. **Develop the business contingency planning policy statement.** A formal policy provides the authority and guidance necessary to develop an effective contingency plan.
2. **Conduct the business impact analysis (BIA).** The business impact analysis helps to identify and prioritize critical IT systems and components.
3. **Identify preventive controls.** These are measures that reduce the effects of system disruptions and can increase system availability and reduce contingency lifecycle costs.
4. **Develop recovery strategies.** Thorough recovery strategies ensure that the system can be recovered quickly and effectively following a disruption.
5. **Develop an IT contingency plan.** The contingency plan should contain detailed guidance and procedures for restoring a damaged system.
6. **Plan testing, training, and exercising.** Testing the plan identifies planning gaps, whereas training prepares recovery personnel for plan activation; both activities improve plan effectiveness and overall agency preparedness.
7. **Plan maintenance.** The plan should be a living document that is updated regularly to remain current with system enhancements.

Developing the IT Business Continuity Plan

Introduction: The table below provides the process steps for developing an IT business continuity plan and can be used throughout the planning process.

Developing the IT Business Continuity Plan

---

1. **Gather all relevant network infrastructure documents** (e.g. network diagrams, equipment configurations, databases).
2. **Obtain copies of existing IT, application listings, and network plans.** If these do not exist, proceed with the following steps. **Note:** Ensure that software as a service (SaaS) or cloud applications are also included in your continuity plan.
3. **Identify what management perceives as the most serious threats** to the IT infrastructure (e.g. fire, human error, loss of power, system failure).
4. **Identify what management perceives as the most serious vulnerabilities** to the infrastructure (e.g. lack of backup power, out-of-date copies of databases).
5. **Review previous history of outages and disruptions and how the firm handled them.**
6. **Identify what management perceives as the most critical IT assets.**
7. **Determine the maximum outage time management can accept if the identified IT assets are unavailable.**
8. **Identify the operational procedures currently used to respond to critical outages.**
9. **Determine when these procedures were last tested to validate their appropriateness.**
10. **Identify emergency response team(s)** for all critical IT infrastructure disruptions; determine their level of training with critical systems, especially in emergencies.
11. **Identify supplier emergency response capabilities.** If they have ever been used; if they were, did they work properly; how much the company is paying for these services; status of service contract; presence of service level agreement (SLA) and if it is used.
12. **Compile results from all assessments into a gap analysis report** that identifies what is currently done versus what ought to be done, with recommendations as to how to achieve the required level of preparedness, and estimated investment required.
13. **Have management review the report and agree on recommended actions.**
14. **Prepare IT disaster recovery plan(s) to address critical IT systems and networks.**
15. **Conduct tests of plans and system recovery assets to validate their operation.**
16. **Update plan documentation to reflect changes.**
17. **Schedule next review/audit of IT business continuity plan capabilities.**

Roles and Responsibilities

First Data has identified the following roles and responsibilities for their Business Continuity Process. As additional background, First Data has six million merchants, the largest in the payments industry. The company handles 45% of all U.S. credit and debit transactions, including handling prepaid gift card processing for many U.S. brands such as Starbucks. It processes around 2,800 transactions per second and $2.2 trillion in card transactions annually and is a good representation to consider for the payments process.

Oversight and Governance

Management: Enterprise Business Continuity is managed by a firm-wide Business Continuity Steering Committee with representation from all major business units at First Data. Compliance with Enterprise Business Continuity program requirements for all business units are tracked with metrics monitored and escalated on a monthly basis.

Audits and Regulation: The Enterprise Business Continuity program is subject to internal and external audit reviews and regulated by the Federal Banking Agency, which includes five banking regulators: the Federal Reserve Board of Governors, the Federal Deposit Insurance Corporation, the National Credit Union Administration, the Office of the Comptroller of the Currency, and the Consumer Financial Protection Bureau. The program is also subject to the legal and regulatory requirements of other countries in which our companies operate.

Business Resiliency

Objectives: The objectives of Business Resiliency include the development of recovery strategies in order to minimize loss to First Data and its clients, continue to serve our customers, ensure the safety of employees, and minimize negative impacts of events. Each First Data business unit is responsible to complete a Business Impact Analysis (BIA) to determine the Recovery Time Objective of the business on an annual basis. The Recovery Time Objective allows First Data to prioritize key businesses for recovery during and after any type of incident.

Responsibility: Each business unit is also responsible to develop and maintain Resiliency Plans on an annual basis. Plans can be used independently or together if the incident affects multiple business units. Each plan includes key elements such as life safety, required resources, equipment, applications, and recovery strategies, including recovery site information and recovery tasks. All plans address high-absenteeism, including pandemic and severe weather events.

Testing: Business Resiliency Plans are required to be tested on a regular basis to ensure an effective program. The firm has a varied testing program, including the testing of recovery solutions such as working from another location (move and resume), working from home, and work load transfer. Our test types include tabletop exercises, simulation exercises, and full disaster recovery tests. Post-exercise reports are created for each event. All testing issues as well as Business Impact Analysis and Business Resiliency Plan compliance are tracked and metrics are provided to senior management.

Disaster Recovery

Focus: Disaster Recovery focuses on restoring the firm's critical systems and applications used by our internal businesses and external clients. Application recovery is prioritized based on the Recovery Time Objective identified in the Business Impact Analysis. First Data maintains Disaster Recovery Procedures for key systems and applications, which provides detailed plans to recover the system or application. These procedures span key personnel, components, and applications that are necessary to minimize the impact to vital business processes following a data center outage.

Team: The Disaster Recovery team manages and coordinates recovery activities and rigorous exercises to demonstrate the firm's ability to recover. Key systems and applications are tested on a regular basis. Follow-up reports are generated and reviewed with all exercise participants and all issues identified are recorded in the firm's risk management tool and tracked through resolution.

Monthly Metrics: Monthly metrics are used to track all Disaster Recovery requirements, including the maintenance of the company's plans and testing of the company's systems and applications. The metrics are socialized to First Data's senior management, which provide a snapshot on the health of the Disaster Recovery Program.

Disaster Recovery and Cloud Providers

Niel Nickolaisen, chief technology officer at O.C. Tanner Company, provides the following considerations for developing a disaster recovery plan with cloud providers. O.C. Tanner Company, an employee recognition company, develops strategic employee recognition and reward solutions that help people to accomplish and appreciate great work for Fortune 100 companies internationally. It offers cloud-based technology, tools, awards, and education services in the areas of social appreciation, performance recognition, service awards, custom awards, event awards, world-class training, and corporate wellbeing. The company's solutions enable companies to create and maintain inspiring cultures and engaging workplaces through employee recognition.

1. **The provider must stratify the services provided into different categories**. Some services are so mission critical that they require redundancy. Other applications are mission critical but require recovery rather than redundancy. Any cloud provider needs to know and design for these differences.
2. **The cloud provider must have the ability to test recovery from a disaster.** Even if the corporate chooses not to do such tests internally, there should be evidence that a provider has done it for others. This evidence should be available.
3. **The cloud provider must demonstrate no single points of failure.** The provider should have a recovery process which is the equivalent of backing up onto the same server. And as a recommended best practice, the provider should follow the same checklists used for the corporate.
4. **The cloud provider must be fiscally viable.**

Metrics for Business Continuity Planning

- Percentage of Downtime
- Number of Days to Recovery
- Frequency of Business Continuity Plan Tests Performed
- Service Level Agreement (SLA) Performance
- Operational Level Agreement (OLA) Performance
- Date of Last Plan Update
- Cloud Computing Plans Reviewed/Obtained

BEST PRACTICE 30: ESTABLISH ESCALATION PROCEDURES

Introduction: Escalation procedures are usually used in conjunction with a closing checklist and establish the criteria for: (1) the types of issues to be escalated, (2) the time frames for escalation, and (3) the materiality or significance the issues that are to be escalated.

A good escalation procedure establishes a roadmap for the types of issues that should be reported to the proper level of management for quicker resolution and action. A well-defined process can also help with accelerating the closing process since the finance and accounting staff doesn't wait until the last minute to report a problem.

However, a poorly defined escalation process may result in the finance and accounting staff reporting too many issues and taking time away from the management team and impacts the cycle time for a faster close. Additional, the executive finance management team may be confronted with problems that lower levels should be able to deal with themselves. This is where cross-training the staff responsible for tasks during the closing process is a critical step.

ROADMAP: 25 STEPS TO SHORTEN THE FISCAL CLOSE

Introduction: This roadmap provides 25 steps that can be implemented to shorten the fiscal closing process.

Roadmap: 25 Steps to Shorten the Fiscal Close

1. **Document Close Practices**
   - Involve the whole organization in understanding the goals and schedule for the fiscal close using checklists, project plans, and good communication. Ensure that roles and responsibilities are documented and well-communicated.
2. **Identify Routine Work and Move It Out of the Closing Crunch**
   - Identify routine work and move it out of the closing crunch. Move recurring allocations and accruals out of the closing process. This alleviates the task of posting journal entries during the close and adding additional tasks to the process.
   - Streamline recurring journal entries by using templates which can easily be updated. These templates can import their data into your accounting system.
3. **Complete Standard Allocations in Advance of Close**
   - Use a standard allocation system with a true-up when something goes out of the established tolerance. This approach moves the standard allocation process out of the fiscal close and can speed up cycle time.
4. **Create Templates for Recurring Reports**
   - Use standardized closing packages for all of your subsidiaries. The subsidiaries use standard templates to reconcile material accounts, which facilitates a more efficient management review.
   - Use standard templates for recurring reports. This makes month-end closing much faster since it streamlines the reporting process. Report writers can streamline and make reports consistent and substantially reduce data entry and the need for reconciliations.
   - Standardizing your management reporting process can result in greater efficiencies in reporting. Potential issues are easily highlighted and surprises during the fiscal close are avoided.

Roadmap: 25 Steps to Shorten the Fiscal Close

5. **Use Accruals and Estimates to Shorten the Close**
   - Using a "not invoiced and not received" report, which is based on purchase orders. This approach supports the accrual process since companies are better able to accrue for all received product and services using accurate data.
   - Many companies use estimates for accruals based on analyzing trends. Some companies use reporting tools and systems to track and record repetitive accruals.
   - Build an understanding of the business so that estimated results can be used during the fiscal closing process.

6. **Cross-Train the Accounting Staff**
   - Cross-training and documentation of all fiscal closing processes can be very beneficial, especially when there is the unexpected absence of a critical associate.

7. **Minimize and Automate Journal Entries During the Closing Process**
   - Automate the journal entry process with a spreadsheet or solution that interfaces to the ERP system.
   - Make greater use of importing tools to upload information into the accounting system. This minimizes duplicate data entry and adds accuracy to the process.
   - To minimize manual data entry during the close, urge staff to have accounts payable invoices entered in a more timely and accurate manner or use electronic invoicing solutions. Some solutions provide purchase order "flip" functionality in which invoices can be directly linked to a purchase order and automatically uploaded to an ERP system.
   - Only use an entry upload process as opposed to performing manual entries. This saves time and accommodates additional reviews to validate accuracy.

8. **Reduce Investigation Levels in a Soft Close Environment**
   - Transition from a monthly hard close to soft monthly closes and quarterly hard closes. This change allows companies to reduce investigation levels and rely on accruals and estimates during the soft close process.

9. **Pare Down Content of Reports**
   - Companies often produce reports with the same data multiple ways and retain all copies. Use one database so that users can create their own reports from standard information.
   - Consider the audiences for your reports and create executive-level reports that have the ability to drill down to obtain additional information.
   - Ask how you can improve the reporting process and implement the suggestions provided.
   - Always provide comments and action plans when producing reports.

10. **Move Routine Inter-Company Accounting Issues Out of the Close**
    - Set a limit for the review of intercompany charges. As an example, move inter-company charges of less than $10,000 out of the close period.

11. **Input All Recurring Journal Entries at One Time**
    - The use of recurring entries and estimates can streamline the fiscal close process.

Roadmap: 25 Steps to Shorten the Fiscal Close

---

12. **Manage the Fiscal Close Like a Project and Establish Clear Accountability for Closing Tasks in a Closing Schedule and Enforce Deadlines**
    - Implement a closing checklist indicating + or – days from the period-end to complete tasks. With a close schedule, all parties impacting the close know the timing of what they have to do. Immediate communication of deviations from the schedule helps keep the close process on track. For planning and communication purposes, many companies establish their closing schedules one year in advance.
    - Use and communicate clear schedules so everyone understands what is expected. Keep a tight closing schedule with all business partners and staff participating in the process.
    - Establish clear accountability for closing tasks and a closing schedule and have frequent communication throughout the closing process to ensure the results of the closing process are timely and accurate as with any key project.
    - The closing process can be a large portion of accounting manager's annual performance objectives, adding additional focus and accountability.
    - Implement a schedule for posting closing entries with duties assigned to specific individuals. Ensure that everyone knows the deadlines and what is needed to meet the deadlines. The schedule should be maintained on the company's network and is updated by the responsible person as tasks are completed, enabling management to review the status of the closing process throughout the cycle and take action in a timely manner.
    - Implement and use a standard closing checklist, closing calendar, and journal-entry responsibility checklist (ad hoc, monthly, quarterly, and specific month). These processes can improve the speed, accuracy, and completeness of the close.
    - During the close, have daily meetings at the end of each day with the auditors. This allows them to tell management what items they see as a roadblock.
13. **Assign Responsibility for Resolving Discrepancies**
    - Train new staff on how to research and resolve discrepancies using current process documentation and checklists.
    - Use timely identification of operating issues and discrepancies in addressing profit/loss.
14. **Develop Partnerships Across Departments to Resolve Recurring Cross-Functional Issues**
    - Following each close, an "Obstacles to Close" or "Postmortem" report is distributed across the organization. This report provides visibility of cross-functional issues and identifies areas for process improvement.
    - Establish cross-departmental communication and support during the fiscal close. By establishing partnerships across departments, many companies were able to set earlier deadlines for information coming from other departments.
15. **Develop and Monitor Close Performance Metrics**
    - Implement and monitor closing metrics as suggested in this toolkit. Gathering the metrics and publishing that information can lead to changes in behavior and supports adherence to deadlines, bottlenecks, and critical paths.
    - Establishing a metrics and monitoring process can highlight and reduce errors during the fiscal close.

Roadmap: 25 Steps to Shorten the Fiscal Close

---

16. **Continuously Improve Closing Processes**
    - By constantly looking at ways to improve the fiscal process, the process can become less cumbersome and easier to manage. As an example, accounting for month-to-month variances in freight costs by assigning the responsibility for identifying and calculating un-invoiced costs to the purchasing agent can help to avoid surprises and speed up the closing process.
    - Continuously improving the closing processes allows companies to prepare accurate financial statements in a timely manner, reduce error rates, and audit findings.
    - Keep track of process improvements recommended and develop a project plan and implementation schedule. Group the process improvements by area such as fiscal close processes, accounting systems, and policies and procedures.

17. **Establish a Closing Date**
    - Establish a closing date by which all expenses and revenue must be posted. Communicate the closing date to everyone who has access to modify the ledger. Close the books for the fiscal period as of the date communicated, prohibiting any further changes to the ledger during the fiscal close.

18. **Use a Trial Balance Report**
    - Start the closing cycle with a trial balance report. Review the balances to identify any anomalies from what is expected. Review the transaction details for any accounts you are uncertain of and note any adjustments that need to be made.

19. **Use Adjusting Entries**
    - Create the adjusting entries to recognize prepaid expenses, accrue outstanding invoices, relieve accruals that have been paid, and recognize depreciation and other amortizations. Post adjusting entries to correct the current balance of any ledger account that reflects expense postings in error.

20. **Utilize an Adjusted Trial Balance Report**
    - Generate an adjusted trial balance report to review the final balances in the ledger. Verify that the trial balance matches on the debit and credit side. Verify that the balances are accurate, checking the account activity if needed. Trial balances will vary from the initial report due to the adjusting entries. This helps you identify any entries that posted incorrectly.

21. **Use Expense Reporting**
    - Create a report to show the final expense activity for the period and year-to-date. Include documentation of the balance sheet, income statement, and depreciation schedules.
    - Save copies of the entire journal entries posted along with the documentation supporting their necessity for audit purposes.

22. **Develop and Implement Financial Closing Strategies**
    - Two overlapping strategies are often at work when organizations have fast monthly, quarterly, and annual accounting closes. These strategies are:
    - **Invest in robust information technology systems.** Companies that follow this strategy have enterprise resource planning (ERP) and business process management systems in place. Then, these businesses share information across a single and unified accounting and fiscal system that features standardized datasets and processes and centralized consolidations.

Roadmap: 25 Steps to Shorten the Fiscal Close

- **Implement best practices.** Managers reorganize processes or tweak procedures inside the accounting and finance function so that their staffs produce accounting information in ways that are faster, smarter, better, and cheaper. With this approach, the operative dynamic is continuous improvement, with managers regularly monitoring and adjusting each component of a close so that efficiency and value rise.

23. **Consider Procedural Best Practices**
    - Use accruals to shorten the close.
    - Create templates for recurring reports.
    - Reduce investigation levels.
    - Minimize journal entries during the closing process.
    - Eliminate or minimize manual data-entry.

24. **Management Best Practices**
    - Establish clear and regular close communication.
    - Develop and monitor close performance metrics.
    - Continuously improve closing processes.
    - Assign responsibility for resolving discrepancies by an established timeline.

25. **Review Unused Accounts in the General Ledger and Minimize Accounting Data**
    - While unused accounts do not necessarily slow the close, they can create the opportunity for fraud, as well as endow financial reports with needless precision. At the same time, a graveyard of unused accounts can be aggravating to senior executives, who often prefer flash reports or quick summaries of business drivers or key developments for their monthly closing signoffs.
    - Minimize accounting data in the core general ledger by limiting code segments to sub-ledgers. This is a somewhat-overlooked opportunity to improve the close process, since keeping the general ledger relatively simple accelerates data rollups, as well as pushes problem resolution into payables, receivables, and other departments that are closer to transactions.
    - Companies can simplify transaction and accounting codes. Such simplification is a small but important change, since it does accelerate data input and speed up the consolidation process.

THE MONTHLY FINANCIAL CLOSE PROCESS CHECKLIST

Introduction: This checklist is a general guide for the fiscal close process checklist and can be modified for use by all types of organizations. As a best practice, many organizations use a checklist to ensure that all the components of the close are properly assigned and occur on schedule. The checklist is a great place to start to determine if there are opportunities to simplify your close by reducing the number of process steps.

AREA/TASK	RESPONSIBILITY	DATE DUE	COMPLETED	REVIEWED
GENERAL CLOSE PROCEDURES				
Controller administers closing instructions on a regular basis to appropriate departments or entities.				
To ensure duplicate journal entries are not posted:				
1. All journal entries made to the GL module are subject to the signature of the Finance Team Lead.				
2. All journal entries made to the GL are assigned a unique Account Reference Number and Batch Number. Note these numbers on the journal entry form.				
The Finance Team Lead reviews the Trial Balance Report and ties the totals to the appropriate Balance Sheet or Income Statement Line Item.				
Periodically validate that the financial system blocks a journal entry if the journal entry does not balance.				
Periodically validate that closing journal entries are blocked from being entered into the books for previous periods. Previous periods in the financial system should be locked to prevent changes.				
CASH				
Obtain bank statements for all accounts.				
Perform reconciliation between bank statement and G/L for all cash accounts.				
Review outstanding checklist for any long outstanding checks. Determine resolution/disposition.				
Review all reconciling items:				
1. Prepare lead schedule.				
2. Prepare list of bank accounts and trading securities for year-end audit confirmation process.				
3. Determine if any cash is considered restricted and/or a compensating balance for appropriate financial statement presentation and footnote disclosure.				

AREA/TASK	RESPONSIBILITY	DATE DUE	COMPLETED	REVIEWED
INVESTMENTS				
Evaluate all investments for proper accounting with reference to SFAS No. 115, and current accounting rules in regard to accounting for equity investments. Update Controller's *investment memo* on a quarterly basis. (See also, Equity Investments below.)				
ACCOUNTS RECEIVABLE				
ACCOUNT ANALYSIS:				
Obtain detail of A/R balances by accounting personnel.				
Reconcile ending A/R balance on *sub-ledger* to G/L.				
Review all reconciling items:				
1. Prepare lead schedule.				
ROLL-FORWARD OF ACCOUNT:				
Prepare roll-forward of A/R activity.				
COLLECTIBILITY REVIEW:				
Create an aged A/R detail. Show A/R in following buckets: 0-30 days, 31-60 days, 61-90 days, and 91+ days. Review long outstanding balances.				
Perform collectibility review of all A/R balances through discussion with relevant parties. Document results of discussion. Determine if any balances require reserves.				

AREA/TASK	RESPONSIBILITY	DATE DUE	COMPLETED	REVIEWED
INVESTMENTS				
ALLOWANCE FOR BAD DEBTS:				
Prepare account analysis showing bad debt allowance.				
Prepare roll-forward of Allowance for Bad Debts account.				
Reconcile beginning balance to G/L and to prior-period financial statement.				
Reconcile Bad Debt Expense to Income Statement.				
Reconcile write-offs to actual write-offs recorded during the period.				
Reconcile ending balance to G/L.				
PREPAID EXPENSES				
Obtain supporting documentation for all additions to Prepaid Assets during the period.				
Ensure amounts are properly classified as Prepaid Assets.				
Prepare account analysis/reconciliation of Prepaid Assets account.				
Review all reconciling items (if any):				
1. Review all asset items for proper classification of short-term vs. long-term.				
OTHER CURRENT ASSETS				
Prepare account analysis of Other Current Assets account.				
Prepare roll-forward of Other Current Assets activity.				
Review all reconciling items (if any):				
Review all asset items for proper classification of short-term vs. long-term.				

AREA/TASK	RESPONSIBILITY	DATE DUE	COMPLETED	REVIEWED
FIXED ASSETS				
ADDITIONS:				
Review new Fixed Asset purchases during period. Obtain related invoices. Ensure invoices have been approved by the responsible budget holder.				
Journal entries related to Fixed Asset disposals are approved by the Finance Team Leader and are supported by appropriate detailed documentation.				
Reconcile additions in roll-forward to detail of purchases during period.				
Ensure all items added to Fixed Assets are properly capitalized.				
Reconcile non-cash acquisitions to Capital Lease or other area(s).				
DISPOSALS:				
Journal entries related to Fixed Asset additions are approved by the Finance Team Leader and are supported by appropriate detailed documentation.				
Tie disposals in roll-forward to detail of assets disposed of during period.				
Ensure journal entries were recorded correctly to remove asset and accumulated depreciation.				
Determine gain or loss recognized on disposals.				
ACCOUNT ANALYSIS:				
Update roll-forward of Fixed Asset by category.				
Agree to fixed assets sub-ledger.				
FOOTNOTE DISCLOSURE:				
Prepare footnote disclosure to show asset classes and related balances.				

AREA/TASK	RESPONSIBILITY	DATE DUE	COMPLETED	REVIEWED
ACCUMULATED DEPRECIATION AND AMORTIZATION				
ACCOUNT ANALYSIS:				
Perform monthly calculation of depreciation expense. Book related entries.				
Prepare roll-forward of accumulated depreciation and amortization accounts.				
ASSETS UNDER CAPITAL LEASE:				
Ensure that assets under Capital Lease are being amortized appropriately.				
FOOTNOTE DISCLOSURE:				
Prepare footnote disclosure to show accumulated depreciation balances as of period-end as well as current period depreciation expense.				
OTHER ASSETS				
Prepare reconciliation of Other Assets account.				
Review all reconciling items (if any):				
1. Review all asset items for proper classification of short-term vs. long-term.				

AREA/TASK	RESPONSIBILITY	DATE DUE	COMPLETED	REVIEWED
GOODWILL				
SFAS No. 142 ANALYSIS:				
Perform annual (or more frequent, if necessary) assessment for impairment.				
ACCOUNT ANALYSIS:				
Discuss with management as to any changes in Goodwill during period.				
Prepare roll-forward of Goodwill account activity.				
Obtain supporting documentation for changes to Goodwill during the period.				
Prepare lead schedule.				
INTANGIBLE ASSETS				
SFAS No. 141 ANALYSIS:				
Perform quarterly assessment for impairment.				
ACCOUNT ANALYSIS:				
Prepare roll-forward of Intangible Asset account activity.				
Obtain supporting documentation for changes to Intangible Assets during the period.				
Prepare lead schedule.				
AMORTIZATION:				
Perform monthly calculation of amortization expense. Book related entries.				

AREA/TASK	RESPONSIBILITY	DATE DUE	COMPLETED	REVIEWED
ACCOUNTS PAYABLE				
CUTOFF:				
Perform A/P cutoff—Three days before period-end.				
ACCOUNT ANALYSIS:				
Obtain A/P sub-ledger detail.				
Reconcile A/P sub-ledger to G/L.				
ACCRUED EXPENSES				
CUTOFF:				
Contact relevant process owners to request information regarding required period-end accruals.				
Contact vendors for outstanding/unbilled amounts as of period-end—External Auditors, Legal, Consultants, Recruiting firms, etc.				
ACCOUNT ANALYSIS:				
Prepare reconciliation of Accrued Expenses accounts. Prepare sub-reconciliations as necessary.				
Document all reconciling items.				
Review all liability items for proper classification of short-term vs. long-term.				

AREA/TASK	RESPONSIBILITY	DATE DUE	COMPLETED	REVIEWED
CAPITAL LEASE OBLIGATION				
SFAS No. 13 ANALYSIS:				
Obtain copies of all new leases entered into during period.				
Perform analysis using SFAS No. 13 criteria.				
Ensure leases are properly accounted for under SFAS No. 13 - capital vs. operating.				
ACCOUNT ANALYSIS:				
Prepare and record journal entries to properly reflect cap lease activity.				
Update roll-forward schedule of Capital Lease Obligation liability.				
Ensure that obligations recorded relate to assets still under ownership.				
Determine proper classification of Capital Lease Obligation as short-term vs. long-term.				
Prepare lead schedule.				
FOOTNOTE DISCLOSURE:				
Prepare footnote disclosure for future commitments.				
OTHER CURRENT LIABILITIES				
Prepare roll-forward of Other Current Liabilities activity.				
Review all reconciling items (if any):				
1. Review all items for proper classification of short-term vs. long-term.				
EQUITY				
Prepare roll-forward of Equity accounts:				
1. Reconcile Net Income in Retained Earnings roll-forward to Income Statement.				
2. Obtain support for all changes in Equity accounts.				

FOREIGN CORRUPT PRACTICES ACT (FCPA)

Introduction: The Foreign Corrupt Practices Act (FCPA) adds a new level of anti-bribery controls to the closing process for global organizations. Under the FCPA's Anti-Bribery Provision, it's unlawful to make a corrupt payment to a foreign official (or political party, political official, or candidate for political office) for the purpose of obtaining business, retaining business, or directing business to any person.

This includes ordering, authorizing, or assisting others to violate or conspire to violate these provisions. This applies not only to a successful corrupt payment—the offer or promise of such payment can also cause violation. Under the Accounting Provision, corporations must make and keep books and records that accurately and fairly reflect the transactions of the corporation. Corporations must devise and maintain an adequate system of internal accounting controls.

The following set of questions can be used to evaluation your risk of potential FCPA violations. It may not necessarily be a key component of your fiscal close, but you may want to review specific disbursement accounts, such as accounts payable, T&E, and payroll, that have large international transactions that are outside the norm. This set of questions can help ensure your company's fiscal results are correct.

Risk Questions	Exposed?
1. Is your company buying or selling products or services internationally?	Yes
2. Are there any suspicions of FCPA violations by company personnel or third-party agents acting on the company's behalf within any of the countries where business is conducted internationally?	Yes
3. Do employees or third-party agents acting on the company's behalf come into contact with foreign officials (for example, customs agents, business licensing officials, government employees, and local political officials)?	Yes
4. Are bribes, entertaining, and gift-giving historically and culturally acceptable in the countries where your company does business?	Yes
5. Are contracts to provide goods or services to foreign governments or state-owned entities a source of revenue for your company?	Yes
6. Have employees who are directly or indirectly responsible for international operations been trained on FCPA issues? Do such employees represent via written confirmation their understanding of and compliance with FCPA policies?	No
7. Does your company have an established, well communicated anti-corruption policy that *specifically addresses* FCPA concerns?	No

Risk Questions	Exposed?
8. Are procedures in place for periodic monitoring of employee and third-party agent compliance with FCPA or anti-bribery laws?	No
9. Does your company use third-party agents, consultants, intermediaries, or distributors when performing business overseas?	Yes
10. Does your company have a robust due diligence process to scrutinize third parties securing international contracts on your company's behalf?	No
11. Is your company doing business in a high-risk FCPA industry such as aerospace and defense, telecommunications, oil, pharmaceuticals, or manufacturing?	Yes
12. Is your company doing business in high-risk countries such as Brazil, China, Russia, India, Nigeria, Afghanistan, Venezuela, or the United Arab Emirates?	Yes
13. Has your company recently merged or are you in the process of merging with a company that does business internationally?	Yes
14. Does your company have or is your company considering a joint venture with a company that does business internationally?	Yes
15. Does your company appropriately account for gifts and entertaining expenses?	No

 ## ACCELERATE YOUR FINANCIAL CLOSE: A 35-STEP ROADMAP

The final tool in our toolkit is a roadmap to help you accelerate your fiscal close. This roadmap is organized into three stages as listed below and provides suggestions to consider when initiating an accelerated close project. This roadmap is a great tool to use to generate ideas for improving your fiscal closing process. Many of the suggestions presented in this roadmap were provided throughout this report.

Stage One: Shorten the Close
Stage Two: Reinvent Procedures
Stage Three: Elevate the Status of Close Participants

Stage One: Shorten the Close

1. Specify your proposal to shorten the close to all levels of management. In doing so, emphasize your goal—finalizing the monthly process and accumulating accounting information faster and at a lower cost.

2. Specify your tactics and approach. The effort takes teamwork, time, commitment, and continuous improvement. And there is no magic formula for accelerating the monthly close.

3. Establish a project team with members from all major groups supporting the closing process. At minimum, these should represent financial reporting, corporate accounting, operations, information technology, and production planning. Ensure the project team has a project manager or leader to plan and lead the effort.

4. Emphasize the roles and responsibilities of each team member. Roles should include providing critical information on closing issues to the accounting group, and making decisions on creating the closing process issues for their departments.

5. Analyze the chart of accounts. It may be obsolete, and many accounts may have inaccurate and incorrect descriptions.

6. Clean up and consolidate your cost centers!

7. Utilize a closing checklist so that the information needed and the deadline for the information are well defined. Update the checklist as needed.

8. Ensure everyone involved in the closing process is properly trained and is aware of the impact they have on the closing process.

9. Require solid closing performance. In particular, demand strict adherence to deadlines as defined in the closing checklist.

10. Implement a remediation plan to focus on areas that impact the closing process.

11. Encourage the use of estimates or tolerances, provided the variance is not significant, to keep your monthly closes moving forward.

12. Standardize internal management and operational reports. Then communicate these changes far in advance so that the new requirements are not surprises.

13. Make sure all levels of the accounting staff understand how their tasks impact the work assigned to your other staff members.

14. Make sure that the closing process is not looked upon as only a "data entry" process.

15. If there are glitches, take the time to understand what happened. Usually, you can figure out what the problem is in a few minutes. Then you can resolve it immediately and prevent the issue from recurring. Be sure to document any closing process issues.

16. Insist on adherence to the system and controls. Allow no deviations and exceptions to avoid a financial restatement.

Stage Two: Reinvent Procedures

17. Agree that it is necessary to reengineer the entire closing process.
18. Break down the closing process into sub-processes. Determine the interdependence between them.
19. Use this process of breaking down activities to identify non-value-adding activities. For example:
    a. Defer the reshuffling of dollars from one general-ledger account to another until the quarterly close. Do the same for your cost centers.
    b. Move your cost allocation off the monthly cycle. Instead, go to fixed rate, budgeted rate, or prior month to develop monthly close entries.
20. Encourage your staff to think ahead. *Example:* Make sure your staff is posting automated accounts payable accruals to the ledger before the first day of the closing.
21. Review information from data entry before the monthly close. This is easier than finding mistakes at crunch time.
22. Determine if the following common non-value-adding activities are slowing your close:
    a. The rule that all entries have to be reviewed and approved by managers before submission. In this case an automated delegation-of-authority process with automated workflow can speed up the approval process.
    b. Waiting to finalize period production until the second day of the closing process.
    c. Finalizing spending the morning of the second day.
    d. Making allocations at the end of the second day, after the spending is finalized.
    e. Permitting inventory-movement entries on the third day and after allocations are reviewed.
23. Review these and other non-value processes. Try to bring them to a culmination within one six-hour window on the first day of the close.
24. Move all preparations for the close immediately before period-end, instead of after.
25. Make sure preliminary spending information is available at the start of the first day after the end of the period.

Stage Three: Elevate the Status of Close Participants

26. Use the 80/20 rule to minimize the amount of work attempted during closing. In particular, focus on the 20% of the information that generates 80% of the work.

27. Eliminate every possible step in the close and then simplify what is left, consolidating like activities or information while meeting reporting requirements.

28. Establish levels of relevancy for data and use these to reduce manual journal-entry line items.

29. Eliminate the need for interdepartmental corrections.

30. Require each accounting staff member to track his or her area's activity during the month, including production. This eliminates the need for a detailed review during the closing process. Such day-to-day monitoring also makes period-ending accruals more accurate.

31. On the last day of the period, make adjustments manually for all relevant receipts, along with period-end timing accruals (utilities, compensation, and so forth).

32. Eliminate the management review requirement before input.

33. Give your staff ownership of the processes in their areas and let them resolve all issues.

34. Make sure processes with different ownership run parallel instead of end to end.

35. Condense the management report into one page of key performance indicators (KPIs). Be sure that your associates can provide drilldown detail for the specific areas supported.

THE FAST CLOSE COMPLIANCE TOOLKIT

Introduction: This toolkit considers several compliance considerations by applicable topic, industry, and process. The toolkit information is provided in the following manner.

- Corporate Compliance Principles and the Role of the Chief Compliance Officer
- Compliance Area and Reference
- Specific Industry Focus
- Process Areas Impacted
- Summary

The fast close compliance toolkit contains information for the following compliance requirements and identifies the business processes impacted. Noncompliance within a specific business process will impact the accuracy of the accumulation of financial transaction results and will create the need for additional due diligence and possible company fines. Adhering to compliance screening requirements will ascertain that employees, suppliers, and customers are not on any compliance watch-lists.

Fast Close Compliance Toolkit Content

- SSEA-18
- The Sarbanes Oxley Act of 2002
- U.S. Sentencing Guidelines
- Foreign Corrupt Practices Act (FCPA)
- The JOBS Act
- Office of Foreign Asset Control (OFAC)
- Bureau of Industry and Security (BIS)
- Foreign Terrorist Organization (FTO)
- Financial Crimes Enforcement Network (FinCEN)
- Gramm-Leach-Bliley Act (GBLA)
- The Federal Financial Institutions Examination Council (FFIEC)
- Bank Secrecy Act (BSA)
- Reg CC
- Reg E
- U.S. Patriot Act and Consumer Identification Program (CIP)
- Office of Inspector General (OIG)
- Health and Insurance Portability and Accountability Act (HIPAA)
- Accountable T&E Plans and Employee Expenses
- IRS Records Retention

Corporate Compliance Principles and the Role of the Chief Compliance Officer

In the document "Corporate Compliance Principles," developed by the National Center for Preventive Law, a compliance program encompasses the set of operational methods that a company uses to ensure its activities adhere to legal requirements and broader company values.

Designing effective compliance programs is an important corporate concern for two reasons. First, public harm and corporate injuries potentially resulting from corporate offenses and deviations from company values justify careful management of offense and misconduct risks. Second, under a number of recently developed legal standards—most notably the Federal Sentencing Guidelines for Organizations, firms with generally effective compliance programs can often significantly reduce or eliminate penalties for offenses that occur despite these programs.

In recent years, both federal and state governments have increased enforcement activities as they relate to corporate conduct and compliance. Publicly traded companies and businesses that operate pursuant to a license, permit, statutory scheme, or government regulatory approval find themselves subject to higher governmental expectations. And corporations that compete in industries of high government interest, such as healthcare and fiscal services, are particularly at risk and are increasingly targeted in both civil and criminal proceedings. Compliance requirements will differ across industries and processes.

The Chief Compliance Officer

Many organizations have implemented the position of chief compliance officer (CCO). This position is defined by the International Association of Risk and Compliance Professionals (IARCP) as follows.

- The chief compliance officer (CCO) of a company is primarily responsible for overseeing and managing compliance within an organization, ensuring that the company and its employees are complying with regulatory requirements and with internal policies and procedures.
- The chief compliance officer (CCO) is the architect and steward of enterprise compliance strategy, structure, and processes.
- As the compliance leader and subject matter expert, the chief compliance officer is responsible for establishing standards and implementing procedures to ensure that the compliance programs throughout the organization are effective and efficient in identifying, preventing, detecting, and correcting noncompliance with applicable rules and regulations.

Controllers should work very closely with the CCOs of their organizations when developing internal control programs and procedures to mitigate compliance risk. Depending on the size of the organization and the assignment of roles and responsibilities, the duties of the CCO and controller can often overlap. Usually, the controller owns the internal program for their organization. And in smaller organizations the controller may be responsible for most CCO duties. In general, the list of duties for the CCO suggests a strong partnership between the controller and CCO.

Duties of the Chief Compliance Officer

- Maintaining current knowledge of laws and regulations, keeping abreast of recent changes
- Developing the annual compliance work-plan that reflects the organization's highest risks that will be monitored by the compliance function as determined by conducting a mandatory annual risk assessment using an enterprise wide approach
- Providing guidance to the board of directors, senior management, staff, and employees on compliance
- Overseeing and monitoring the implementation of the compliance program and working with the controller of the organization to develop the appropriate internal controls program
- Reporting on a regular basis on the progress of implementation, and assisting these components in establishing methods to improve efficiency and quality of services, and to reduce the vulnerability to fraud, abuse, and waste
- Periodically revising the program in light of changes in the needs of the organization and in the law and policies and procedures of government
- Responding to government investigations and queries as the principal point of contact
- Monitoring external audit review processes, maintaining awareness of compliance issues, and in conjunction with the Office of General Counsel and senior management, responding to administrative inquiries related to compliance issues or audits

The Fast Close Compliance Toolkit

Compliance Area and Reference	Specific Industry Focus	Process Areas Impacted	Summary
SSAE-18 https://www.ssae-16.com/soc-1-report/the-ssae-18-audit-standard/	All Global Service Providers	Payroll Processing Benefits Providers Business Process Outsourcing (BPO) Organizations Loan Servicing Organizations that Process Client Data Data Center Co-Location/Network Monitoring Services Software as a Service (SaaS) Medical Claims Processors	**Overview** SSAE 18 is a series of enhancements aimed to increase the usefulness and quality of SOC reports, now, superseding SSAE 16, and, obviously the relic of audit reports, SAS 70. The changes made to the standard this time around will require companies to take more control and ownership of their own internal controls around the identification and classification of risk and appropriate management of third-party vendor relationships. These changes, while not overly burdensome, will help close the loop on key areas that industry professionals noted gaps in many service organization's reports. SSAE18 is now effective as of May 1, 2017, and if you have not made the necessary adjustments required, now is the time to find a quality provider to discuss the proper steps. All organizations are now required to issue their System and Organization Controls (SOC) Report under the SSAE-18 standard in an SOC 1 Report. The SOC 1 report produced will look and feel very similar to the one issued under SSAE-16, it will just contain a couple additional sections and controls to further enhance the content and quality, and thus, the ability for third parties to rely on. **What's New in SSAE 18?** As mentioned above, there are a couple key changes that companies currently performing a SOC 1 or 2, or, will be performing one in the near future, need to take into consideration this year and going forward. Service Organizations will need to implement a formal Third Party Vendor Management Program.

The Fast Close Compliance Toolkit

Compliance Area and Reference	Specific Industry Focus	Process Areas Impacted	Summary
			Service Organizations will need to implement a formal Annual Risk Assessment process.
			In addition to the control based changes, your SOC report should also now contain two additional sections describing the risk assessment process, as well as the Subservice Organizations that play a role in the overall operation of the system and the corresponding controls they impact or have complete ownership of. These two components were typically present in SOC 2 reports previously, but not formally required. Now this concept is being formalized and extended to all SOC reports going forward.
			Now, for companies that have not previously undergone a SOC 1 audit because their service/operations were not fiscally significant, SSAE 18 expands the definition of what is allowed to be reported on to include an entity's compliance with certain laws or regulations, contractual arrangements, or another set of defined agreed-upon procedures—just about any outsourced service where third-party validation would be beneficial and add assurance. This now allows for an official, independent review of a wide-range of operations under a trusted and consistent set of auditing and reporting guidelines.

The Fast Close Compliance Toolkit

Compliance Area and Reference	Specific Industry Focus	Process Areas Impacted	Summary
The Sarbanes Oxley Act of 2002 http://www.soxlaw.com/ www.sec.gov	All Public Companies	All Financial Transactions	Congress reacted to corporate fiscal scandals, including those affecting Enron, Arthur Andersen, and WorldCom, by passing the Sarbanes Oxley Act of 2002. This Act, often referred to as SOX or Sarbox, is designed to "protect investors by improving the accuracy and reliability of corporate disclosures made pursuant to the securities laws." The Act provides for new levels of auditor independence; personal accountability for CEOs and CFOs; additional accountability for corporate Boards; increased criminal and civil penalties for securities violations; increased disclosure regarding executive compensation, insider trading and financial statements; and certification of internal audit work by external auditors.
U.S. Sentencing Guidelines http://www.ussc.gov/guidelines/index.cfm	All U.S. Corporations	All Financial Transactions	The U.S. government would also appear to believe that a company's ethics and compliance culture are set by the very top levels of management because the U.S. Sentencing Guidelines states: *"High-level personnel and substantial authority personnel of the organization shall be knowledgeable about the content and operation of the compliance and ethics program … and shall promote an organizational culture that encourages ethical conduct and a commitment to compliance with the law."* While the Guidelines apply to all corporations, the larger the organization the more formal the program should be and the greater the penalty for failure to comply. Formal policies and procedures and extensive communication programs are expected of a large publicly traded corporation. The expectations are not as extensive for a small business.

The Fast Close Compliance Toolkit

Compliance Area and Reference	Specific Industry Focus	Process Areas Impacted	Summary
Foreign Corrupt Practices Act (FCPA) http://www .justice.gov/ criminal/ fraud/fcpa/	All U.S. Industries	**Accounts Receivable** Procurement **Accounts Payable,** T&E Payroll	The Foreign Corrupt Practices Act of 1977, as amended, 15 U.S.C. §§ 78dd-1, et seq. ("FCPA"), was enacted for the purpose of making it unlawful for certain classes of persons and entities to make payments to foreign government officials to assist in obtaining or retaining business. Specifically, the anti-bribery provisions of the FCPA prohibit the willful use of the mails or any means of instrumentality of interstate commerce corruptly in furtherance of any offer, payment, promise to pay, or authorization of the payment of money or anything of value to any person, while knowing that all or a portion of such money or thing of value will be offered, given or promised, directly or indirectly, to a foreign official to influence the foreign official in his or her official capacity, induce the foreign official to do or omit to do an act in violation of his or her lawful duty, or to secure any improper advantage in order to assist in obtaining or retaining business for or with, or directing business to, any person. The FCPA also requires companies whose securities are listed in the United States to meet its accounting provisions. See 15 U.S.C. § 78m. These accounting provisions, which were designed to operate in tandem with the anti-bribery provisions of the FCPA, require corporations covered by the provisions to (a) make and keep books and records that accurately and fairly reflect the transactions of the corporation and (b) devise and maintain an adequate system of internal accounting controls.

The Fast Close Compliance Toolkit

Compliance Area and Reference	Specific Industry Focus	Process Areas Impacted	Summary
The JOBS Act http://majority leader.gov/ uploadedfiles/ JOBSACTOne Pager.pdf	**Startup Companies**	**Investors**	"Simply, the JOBS Act will make funding more accessible for startups by allowing non-accredited investors to participate in the funding rounds, and this alone, I believe will be the main factor driving the increase in new companies being founded. And with new companies comes the need to hire staff. Without a doubt, this will help the current unemployment rate," said Tanya Prive, founder of *Rock The Post*, a social networking platform for entrepreneurs to fund and swap resources.
Office of Foreign Asset Control (OFAC) http://www .treasury.gov/ about/ organizational- structure/ offices/Pages/ Office-of- Foreign- Assets- Control.aspx	**All U.S. Industries**	**Accounts Receivable** **Procurement** **Accounts Payable** **T&E** **Payroll**	The Office of Foreign Assets Control (OFAC) of the U.S. Department of the Treasury administers and enforces economic and trade sanctions based on U.S. foreign policy and national security goals against targeted foreign countries and regimes, terrorists, international narcotics traffickers, those engaged in activities related to the proliferation of weapons of mass destruction, and other threats to the national security, foreign policy, or economy of the United States. OFAC acts under Presidential national emergency powers, as well as authority granted by specific legislation, to impose controls on transactions and freeze assets under U.S. jurisdiction. Many of the sanctions are based on United Nations and other international mandates, are multilateral in scope, and involve close cooperation with allied governments.

The Fast Close Compliance Toolkit

Compliance Area and Reference	Specific Industry Focus	Process Areas Impacted	Summary
			Various sanctions programs administered by OFAC prohibit U.S. citizens, permanent residents of the U.S. and U.S.-based businesses, including U.S. branches of foreign companies, from engaging in business or fiscal transactions with any party included on OFAC's Specially Designated Nationals List (SDN List). The SDN List, which contains thousands of names, includes individuals, banks, businesses, vessels and other organizations that have been targeted and blocked by the U.S. Government for various policy reasons, such as terrorism, drug trafficking, and weapons of mass destruction proliferators. Because of the ever-changing foreign policy landscape, OFAC frequently makes changes to the SDN List.
Bureau of Industry and Security (BIS) http://www.bis .doc.gov/	All Industries	Accounts Receivable Logistics	The United States Department of Commerce's Bureau of Industry and Security (BIS), formerly known as the Bureau of Export Administration, is responsible for administering and enforcing export controls on U.S. commercial products, software, and technology. BIS is also responsible for overseeing export controls on "dual-use" items that can be used in weapons of mass destruction applications, terrorist activities, or human rights abuses.

The Fast Close Compliance Toolkit

Compliance Area and Reference	Specific Industry Focus	Process Areas Impacted	Summary
			In addition to enforcing the Export Administration Regulations (EAR), BIS is responsible for issuing and administering several restricted party lists that apply to export and re-export transactions for which the agency has jurisdiction. These lists, which change frequently, include the following: ■ Denied Persons List—Includes the names of individuals and companies that have been denied export privileges by BIS, usually due to a violation of U.S. export control laws. U.S. persons and companies are generally prohibited from engaging in export transactions with parties named on the Denied Persons List. ■ Entity List—Identifies the names of companies, individuals, government agencies and research institutions that trigger export and re-export license requirements. U.S. companies need to ensure that the appropriate export licenses are in place before proceeding with transactions with parties on the Entity List. ■ Unverified List—Includes the names of foreign parties that BIS have been unable to conduct a pre-license check or post-shipment verification. Potential transactions with parties on the Unverified List are a "red flag" that must be addressed and resolved before proceeding with the export. Significant civil and criminal fines and other penalties can be imposed on persons or companies engaging in prohibited transactions with parties included on the Denied Persons and Entity Lists. Civil penalties can also be imposed on export transactions with such parties even if such activity occurred inadvertently.

The Fast Close Compliance Toolkit

Compliance Area and Reference	Specific Industry Focus	Process Areas Impacted	Summary
Foreign Terrorist Organization (FTO) http://www.state.gov/j/ct/rls/other/des/123085.htm	All U.S. Industries	**Accounts Receivable** **Procurement** **Accounts Payable** **T&E** **Payroll**	Foreign Terrorist Organizations (FTOs) are foreign organizations that are designated by the Secretary of State in accordance with section 219 of the Immigration and Nationality Act (INA), as amended. FTO designations play a critical role in our fight against terrorism and are an effective means of curtailing support for terrorist activities and pressuring groups to get out of the terrorism business.
Financial Crimes Enforcement Network (FinCEN) http://www.fincen.gov/	Financial Institutions	**ACH, Wires, Checks, and Deposits**	When the USA PATRIOT Act of 2001 was enacted, the act's Section 314(a) became a critical tool for investigating persons suspected of terrorism and/or money laundering. With the Financial Crimes Enforcement Network (FinCEN) as the conduit, 314(a) enables law enforcement to solicit information from fiscal institutions related to such investigations through what is known as the FinCEN 314 list. The highly confidential and involved FinCEN compliance process depends upon the cooperation of three critical groups: 1. Federal, state, local, and foreign law enforcement agencies send FinCEN their requests for information regarding subjects suspected of terrorism or money laundering. 2. FinCEN reviews these requests and every two weeks sends its FinCEN list via a secure internet site to fiscal institutions across the country. 3. Financial institutions must promptly search their entire customer database for any accounts maintained within the last 12 months and any transactions conducted within the last 6 months by named subjects on the FinCEN list.

The Fast Close Compliance Toolkit

Compliance Area and Reference	Specific Industry Focus	Process Areas Impacted	Summary
Gramm-Leach-Bliley Act (GLBA) http://business.ftc.gov/privacy-and-security/gramm-leach-bliley-act	Per GLBA, the term *fiscal institution* covers many parallel sectors such as tax preparers, credit counselors, debt collectors, automobile dealers, and much more. In general, if a business collects and shares personal information about consumers to whom they extend or arrange credit, they have an obligation to GLBA.	Transactions dealing with consumers' personal fiscal information	Three integral pieces of the 1999 Gramm-Leach-Bliley Act (GLBA) focus on the information security of consumers' personal fiscal information. The Financial Privacy Rule, the Safeguards Rule, and the Pre-texting Provisions together determine how fiscal institutions can collect this information and how they must ensure the security and confidentiality of it. To fulfill their GLBA compliance, all fiscal institutions must: ■ Provide notice to customers about its privacy requirements regarding their personal fiscal information (Financial Privacy) ■ Establish, implement, and maintain an Information Security Program that secures and protects consumers' personal fiscal information from anticipated threats and/or unauthorized access (Safeguards) ■ Ensure that consumers' personal fiscal information is not being collected under false pretenses (Pretexting)

The Fast Close Compliance Toolkit

Compliance Area and Reference	Specific Industry Focus	Process Areas Impacted	Summary
The Federal Financial Institutions Examination Council (FFIEC) http://www.ffiec.gov/	**Financial Institutions**	**Business Continuity Planning, Development and Acquisition, Electronic Banking, Fedline®, Information Security, IT Audit, IT Management, Operations, Outsourcing Technology Services, Retail Payment Systems, Supervision of Technology Service Providers, and Wholesale Payment Systems**	The Federal Financial Institutions Examination Council (FFIEC) is a five-member agency responsible for establishing consistent guidelines and uniform practices and principals for fiscal institutions. The member agencies include the Board of Governors of the Federal Reserve System (FRB), the Federal Deposit Insurance Corporation (FDIC), the National Credit Union Administration (NCUA), the Office of the Comptroller of the Currency (OCC), and the Office of Thrift Supervision (OTS). In 2004, the FFIEC updated its information technology examination manual to account for the ever-quickening pace of changes and advancements in technology occurring at fiscal institutions and technology service providers. The result is the FFIEC IT Examination Handbook, a compilation of 12 booklets which can be updated individually as needed by the Council.

The Fast Close Compliance Toolkit

Compliance Area and Reference	Specific Industry Focus	Process Areas Impacted	Summary
Reg CC http://www.federalreserve.gov/pubs/regcc/regcc.htm	Financial Institutions	Deposits to Financial Institutions	In response to consumer complaints about lengthy deposit hold times, Congress passed the Expedited Funds Availability (EFA) Act in 1987, ushering in Regulation CC (Reg CC). Reg CC sets fair and uniform guidelines and required disclosures for how deposited funds are handled and credited to customers' accounts. It also gives fiscal institutions the right to delay availability in situations which pose a high risk of fraud. Sub-part B of Regulation CC Compliance deals specifically with this Funds Availability, and therefore presents the most challenges for fiscal institutions. It stipulates by deposit type the amount of time that institutions can hold a deposit either under normal availability or, if specific criteria are met, under an extension of normal availability.
Reg E http://www.fdic.gov/regulations/laws/rules/6500-3100.html	Financial Institutions	All EFT Transactions	Since 1978, when Congress passed the Electronic Fund Transfers Act (EFTA), better known as Regulation E (Reg E), fiscal institutions have been responsible for properly investigating consumer claims of electronic fund transfer (EFT) errors. Those investigations must follow very specific error resolution procedures. At the time that Reg E was enacted, paper-based payments far outnumbered electronic fund transfer payments. Today, the exact opposite is true with electronic payments representing over 66% of all payments. The rise in EFTs has been accompanied by a parallel rise in EFT error claims, making Reg E compliance that much more difficult for fiscal institutions to follow.

The Fast Close Compliance Toolkit

Compliance Area and Reference	Specific Industry Focus	Process Areas Impacted	Summary
			Accurately complying with Reg E error resolution procedures requires fiscal institutions and their employees to recognize the following milestones and proceed accordingly with each claim: ▪ When the official notice of a claim has occurred so that it can be investigated and resolved within the Reg E specified time period ▪ When to issue provisional credit to the customer during an investigation ▪ When to debit the customer's account if the investigation shows that no error occurred ▪ When and how the customer should be notified throughout the investigation
U.S. Patriot Act and Consumer Identification Program (CIP) http://www .fincen.gov/ statutes_regs/ patriot/	Financial Institutions	Consumer Bank Account Information	Section 326 compliance requires that CIP procedures should: ▪ Verify the identity of any person seeking to open an account using documentary and non-documentary verification. ▪ Maintain records of that CIP verification process for five years after the account is closed. ▪ Compare the customer's name against the government's list of known or suspected terrorists. ▪ Provide customers with adequate notice of the requirements for customer identification. The U.S. Treasury Department considers Section 326's customer identification and recordkeeping requirements as vital tools in its fight against criminal enterprises such as terrorism and the growing threat from identity theft. Financial institutions play a significant role in that fight through their CIP compliance.

The Fast Close Compliance Toolkit

Compliance Area and Reference	Specific Industry Focus	Process Areas Impacted	Summary
Office of Inspector General (OIG) http://oig.hhs.gov/	Hospitals, Healthcare Systems, and Healthcare Insurance Companies	Accounts Receivable, Patient Billing	**Office of Inspector General's (OIG)** mission is to protect the integrity of **Department of Health & Human Services (HHS)** programs as well as the health and welfare of program beneficiaries. Since its 1976 establishment, OIG has been at the forefront of the Nation's efforts to fight waste, fraud, and abuse in Medicare, Medicaid, and more than 300 other HHS programs. HHS OIG is the largest inspector general's office in the federal government, with more than 1,700 employees dedicated to combating fraud, waste, and abuse and to improving the efficiency of HHS programs. A majority of OIG's resources goes toward the oversight of Medicare and Medicaid—programs that represent a significant part of the federal budget and that affect this country's most vulnerable citizens. OIG's oversight extends to programs under other HHS institutions, including the Centers for Disease Control and Prevention, National Institutes of Health, and the Food and Drug Administration.

The Fast Close Compliance Toolkit

Compliance Area and Reference	Specific Industry Focus	Process Areas Impacted	Summary
Health and Insurance Portability and Accountability Act (HIPAA) http://www.hhs.gov/ocr/privacy/	HIPAA applies to all healthcare providers, health plans, health clearinghouses, and those entities which interact with them by exchanging PHI. Information.	Transactions that contain patient or employee health information	On August 21, 1996, Congress passed the Health and Insurance Portability and Accountability Act, better known as HIPAA. Two primary outcomes of HIPAA are its Privacy Rule and Security Rule, both of which work to protect patient health information. The goal of these uniform standards is to promote the secure flow of health information while at the same time supporting the highest level of patient care. The Privacy Rule identifies what patient information is to be protected. This Protected Health Information (PHI) includes data that identifies or could identify the patient, such as their name, address, date of birth, or Social Security number. The Security Rule specifically protests PHI that is created, received, maintained, or transmitted electronically.

The Fast Close Compliance Toolkit

Compliance Area and Reference	Specific Industry Focus	Process Areas Impacted	Summary
Accountable T&E Plans and Employee Expenses https://www.irs.gov/publications/p463	All Industries	T&E	▪ Car expenses. The cost of using your car as an employee, whether measured using actual expenses or the standard mileage rate, will no longer be allowed to be claimed as an unreimbursed employee travel expense as a miscellaneous itemized deduction due to the suspension of miscellaneous itemized deductions that are subject to the 2% floor under section 67. The suspension applies to tax years beginning after December 2017, and before January 2026. Deductions for expenses that are deductible in determining adjusted gross income are not suspended. For example, Armed Forces reservists, qualified performing artists, and fee-basis state or local government officials are allowed to deduct unreimbursed employee travel expenses as an adjustment to total income on Schedule 1 (Form 1040), line 24. ▪ Standard mileage rate. For 2018, the standard mileage rate for the cost of operating your car for business use is 54.5 cents (0.545) per mile. Car expenses and use of the standard mileage rate are explained in Chapter 4. ▪ Depreciation limits on cars, trucks, and vans. For 2018, the first-year limit on depreciation, special depreciation allowance, and section 179 deduction for vehicles acquired before September 28, 2017, and placed in service during 2018 is $16,400. The first-year limit on depreciation, special depreciation allowance, and section 179 deduction for vehicles acquired after September 27, 2017, and placed in service during 2018 is $18,000. If you elect not to claim a special depreciation allowance for a vehicle placed in service in 2018, the amount is $10,000. Depreciation limits are explained in Chapter 4.

The Fast Close Compliance Toolkit

Compliance Area and Reference	Specific Industry Focus	Process Areas Impacted	Summary
			■ Meals and entertainment. For 2018, the treatment of certain meals and entertainment expenses was changed. In general, entertainment expenses are no longer deductible. The cost of business meals generally remains deductible, subject to the 50% limitation. See section 274 for additional information on the changes.
			■ Section 179 deduction. The maximum amount you can elect to deduct for most section 179 property (including cars, trucks, and vans) you placed in service in tax years beginning in 2018 is $1,000,000. This limit is reduced by the amount by which the cost of section 179 property placed in service during the tax year exceeds $2,500,000. Section 179 deduction is explained in Chapter 4.
			■ Special depreciation allowance. For 2018, the first year special ("bonus") depreciation allowance on qualified property (including cars, trucks, and vans) is 100% for qualified property acquired and placed in service after September 27, 2017, and placed in service before January 2023, and is reduced 20% each year after for property placed in service before January 2027. Special depreciation allowance is explained in Chapter 4.

The Fast Close Compliance Toolkit

Compliance Area and Reference	Specific Industry Focus	Process Areas Impacted	Summary
Know Your Customer (KYC) https://www.forbes.com/sites/forbestechcouncil/2018/07/10/know-your-customer-kyc-will-be-a-great-thing-when-it-works/#7f76c67e8dbb	Global Companies	Customer and Supplier Impacting Transactions	KYC started out as one of the least controversial parts of the Patriot Act. Its anti-money laundering (AML) goal is understandable and clearly needed. Its requirements—having banks verify customers are who they say they are, confirm they're not on any prohibited lists and assessing their risk factors—are remarkably straightforward. Primarily because the law didn't provide a standard for what types of information should be used to verify customers. Regulators seem to be doing this on purpose. The reasoning seems to be that if banks get clear guidelines on what constitutes adequate KYC, they will never look any further than the minimum requirements. The result is each fiscal institution, operating in fear of massive fines, has its own procedures and requirements for conducting due diligence.

The Fast Close Compliance Toolkit

Compliance Area and Reference	Specific Industry Focus	Process Areas Impacted	Summary
Anti-Money Laundering (AML) Requirements	Financial Institutions	**Bank Secrecy Act regulations require fiscal institutions to strictly record and/or report on cash purchases of negotiable instruments, cash transactions exceeding $10,000**	Firms must comply with the Bank Secrecy Act and its implementing regulations ("Anti-Money Laundering rules"). The purpose of the AML rules is to help detect and report suspicious activity including the predicate offenses to money laundering and terrorist financing, such as securities fraud and market manipulation. FINRA reviews a firm's compliance with AML rules under FINRA Rule 3310, which sets forth minimum standards for a firm's written AML compliance program. The basic tenets of an AML compliance program under FINRA 3310 include the following: The program has to be approved in writing by a senior manager. It must be reasonably designed to ensure the firm detects and reports suspicious activity. It must be reasonably designed to achieve compliance with the AML Rules, including, among others, having a risk-based customer identification program (CIP) that enables the firm to form a reasonable belief that it knows the true identity of its customers. It must be independently tested to ensure proper implementation of the program. Each FINRA member firm must submit contact information for its AML Compliance Officer through the FINRA Contact System (FCS). Ongoing training must be provided to appropriate personnel.

THE M&A DUE DILIGENCE CHECKLIST

Introduction: The following due diligence checklist should be used as a master list of possible due diligence items that should be investigated when initiating an M&A activity. It is not always necessary to use the entire list but to select only those items that appear to be most relevant to the current acquisition target.

The analysis of specific GL accounts and accurate reporting of fiscal results for both the organizations are the drivers of this checklist. Inaccurate fiscal close information will impact and delay the results of the due diligence process. A faster close will provide the financial information needed for the M&A due diligence process in a more timely manner.

The M&A Due Diligence Checklist

Synergies
- Itemize the synergies that will be created by the acquisition. Split the synergies list into those that are based on identifiable cost reductions and those based on possible revenue increases.
- How well do the products, personnel, and geographic coverage of the acquirer and the company being acquired fit together?

Market Overview
- What is the size of the market?
- How is the market segmented?
- What is the market's projected growth and profitability?
- What are the factors affecting growth and profitability?
- What are the trends in the number of competitors and their size, product innovation, distribution, finances, regulation, and product liability?

Corporate Overview
- What are the company's core competencies?
- Does the company maintain any strategic alliances?
- When and where was the company founded, and by whom?
- What is its history of product development?
- What is the history of the management team?
- Has the corporate location changed?
- Have there been ownership changes?
- Have there been acquisitions or divestitures?
- What is its fiscal history?

Culture
- What type of command structure is used? Does it vary by department?
- Is there a set of standard policies and procedures that govern most processes? How closely do employees adhere to it?
- What practices does the company use to retain employees?
- What types of social functions do employees engage in as a group?

The M&A Due Diligence Checklist

- Does the company generally promote from within or from the outside?
- What types of training does the company require of its employees?
- What types of indoctrination programs are used for new employees?
- What types of awards and ceremonies are used to recognize employee achievements?
- What level of customer service is the company accustomed to provide? Does it support "above and beyond" levels of support, and publicize these efforts?
- What dress code does it allow? Does this vary by location?
- What type of feedback mechanisms are used to discuss issues about employee performance?
- How does the company disseminate information to its employees? Is it a more formal method, such as a monthly newsletter, or more informal employee meetings?
- What is the physical environment? Does the company emphasize low costs with cheap furnishings or more expensive surroundings?
- Is there a sense of urgency in completing tasks, or is the environment more relaxed?

Employees

- If applicable, obtain a list of all employees, their current compensation, and compensation for the prior year, date of hire, date of birth, race, sex, and job titles. Be sure to keep this information confidential.
- Obtain a list of all inactive employees, stating the reason for their inactive status and the prognosis for their return.
- Obtain copies of the I-9 forms for all active employees.
- Obtain copies of any employment agreements.
- Obtain copies of performance evaluation criteria and bonus plans.
- Obtain copies of any non-compete, intellectual property, and/or confidentiality agreements. Also obtain copies of non-compete agreements that currently apply to terminated employees.
- Obtain copies of any salesperson compensation agreements.
- Obtain copies of any director compensation agreements.
- Summarize any loan amounts and terms to officers, directors, or employees.
- Obtain any union labor agreements.
- Determine the number of states to which payroll taxes must be paid.
- Obtain a copy of the employee manual.
- Conduct background investigations on principal employees.
- Summarize the names, ages, titles, education, experience, and professional biographies of the senior management team.
- Obtain copies of employee resumes.
- What has the employee turnover rate been for the past two years?
- Obtain a list of all involuntary terminations within the past year, stating the reason for termination and the age, sex, race, and disability status of each person terminated.
- Obtain a copy of the organization chart.

The M&A Due Diligence Checklist

Benefits

- Review accrued 401k benefits. What is the company contribution percentage? What is the level of employee participation?
- Obtain copies of all pension plan documents, amendments, and letters of determination.
- Obtain copies of the pension assets, liabilities, expenses, and audits for the past three years.
- Determine the funding status of the company pension plan, and the ten-year projected cash expense associated with it.
- Itemize all fringe benefits, along with current and projected employee eligibility for and participation in each one.
- Obtain a list of all former employees using COBRA coverage, and the dates on which their access to COBRA coverage expires.
- Itemize all executive perquisites above the standard benefits package, and the extent of these expenses for the past two years.

Intellectual Property

- Review all current patent, trademark, service mark, trade name, and copyright agreements, and note renewal dates.
- Obtain an itemization of all pending patent applications.
- Determine annual patent renewal costs.
- Determine the current patent-related revenue stream.
- Document the patent application process. Have any potential patents not been applied for?
- List all trademark and service mark registrations and pending applications for registration. Verify that all affidavits of use and renewal applications have been filed, and prosecution of all pending applications is current.
- List all unregistered trademarks and service marks used by the organization.
- Collect and catalog copies of all toolkits and check for unlisted trademarks and service marks, proper notification.
- List all copyright registrations.
- List all registered designs.
- Does the company have any information that provides a competitive advantage? If so, verify that the information is marked as "confidential."
- Have all employees executed Invention Assignment and Confidentiality agreements?
- Obtain copies of all licenses of intellectual property in which the company is the licensor or licensee.
- List all lawsuits pertaining to intellectual property in which the organization is a party.

Brands

- Review any branding strategy documents. Does the company have a long-term plan for brand support?
- Review budgeted and actual expenditures for customer support, marketing, and quality assurance related to branding.
- What types of advertising and promotion are used?
- Ensure that the company has clear title to any branded names.
- How well is the brand supported on the company website?
- Note the amount and trend of any legal fees needed to stop brand encroachment.

The M&A Due Diligence Checklist

Risk Management

- Is there a risk management officer? What is this person's job description?
- Does the company have an overall risk mitigation plan that it updates regularly?
- Review all corporate insurance, using a schedule from the company's insurance agency. If there is material pending litigation, determine the extent of insurance coverage and obtain insurance company confirmation. Note whether insurance terms are for "claims made" or "claims incurred," as well as the amounts of deductibles.
- Have aggregate insurance amounts been penetrated, or is there a history of coming close to the aggregate totals?
- Have there been substantial premium adjustments in the past?
- To what extent does the company self-insure its activities? Are there uninsured risks that the company does not appear to be aware of or is ignoring?

Capacity

- Determine the facility overhead cost required for minimum, standard, and maximum capacity.
- Ascertain the amount of capital replacements needed in the near future.
- Determine the periodic maintenance cost of existing equipment.
- Determine the maximum sustainable production capacity by production line.
- Estimate the cost of modifications needed to increase the capacity of each production line or facility.

Assets

- Verify bank reconciliations for all bank accounts harboring significant cash balances.
- Obtain current detail of accounts receivable.
- Determine the days of receivables outstanding and the probable amount of bad debt. Review the allowance for doubtful accounts calculation.
- Obtain a list of all accounts and notes receivable from employees.
- Obtain a list of all inventory items, and discuss the obsolescence reserve. Determine the valuation method used.
- Obtain the current fixed asset listing, as well as depreciation calculations. Audit the largest items to verify their existence.
- Appraise the value of the most expensive fixed assets.
- Obtain an itemized list of all assets that are not receivables or fixed assets.
- Ascertain the existence of any liens against company assets.
- Obtain any maintenance agreements on company equipment.
- Is there an upcoming need to replace assets?
- Discuss whether there are any plans to close, relocate, or expand any facilities.
- Itemize all capitalized research and development or software development expenses.
- Determine the value of any net operating loss carryforward assets.

Liabilities

- Review the current accounts payable listing.
- Obtain a list of all accounts payable to employees.
- Review the terms of any lines of credit.
- Review the amount and terms of any other debt agreements. Review covenants in the debt agreements, and determine if the company has breached the covenants in the past, or is likely to do so in the near future.

The M&A Due Diligence Checklist

- Look for unrecorded debt.
- Verify wage and tax remittances to all government entities, and that there are no unpaid amounts.
- Review the sufficiency of accruals for wages, vacation time, legal expenses, insurance, property taxes, and commissions.
- Obtain copies of all unexpired purchasing commitments (purchase orders, etc.).
- Investigate any potential warranty, environmental, legal, and regulatory noncompliance issues.

Equity

- Obtain a shareholder list that notes the number of shares held and any special voting rights.
- Review all board resolutions authorizing the issuance of stock to ensure that all shares are validly issued.
- Review all convertible debt agreements to which the company or any subsidiary is a party. Note any restrictions on dividends, on incurring extra debt, and on issuing additional capital stock. Note any unusual consent or default provisions. Note the conversion trigger points.
- Review any disclosure documents used in the private placement of securities or loan applications during the preceding five years.
- Review all documents affecting ownership, voting, or rights to acquire the company's stock for required disclosure and significance to the purchase transactions, such as warrants, options, security holder agreements, registration rights agreements, shareholder rights, or poison pill plans.

Profitability

- Obtain audited financial statements for the last three years.
- Obtain monthly financial statements for the current year.
- Obtain copies of federal tax returns for the last three years.
- Determine profitability by product, customer, and segment.
- What are the revenues and profits per employee?
- What is the direct materials expense impact as a percentage of revenue?
- How have revenues, costs, and profits been trending for the past three years?
- How many staff are directly traceable to the servicing of specific customer accounts?
- Are there any delayed expenses? Has the customer avoided necessary maintenance expenditures or wage increases in order to boost profitability?
- Has the company capitalized a disproportionate amount of expenses?
- Obtain the budgets for the past three years. Does the company meet its budgetgoals or are there significant variances?

Cash Flow

- Develop a cash forecast for the next six months. Will the company absorb cash?
- Review the trend line of work capital for the past year. How is it changing in relation to total sales?
- Categorize working capital by segment, product line, and customer. What parts of the business are absorbing the most cash?
- Determine historical and projected capital expenditure requirements. Does the company have enough cash to pay for its capital investment needs?

The M&A Due Diligence Checklist

Customers

- How concentrated are sales among the top customers?
- What is the distribution of sales among the various products and services?
- What is the current sales backlog by customer?
- What is the seasonality of sales? Are sales unusually subject to changes in the business cycle?
- What is the fiscal condition of key customers? Does it appear that their businesses are sufficiently robust to continue supporting purchases from the company?
- How long has the company had sales relationships with its key customers?
- Which new customers is the company actively pursuing, and how much potential revenue and profit do they represent?
- How profitable is each of the key customer accounts? Do any customers require a disproportionate amount of servicing, or require special terms and conditions?
- Itemize any customer contracts that are coming up for renewal and likely changes to the key terms of those agreements.
- Is there a history of complaints from any customers? How profitable are the customers who appear to be the most dissatisfied?
- Obtain a list of all customers who have stopped doing business with the company in the last three years.

Sales Activity

- Determine the amount of ongoing maintenance revenue from standard products.
- Obtain copies of all outstanding proposals, bids, and offers pending award.
- Obtain copies of all existing contracts for products or services, including warranty and guarantee work.
- What is the sales strategy (e.g. add customers, increase support, increase penetration into existing customer base, pricing, etc.)?
- How does the company promote its products and services (advertising, trade shows, etc.)?
- What is the structure of the sales organization? Are there independent sales representatives?
- Obtain the sales organization chart.
- How many sales personnel are in each sales position?
- What is the sales force's geographic coverage?
- What is the sales force's compensation, split by base pay and commission?
- What were the sales per salesperson for the past year?
- What was the sales expense per salesperson for the past year?
- What is the sales projection by product for the next 12 months?
- Into what category do customers fall—end users, retailers, OEMs, wholesalers, and/or distributors?
- How many customers are there for each product, industry, and geographic region?
- What is the average order size?
- Does the company have an Internet store? Does the site accept online payments and orders? What percentage of total sales comes through this medium?
- What is the structure of the technical support group? How many people are in it, and what is their compensation?

The M&A Due Diligence Checklist

- Does the company use email for marketing notifications to customers?
- What are the proportions of sales by distribution channel?
- How many customers can the company potentially market its products to? What would be the volume by customer?
- What is the company's market share? What is the trend?
- Are there new markets in which the products can be sold?

Product Development

- Which products are nearing the end of their useful lives, and how much revenue is attached to them?
- Obtain a list of development projects in the product pipeline. What is the estimated remaining time and expense required to launch each one?
- What attributes make the company's new products unique?
- Have any products been in the development pipeline for a long time that have no immediate prospects for product launch?
- Who are the key development personnel? What is their tenure and educational background?
- Does the company primarily use incremental product improvements, or engage in major new product development projects?
- How much money is invested annually in development? As a proportion of sales? How does this spending compare to that of competitors?
- Does the company have a history of issuing inadequately engineered products that fail? Is this finding supported by warranty claim records?
- Is there a product development plan? Does it tend to target low-cost products, ones with special features, or some other strategy? How closely does the development team adhere to it?
- Does the company use target costing to achieve predetermined profitability targets?
- Does it design products that avoid constrained resources?

Production Process

- Does the company have a push or pull manufacturing system?
- Does the company practice constraint management techniques?
- Does the company use work cells or continuous assembly lines?
- Is there an adequate industrial engineering staff? Does it have an ongoing plan for process improvement?
- What is the production area safety record? What types of problems have caused safety failures in the past?
- What issues have caused shipping delays in the past?
- What is the history of product rework, and why have rework problems arisen?

Information Technology (IT)

- What systems use third-party software, and which ones use custom-built solutions? Are the third-party systems under maintenance contracts, and are the most recent versions installed?
- To what degree have third-party systems been modified? Have they been so altered that they can no longer be upgraded?
- Are user computers monitored for unauthorized software installations?

The M&A Due Diligence Checklist

- What is the level of difficulty anticipated to integrate the company's databases into the buyer's systems?
- Are there adequate backup systems in place with offsite storage, both for the corporate-level databases and for individual computers?
- What is the level of security required for access to the company's servers?

Internet and Firewall

- Does the company use the Internet for internal use as an interactive part of operations? What functions are used in this manner? Does the company use cloud computing and Software as a Service (SaaS) applications?
- Has the company's firewall ever been penetrated, and how sensitive is the information stored on the company network's publicly available segments? Does the company have any cybersecurity concerns?
- Does the company provide technical support information through its website?
- Are website usage statistics tracked? If so, how are they used for management decisions?
- In what way could operational costs decrease if the company's customers interacted with it through the Internet?

Legal Issues

- Obtain the articles of incorporation and bylaws. Review for the existence of preemptive rights, rights of first refusal, registration rights, or any other rights related to the issuance or registration of securities.
- Review the bylaws for any unusual provisions affecting shareholder rights or restrictions on ownership, transfer, or voting of shares.
- Obtain certificates of good standing for the company and all significant subsidiaries.
- Review the articles of incorporation and bylaws of each significant subsidiary. Determine if there are restrictions on dividends to the company. For each subsidiary, review the minutes of the board of directors for matters requiring disclosure.
- Obtain a list of all states in which the company is qualified to do business and a list of those states in which it maintains significant operations. Determine if there is any state where the company is not qualified but should be qualified to do business
- Obtain the minutes from all shareholder meetings for the past five years. Review for proper notice prior to meetings, the existence of a quorum, and proper voting procedures; verify that stock issuances have been authorized; verify that insider transactions have been approved; verify that officers have been properly elected; verify that shares are properly approved and reserved for stock option and purchase plans.
- Obtain the minutes of the Executive Committee and Audit Committee for the past five years, as well as the minutes of any other special board committees. Review all documents.

The M&A Due Diligence Checklist

- Review all contracts that are important to operations. Also review any contracts with shareholders or officers. In particular, look for the following provisions:
  - Default or termination provisions
  - Restrictions on company action
  - Consent requirements
  - Termination provisions in employment contracts
  - Ownership of technology
  - Cancellation provisions in major supply and customer contracts
  - Unusual warranties or the absence of protective provisions
- Obtain copies of all asset leases, and review for term, early payment, and bargain purchase clauses.
- Obtain copies of all office space lease agreements, and review for term and renewal provisions.
- Review all related-party transactions for the past three years.
- Review the terms of any outbound or inbound royalty agreements.
- Was any company software (either used internally or resold) obtained from another company? If so, what are the terms under which the code is licensed? Are there any associated royalty payments?
- Review all legal invoices for the past two years.
- Review all pending and threatened legal proceedings to which the company or any of its subsidiaries is a party. Describe principal parties, allegations, and relief sought. This includes any governmental or environmental proceedings. Obtain copies of existing consent decrees or significant settlement agreements relating to the company or its subsidiaries.
- If the company is publicly held, obtain all periodic filings for the past five years, including the 10K, 10Q, 8K, and Schedule 13D.
- Review all annual and quarterly reports to shareholders.
- Review the auditors' letter to management concerning internal accounting controls and procedures, as well as any management responses.
- Review any reports of outside consultants or analysts concerning the company.
- Research any press releases or articles about the company within the past year.
- Review all related-party transactions for the past three years.
- Review the terms of any outbound or inbound royalty agreements.
- Was any company software (either used internally or resold) obtained from another company? If so, what are the terms under which the code is licensed? Are there any associated royalty payments?
- Review title insurance for any significant land parcels owned by the company.

Regulatory Compliance

- Review the company's correspondence with the Securities and Exchange Commission (SEC), any national exchange, or state securities commission—other than routine transmittals—for the past five years. Determine if there are or were any enforcement or disciplinary actions or any ongoing investigations or suggestions of violations by any of these entities.

The M&A Due Diligence Checklist

- Review any correspondence during the past five years with the Environmental Protection Agency, Federal Trade Commission, Occupational Safety and Health Administration, Equal Employment Opportunity Commission, or Internal Revenue Service. Determine if there are any ongoing investigations or suggestions of violations by any of these agencies.
- Review any required regulatory compliance and verify that necessary licenses and permits have been maintained, as well as ongoing filings and reports.
- If there is a General Service Administration schedule? If so, when does it come up for renewal?
- Obtain copies of the most recently filed EEO-1 and VETS-100 forms.
- Obtain copies of any affirmative action plans.
- Obtain copies of any open charges of discrimination, complaints, or related litigation, or any such cases that have been closed within the past five years.

Policies and Procedures

- Obtain the accounting policies and procedures manual.
- Review all key accounting policies to ensure that they comply with generally accepted accounting principles.
- Obtain the standard offer letter format, the standard termination letter format, and the employment application form.
- Obtain the human resources policies relating to sexual harassment, background investigations, and drug testing.

The Purchase Transaction

- If the transaction involves the issuance of stock, are there sufficient authorized shares for the offering, including any conversion rights, taking into account any shares reserved for issuance pursuant to outstanding options, warrants, convertible securities, and employee benefit plans?

Red Flag Events

- Are there concerns with the fiscal closing process such as timeliness, the number of adjusting entries, and financial statement misstatements?
- Has an auditor resigned within the past three years?
- Is there evidence of continual changes in accounting methods?
- Are there unusually complex business arrangements that do not appear to have a business purpose?
- Is the company continually exceeding its loan covenant targets by very small amounts?
- Do any of the principals have criminal records?
- Have there recently been significant insider stock sales?
- Is the internal audit team subjected to significant scope restrictions?
- Are a large proportion of monthly sales completed during the last few days of each month?
- Has the company tried to sell itself in the past and failed?
- Has the company received major warnings from regulatory agencies?
- Does the company appear to manipulate reserve accounts in order to smooth or enhance its reported earnings?

FINANCE AND ACCOUNTING KEY BUSINESS PARTNERSHIPS MATRIX

Introduction: To enable a seamless fiscal closing process, finance and accounting executives should consider building business partnerships with the organizations included in the table below. This matrix was developed to provide a listing of potential business partnership organizations and can be used to ensure that all applicable departments are identified as stakeholders that impact the fiscal close.

The matrix also includes the areas of influence that will drive the business partnership. Although the areas of influence will change in public and private companies, the value of a business partnership can influence good communication across the company and will ensure complete data for financial reporting.

Suggested Business Partnership Organizations	Areas of Influence

HR and Benefits	▪ Allocations
	▪ HR and Payroll Internal Controls
	▪ Entity Level Controls
	▪ HR Policies
	▪ Controller Staff Development and Training Programs
	▪ Benefit Plan Decision Making
	▪ Pension Plan Investment Analysis
	▪ SSAE 18—SSAE 18 addresses the importance of accurately disclosing the relationship between the service organization and the subservice organization. Under SSAE 18 a service organization should:
	  ▪ Identify all subservice organizations used in providing the services.
	  ▪ Include a description of any subservice organization controls (referred to as Complementary Subservice Organization Controls) that the service organization relies on to provide the primary services to its customers.
	▪ Sarbanes Oxley 302 and 404

Facilities	▪ Allocations
	▪ Physical Security Controls
	▪ Facility Strategy
	  ▪ Closing Old Facilities
	  ▪ Building New Facilities
	▪ Capital Budgets

Suggested Business Partnership Organizations	Areas of Influence
Supply Chain	▪ Depreciation Analysis ▪ Risk Management ▪ Insurance Plans ▪ Asset Impairment ▪ Sarbanes Oxley 302 and 404 ▪ Supply Chain Internal Controls ▪ Supply Chain Strategy ▪ Logistics Outsourcing Strategy ▪ Inventory Control and Accounting ▪ Inventory Fraud Detection and Prevention ▪ Operational Metrics and Reporting ▪ Risk Management ▪ SSAE 18 ▪ Sarbanes Oxley 302 and 404
Legal and Risk Management	▪ Allocations ▪ Entity-Level Controls ▪ Risk Management ▪ Insurance ▪ Record Management ▪ Contract Compliance ▪ Regulatory Compliance Issues ▪ Fraud Detection and Prevention ▪ Sarbanes Oxley 302 and 404
Compliance	▪ Regulatory Compliance Applicable to the Organization. ▪ Address Compliance Issues and Ensure the Implementation of Corrective Action Plans ▪ Sarbanes Oxley 302 and 404
Internal Audit	▪ Control Self-Assessment and Internal Controls Programs. ▪ Address Control Issues and Ensure the Implementation of Corrective Action Plans ▪ Recommend Audit Plan and Focus ▪ Sarbanes Oxley 302 and 404
Ethics and Compliance	▪ Entity-Level Controls ▪ Entity-Level Control Questionnaire ▪ Ethics Hotline Issues ▪ Whistleblower Protection ▪ Fraud Detection and Prevention ▪ Tone at the Top ▪ Sarbanes Oxley 302 and 404

Suggested Business Partnership Organizations	Areas of Influence
Security and Investigations	▪ Ethics Hotline Issues ▪ Fraud Detection and Prevention—Financial Statement Fraud ▪ Security Controls ▪ Physical Security ▪ Protection of company data

Information Technology	▪ Allocations
	▪ Develop IT Strategy
	▪ IT Controls
	  ▪ System Access Controls
	▪ Reporting and Metrics
	▪ Selection of ERP Systems
	  ▪ Cost Analysis
	  ▪ Functionality
	▪ Financial Systems
	▪ Capital Budget
	▪ Asset Impairment
	▪ IT Business Continuity Plan
	▪ SSAE 18
	▪ Sarbanes Oxley 302 and 404

FISCAL CLOSE RISKS AND CHALLENGES

Introduction: The risks and challenges represent the items that can go wrong within the financial close process. Although there are different reporting requirements and levels of complexity across industries and companies, the risks and challenges are very similar. This tool groups the risks and challenges for the closing process into three areas as listed below:

1. Operational
2. Accumulation of Financial Information
3. Processing and Reporting of Financial Information

Operational

1. Close process exceeding targeted benchmark.
2. Finance resembles a firedrill during the close.
3. All other finance activity shuts down during the close.
4. Reports are too late, too difficult to understand, overly complex, suspect, or often revised.

5. The financial close process never seems to end.
6. Differences between internal and external financial reports and conflicting internal report requirements.
7. Multiple systems and data warehouses used during the close process.
8. There is no clear ownership of the data.
9. Reports are usually created in spreadsheets.
10. Financial hierarchy is too complex.
11. Limited capacity or ability to report operational metrics or KPIs.
12. There are too many cost centers—many are inactive and can be consolidated.
13. Disparate and disconnected business and financial systems.
14. Multiple, nonstandard, or overly complex charts of accounts (the basic "bones" of the accounting system).
15. Too many adjusting entries.
16. No time to worry about financial close internal controls or risk analysis.

Accumulation of Financial Information

1. The financial statements issued to the public may not be prepared in accordance with GAAP.
2. Reports may not be accurate, and critical decisions may be based on erroneous information.
3. Policies and procedures may not be properly or consistently applied by or between the organization's operating units.
4. SEC and other governmental reporting requirements and/or loan restrictions may be violated. Exposure to shareholder litigation increases substantially due to improper reporting.
5. Journal entries may be incorrectly prepared, duplicated, omitted, or made for the purposes of misstating account balances to conceal irregularities or shortages.
6. The financial statements issued to the public may not be prepared in accordance with GAAP.
7. Accountability over recorded transactions may not be maintained.
8. Amounts could be accrued for expenses that are not likely to occur in order to generate "funding" sources for future periods.

Processing and Reporting of Financial Information

1. Financial statements may be misstated as journal entries may be omitted, recorded in the wrong period, duplicated, and/or incorrectly made.
2. The financial statements issued to the public may not be prepared in accordance with GAAP applied on a consistent basis.
3. Reports may not be accurate, and critical decisions may then be based on erroneous information.

4. SEC and other governmental reporting requirements and/or loan restrictions may be violated. Exposure to litigation increases substantially due to improper financial reporting.
5. Confidential and proprietary information may be reviewed and disclosed by unauthorized individuals. The organization's competitive position and reputation may be adversely affected.
6. Records may be destroyed or altered. This may result in the inability to prepare accurate and reliable financial statements.
7. Financial information required for budgeting, forecasting, or analysis may not be available.
8. Policies and procedures may not be properly or consistently applied by or between operating units. Financial statements may be prepared inaccurately or untimely.
9. The risk of error in the accumulation and reporting of financial information is increased.
10. The company may be exposed to litigation due to inadequate record maintenance.
11. Errors and omissions in physical safeguarding, authorization, and transaction processing may go undetected and uncorrected. Financial statements and records may be prepared inaccurately or untimely.

FISCAL CLOSE STANDARDS OF INTERNAL CONTROL

Introduction: The fiscal closing process encompasses the functions involved in ensuring that U.S. GAAP is followed by the organization, which includes preparing journal entries and posting to the general ledger; gathering and consolidating the information required for the preparation of financial statements and other external financial reports; and preparing and reviewing the financial statements and other external reports.

In management's selection of procedures and techniques of control, the degree of control implemented is a matter of reasonable business judgment. The common guideline that should be used in determining the degree of internal controls implementation is that the cost of a control should not exceed the benefit derived. However, there is a minimum set of controls that should exist within a business environment. The internal control standards listed here represent the minimum controls to be considered for the fiscal closing process.

The specific functions or activities included in this checklist are:

- Accumulation of Financial Information
- Processing and Reporting of Financial Information

Accumulation of Financial Reporting Information

1. **Policy and Procedures:** Accounting policies and procedures must be developed and documented in accordance with U.S. GAAP and Corporate Policy. These policies and procedures must be followed regardless of "materiality." A current version of the abovementioned policies and procedures should be readily available in all company locations.
2. **Policy Changes:** New accounting policies or changes to existing policies should be properly researched, reviewed, documented, and communicated on a timely basis. The controller must authorize all changes in accounting policies. Local finance management may also develop tailored policies and procedures. Those conflicting with corporate policy must be approved in writing the corporate controller.
3. **Journal Entries:** Journal entries must be accurately input to the general ledger in the correct accounting period. Processes should be in place to ensure the accuracy of journal entry postings to the general ledger.
4. **Documented Journal Entries:** All manual general ledger journal entries must be documented, reviewed, and approved by financial supervision. A process should also be in place to identify manual journal entries so that it may be determined if any were omitted or duplicated.
5. **Standardized Journal Entries:** Standardized (i.e. system calculated and posted) general ledger journal entries must be utilized whenever possible. When the journal entry is established, the process for calculation must be reviewed, approved, and documented by local financial management. A process should also be in place to identify standardized journal entries so that it may be determined if any were omitted, duplicated, or have unreasonable values.
6. **Nonstandard Transactions:** Policies must be established to review and approve the accounting treatment of general ledger journal entries that do not occur on a regular basis.
7. **Contra Asset Accounts:** Contra-asset accounts should be utilized where necessary to maintain both proper asset valuation and detailed accounting records (e.g. receivables, inventory, and property).
8. **Monthly Accruals:** On a monthly basis, an accrual must be made of all known liabilities that have not been processed for payment or recorded in the accounting records, as determined by corporate policy. A quarterly review and evaluation should be conducted at the operating unit reporting level to determine if any existing contingent liabilities should be recorded in accordance with U.S. GAAP requirements.
9. **Asset Account Reviews:** All noncurrent asset accounts should be reviewed at least annually to ensure values do not exceed the lower of cost or market value. All current asset accounts should be reviewed at least quarterly to ensure that values do not exceed the lower of cost or market value.

Processing and Reporting of Financial Information

1. **Journal Entry Processing:** Controls must be established to ensure all journal entries have been processed and posted once they have been input into the system. Transaction error registers should be generated and significant discrepancies resolved prior to period close.
2. **Reporting Schedules and Cutoffs:** Adherence to monthly, quarterly, and annual closing and reporting schedules and cutoffs must be strict and consistent.
3. **General Ledger Reconciliations:** General ledger balances must be reconciled (contents are known and status is current) to the subsidiary ledgers or other supporting records on a timely basis. Any differences must be promptly resolved and recorded, generally by the next monthly reporting interval. All unexplained differences, however, must be reported to appropriate financial management as soon as discovered even if not yet resolved.
4. **Suspense Account Transactions:** Clearing and suspense account transactions, including the transfer of expense, income, or capital, must be resolved on a timely basis. Proper recognition of income or expense for these accounts must be made on at least a quarterly basis and on a monthly basis where possible.
5. **General Ledger Adjustments:** Consolidation, reclassification, and other adjustments to the general ledger balances must be adequately explained and documented. Such adjustments must be approved by the appropriate controller/manager or authorized designee.
6. **Financial Report Preparation:** Procedures and responsibilities must be established and maintained to ensure timely and accurate preparation, review, and approval of external financial reports, including reports to governmental and regulatory bodies. These procedures must also ensure that such reports comply with the established requirements for financial information and related disclosures.
7. **Access to Accounting and Finance Records, Documents, and Information Systems:** These must be safeguarded and access granted only on the principle of "need to know."
8. **Records Management:** Accounting and financial records must be complete, well organized, and retained in accordance with Corporate Policy on Records Management and tax requirements. Sufficient records must be kept in a secure but accessible environment to accurately and completely support all non-fixed assets and all liabilities.
9. **Financial Results:** Only authorized individuals must be given the responsibility to discuss financial results with individuals outside of the Company.
10. **Financial Reporting Requirements:** All operating units must comply with the current financial reporting requirements established by the corporate controller.
11. **Legal Financial Reporting Requirements:** Adherence to all legal reporting requirements (e.g. tax returns, statutory audits, etc.) must be strict and consistent.
12. **Financial Statement Translation:** Foreign financial statements must be translated in accordance with U.S. GAAP and corporate policy.
13. **General Ledger Accounts Definitions:** Current definitions must be documented and maintained for all ledger accounts.
14. **General Ledger Account Owners:** Lists of ledger account owners must be kept current and cost center managers shall have responsibility for the accuracy of the account balance.

15. **Actual-to-Forecast Comparisons:** Comparisons and explanations of actual financial information to forecast information must be routinely completed according to established policies and procedures; all significant variances must be researched and reflected in revised estimates/plans as appropriate in a timely way. Uniformly defined (same methodology) balance sheet performance measures must be established and actual performance measured against forecast on a monthly basis.
16. **Related-Party Transactions:** Related-party transactions should be reported in accordance with GAAP.

 ## THE FISCAL CLOSE DASHBOARD

Introduction: Measuring the results of your financial close to determine if you're achieving your goal of timely, accurate, and consistent data requires a constant review of your progress. You may be closing the books much sooner, but there could be several more adjusting entries and review errors.

I suggest that a member of the finance and accounting team is assigned the responsibility of reviewing the results of the close and tracking the metrics listed below. The results can be incorporated into a closing dashboard and communicated during your post-close review or follow-up process. The intent of tracking these metrics is to focus on a plan for continuous process improvement as a faster and efficient close is achieved.

The Fiscal Close Dashboard

1. **Gross number of adjusting entries:** Transaction errors must be corrected, and their correction delays the closing process. Thus, investigating the gross number of adjusting entries can be used to track down issues that are delaying the close.
2. **Review errors:** Note the types of errors found during the initial review of the financial statements. This information can be used to track down and correct underlying problems that can be prevented during future closing processes.
3. **Completion times:** Further refine the duration of the closing process to focus on each category of activities that must be completed, to understand not only how long they take, but also how they are impacted by other steps in the closing process. Some of these measurements by activity type are:
   - Time for subsidiaries to forward their results to corporate headquarters
   - Time to close the processing of period-end cash
   - Time to finish processing accounts payable
   - Time to issue billings to customers
   - Time to close payroll and record accrued wages
   - Time to count and value ending inventory
   - Time to issue related management reports

THE CONTROLLER'S DASHBOARD

Introduction: This dashboard provides 18 metrics that a controller may look at when implementing a scorecard to represent the results of the financial processes within his or her organization.

This dashboard can be used as a menu to choose from since many companies start with a list of 5 to 10 metrics or key performance indicators (KPIs) and continue to expand the list as additional analytical needs are identified based on the data available.

The Controller's Dashboard

1. DSO—Average Collection Period for Accounts Receivable
2. DPO—Average Payment Period for Accounts Payable
3. Total Annual Banking Fees
4. Average Number of Error Transactions per Month by:
   a. Accounts Receivable
   b. Accounts Payable
   c. T&E
   d. Payroll
   e. Treasury
   f. General Ledger
5. Average Return on Short-Term Investments
6. Averages Cost of Short-Term Borrowed Capita
7. Achievement of Working Capital Goals
8. Achievement of Financial Compliance Goals
9. Number of Finance and Accounting FTEs
10. Number of Days to Collect Financial Data Needed for the Closing Process
11. Number of Days to Close
12. Number of Days to Report Global Cash Position
13. Total Treasury Cost Divided by Revenue
14. Average Consolidated Cash Positions
15. Total Managed Annual Cash Flows
16. Accuracy of Global Forecasting
17. Annual Company Revenue
18. Internal Control Weaknesses

THE DETAILED FISCAL CLOSE SCORECARD

Introduction: This scorecard provides four sets of metrics that should be considered during the fiscal closing process.

1. Account Quality and Reconciliation
2. Quality of the Fiscal Close

3. Headcount and Workload Balance
4. Fiscal Close Cycle Times and Ratios

The scorecard provides information that will enable finance and accounting professionals to analyze the details of their closing processes and allows finance executives to determine the root cause of any problem. The delays in completing your financial statements could be due to the following factors:

- Too many consolidation points;
- A nonstandard chart of accounts;
- Too many manual journal entries and corrections; or
- A large number of post-close or management entries.

I recommend that this scorecard is prepared on a monthly, quarterly, or annually basis. It can be easily customized to fit your business. We recommend trend analysis to compare results from period to period. Additionally, your scorecard results can be used to benchmark fiscal closing results with other organizations.

Detailed Fiscal Close Scorecard

1. **Account Quality and Reconciliation**
   1. Use of Standard Chart of Accounts
   2. Number of Categories of Accounts
   3. Number of General Ledgers
   4. Number of Consolidation Entities
   5. Number of General Ledger Accounts
   6. Number of Duplicate General Ledger Accounts
   7. Number of Manual Journal Entries
   8. Number of Manual Journal Entry Corrections
   9. Number of Post-Close or Management Entries
   10. Number of Times Financial Information Is Updated During the Cycle
   11. Number of Systems Issues Reported During the Cycle
   12. Number of Internal Control/Fraud Issues Identified

2. **Quality of the Fiscal Close**
   1. Use of Standard Closing Schedule(s)
   2. Use of Financial Close Policies and Procedures and Submission Guidelines
   3. Number of Spreadsheets Used to Support the Closing Cycle
   4. Number of Issues/Errors Reported During Each Closing Cycle
   5. Cycle Time Required for Issue Resolution
   6. Time Spent Resolving Quality Issues
   7. Average Number of Open Issues After Each Closing Cycle
   8. Number/Percentage of Late Submissions
   9. Number/Percentage of Electronic Submissions

Detailed Fiscal Close Scorecard

---

    10. Ratio of Electronic/Manual Submission
    11. Volume of Submissions
       a. Other Ledgers or Sub-ledgers
       b. Cost Accounting
       c. Tax
       d. Investment Accounting and Reporting
       e. Actuarial
       f. Outsourced Processes (Third Parties)
       g. Other

3. **Headcount and Workload Balance**
    1. Number of FTEs Involved in the Fiscal Closing Cycle
       a. Submission
       b. Analysis
       c. Reporting
          i. Internal
          ii. External
       d. Reconciliation
    2. Use of Temporary Employees During the Financial Closing Cycle

4. **Fiscal Close Cycle Times and Ratios**
    1. **Cycle Time**—Average number of business days it takes to close the general ledger and process the financial statements.
    2. **Closing Ratio**—Average time spent on closing the books vs. average time spent on analyzing the results.
    3. **Closing Headcount**—Number of FTEs needed to close the books within the closing period.
    4. **Real-Time Data**—Number of business days required to process financial reports after the general ledgers are closed.
    5. **Closing Type:**
       a. By Company Code
       b. By Ledger Amount
       c. By Account Code
       d. By Accruals
       e. By GAAP

 ## THE PROJECT MANAGEMENT TOOLKIT

Introduction: Project management applies operational, business, and management knowledge to the identification of project activities that are required to complete deliverables within timelines and cost estimates. Project management disciplines should be used during the fiscal close to enable repeatable processes and ultimately a streamlined closing process.

The Project Management Institute (PMI) defines a *project* as follows:

A project is *temporary* in that it has a defined beginning and end in time, and therefore defined scope and resources.
　　And a project is *unique* in that it is not a routine operation, but a specific set of operations designed to accomplish a singular goal.[i]

These definitions of a project describe the fiscal closing process.

What Is Project Management?

According to PMI, project management is the application of knowledge, skills, tools, and techniques to project activities to meet project requirements. Project management is accomplished through the use of processes as listed below and as depicted in the following diagram.

- Initiating
- Planning
- Executing
- Controlling
- Closing

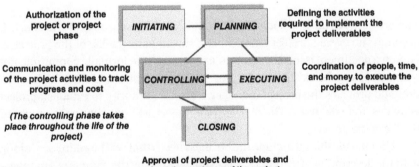

Source: This chart was developed using material from the Project Management Institute's (PMI) Project Management Body of Knowledge (PMBOK), 3th edition.

---

[i] Project Management Institute (PMI), "What Is Project Management?" Accessed March 30, 2019. https://www.pmi.org/about/learn-about-pmi/what-is-project-management.

Other Project Management Components, Considerations, and Definitions

Other components, considerations, and definitions for the project management discipline are included below.

Project Life Cycle

A project life cycle defines the beginning and end of a project and establishes phases for project management. A project life cycle is defined by the type of project. The life cycle for a software implementation project will differ from a construction project.

Project Scope

The project scope forms the boundaries for the deliverables of the project and can be the service level agreement (SLA) between the project management team and the project sponsor. The project scope identifies both the project objectives and project deliverables. The project scope process includes the project charter, the project mission, and the initial descriptions of project constraints and assumptions, which are described.

Project Charter

The project charter is a document that describes the purpose of the effort. It becomes the overall project team charter throughout the life of the project. It is often a document issued by senior management that formally communicates and authorizes the existence of a project. The charter establishes the foundation and provides the project manager with the authority to establish project activities and resources. The charter of a project will not change throughout the life of the project.

The charter should include the business needs that will be addressed, along with the description of the effort. It is usually issued by the company's management team or sponsor in the initial communication process that "kicks off" the effort.

Project Mission Statement

The project mission statement is a short statement that includes the primary deliverables of the project and the expected outcome.

Program Management Office (PMO)

PMOs can help both public and private organizations by providing the structure needed to both standardize project management practices and track large initiatives or multiple projects.

Project Constraints and Assumptions

The tools and techniques for scope planning include cost analysis and identification and analysis of alternatives. The outputs of the process include the scope statement, project justification, project deliverables, and project objectives. The scope will include supporting detail and a scope management plan. The scope management plan is important since it defines how project scope changes will be identified, prioritized, and managed. Changes in scope are a major challenge in the project management process. If the scope is not properly managed, timeline, cost, and deliverables can be jeopardized.

The Project Budgeting Process

The project budgeting process includes resource planning, cost estimating, cost budgeting, and cost control.

Resource Planning

Resource planning is defined as "determining what physical resources (people, equipment, materials) and what quantities of each should be used and when they would be needed to perform project activities." The primary requirement for the resource planning process is the work breakdown structure (WBS). The WBS is a grouping of project elements that organizes the requirements of the project scope. The WBS defines a hierarchy of project activities required to complete the project.

Cost Estimating

Cost estimating develops an approximate cost plan for the resources and activities needed to complete the project. The WBS and resources rates are key inputs into the cost estimate. The outputs of the cost estimate process are the quantitative assessment, likely costs, cost for all resources, and the degree of accuracy.

Cost Control

Once the cost estimate is established, a cost control process is implemented. Cost control focuses on monitoring cost performance, ensuring changes are recorded accurately and unauthorized changes are prohibited, informing stakeholders of cost changes, maintaining expected costs with acceptable limits, and documenting the reasons for favorable or unfavorable cost variances.

Developing a Project Plan

A *project plan*, according to the Project Management Institute (PMI) Project Management Body of Knowledge (PMBOK), is:

> ... a formal, approved document used to guide both project execution and project control. The primary uses of the project plan are to document planning assumptions and decisions, facilitate communication among stakeholders, and document approved scope, cost, and schedule baselines. A project plan may be summarized or detailed.[ii]

Project Planning Process Steps

Project Planning Process Steps
1. Define the Scope
2. Determine Available Resources
3. Check the Timeline
4. Assemble Your Project Team
5. List the Big Steps
6. List the Smaller Steps and Define the Work Breakdown Structure (WBS)
7. Develop a Preliminary Plan
8. Create Your Baseline Plan
9. Request Project Adjustments
10. Work Your Plan, But Don't Die for It
11. Monitor Your Team's Progress
12. Document Everything

[ii] Ibid.

Glossary

Access Controls   These are the procedures and controls that limit or detect access to critical network assets to guard against loss of integrity, confidentiality, accountability, or availability. Access controls provide reasonable assurance that critical resources are protected against unauthorized modification, disclosure, loss, or impairment.

Account Number   Defines the accounting transaction type for the transaction and includes a system-generated number tied to a company's chart of accounts.

Accounting Policy   Basic concepts, assumptions, policies, methods, and practices used by a company for maintaining accounting principles and summarization into financial statements as prescribed by GAAP. A policy can be described as *what* needs to happen to ensure that accounting cycles are working within boundaries of internal control.

Accounting Procedure   The routine steps in processing accounting data during an accounting period. In sequence, (1) occurrence of the transaction, (2) classification of each transaction in chronological order (journalizing), (3) recording the classified data in ledger accounts (posting), (4) preparation of financial statements, and (5) closing of nominal accounts. A procedure ensures that a policy is properly executed and explains *how*. Other procedures or policies will be referenced if applicable.

Accruals   Accruals are adjustments for (1) revenues that have been earned but are not yet recorded in the accounts, and (2) expenses that have been incurred but are not yet recorded in the accounts. The accruals need to be added via adjusting entries so that the financial statements report these amounts.[i]

Assertions   Financial statement assertions are claims made by an organization's management regarding its financial statements. The assertions form a

---

[i] Accounting Coach, "What Are Accruals?" Accessed January 1, 2019. https://www.accounting coach.com/blog/what-are-accruals.

theoretical basis from which external auditors develop a set of audit procedures and all of the information contained within the financial statements has been accurately recorded.

Audit Committee   The audit committee's role includes: the oversight of financial reporting; the monitoring of accounting policies; the oversight of any external auditors; regulatory compliance; and discussion of risk management policies with management. The audit committee may approve and review the status of the company's annual internal audit plan and is usually apprised of any suspicions of fraud reported via the ethics hotline or other means.

Balanced Scorecard   The balanced scorecard is a strategic planning and management system that is used extensively in business and industry, government, and nonprofit organizations worldwide to align business activities to the vision and strategy of the organization, improve internal and external communications, and monitor organization performance against strategic goals. The balanced scorecard is a management system (not only a measurement system) that enables organizations to clarify their vision and strategy and translate them into action. It provides feedback around both the internal business processes and external outcomes in order to continuously improve strategic performance and results. When fully deployed, the balanced scorecard transforms strategic planning from an academic exercise into the nerve center of an enterprise.

It was originated by Drs. Robert Kaplan (Harvard Business School) and David Norton as a performance measurement framework that added strategic non-fiscal performance measures to traditional fiscal metrics to give managers and executives a more "balanced" view of organizational performance.

Benchmarking   According to Wikipedia, benchmarking is the practice of comparing business processes and performance metrics to industry bests and best practices from other companies. Dimensions typically measured are quality, time, and cost.[ii]

Best Practices   Implementation of the highest quality, most advantageous, repeatable processes achieved by applying the experiences of those with the acquired skill or proficiency. Best practices are achieved by implementing processes, templates, and checklists that will improve cycle time, reduce cost, and provide the foundation for continuous improvement.

Budget Process   A budget process refers to the process by which companies create, communicate and approve an annual budget. Most companies track

---

[ii] Wikipedia, "Benchmarking." Accessed March 2, 2019. https://en.wikipedia.org/wiki/Benchmarking.

results on a monthly basis through internal reporting processes where actual expenses are compared with the approved budget for a cost center or operating unit. This monthly review will identify excessive spending that could reflect a control issue.

Business Continuity Planning   This is the process of developing advance arrangements and procedures that enable an organization to respond to an event in such a manner that critical business functions continue with planned levels of interruption or essential change.

Business Continuity Program   This is an ongoing program supported and funded by executive staff to ensure business continuity requirements are assessed, resources are allocated, and recovery strategies and procedures are completed and tested.

Change in Accounting Principle   When a company adopts an alternative generally accepted accounting principle from a previously used principle to account for the same type of transaction or event, that action is called a change in accounting principle. The term *accounting principle* includes not only accounting principles and practices but also the methods of applying them.

The initial adoption of an accounting principle in recognition of events or transactions occurring for the first time or that were previously immaterial in their effect is not considered a change in accounting principle. A change in accounting principle differs from a change in accounting estimate in that a change in accounting estimate results when new events occur, more experience is acquired, or additional information is obtained that affects the previously determined estimate.

Common Chart of Accounts   A common chart of accounts is a numbered list of the accounts that comprise a company's general ledger. A company should establish accounting policies and rules for the use of specific account numbers. As a best practice, a simplified chart of accounts will enable a faster close. The accounting department should monitor the use of accounts and identify and correct any anomalies or unused accounts.

Company Code   The business transactions relevant for financial accounting are entered, saved, and evaluated at company code level. You usually create a legally independent company in your ERP system (e.g. the applicable ERP system) with one company code.

Compensating Controls   In some cases, an employee will perform all activities within a process. In this scenario, segregation of duties does not exist and risk cannot be identified or mitigated in a timely manner. As a result, the implementation of additional compensating controls should be considered.

A compensating control reduces the vulnerabilities in ineffectively segregated functions. A compensating control can reduce the risk of errors, omissions, irregularities, and deficiencies, which can improve the overall business process. However, it should be noted that many companies include compensating controls in their internal controls programs as additional measures to reduce risk. These controls can be embedded in continuous controls monitoring (CCM) and controls self-assessment (CSA) processes. Continuous controls monitoring (CCM) refers to the use of automated tools and various technologies to ensure the continuous monitoring of fiscal transactions and other types of transactional applications to reduce and mitigate risk. A CCM process includes the validation of authorizations, systems access, system configurations, and business process settings.

Consolidation Software   According to E&Y, consolidation can make the reporting process more complicated and can introduce stringent timelines for many organizations. An effective and consistent reporting process requires a reliable database. This is often achieved by using dedicated consolidation and reporting software. This software allows for an automated process, a reliable audit trail, and a protected database.

Contingency Plan   Contingency plans are defined as a set of measures to deal with emergencies caused by failures due to human action or natural disasters that impact the operation of a company. Contingency planning includes the prearranged plans and procedures that critical business functions will execute to ensure business continuity until computer and telecommunications facilities are reestablished following a disaster.

Continuous Auditing (CA)   CA is an automatic method used to perform auditing activities, such as control and risk assessments, on a more frequent basis. Technology plays a key role in continuous audit activities by helping to automate the identification of exceptions or anomalies, analyze patterns within the digits of key numeric fields, review trends, and test controls, among other activities.

The "continuous" aspect of continuous auditing and reporting refers to the real-time or near-real-time capability for fiscal information to be checked and shared. Not only does it indicate that the integrity of information can be evaluated at any given point of time, it also means that the information is able to be verified constantly for errors, fraud, and inefficiencies. It is the most detailed audit.[iii]

[iii] Wikipedia, "Continuous Auditing." Accessed March 2, 2019. https://en.wikipedia.org/wiki/Continuous_auditing.

Continuous Controls Monitoring (CCM)   According to Gartner, continuous controls monitoring (CCM) is a set of technologies to reduce business losses through continuous monitoring and reducing the cost of audits through continuous auditing of the controls in fiscal and other transactional applications.[iv]

Contra Revenue   Contra revenue is a deduction from the gross revenue reported by a business, which results in net revenue. Contra revenue transactions are recorded in one or more contra revenue accounts, which usually have a debit balance (as opposed to the credit balance in the typical revenue account).[v]

Cost Center   The designated accounting location, in which costs are incurred, defined as a subunit of a legal entity and in some cases the business unit depending on how the business unit code is utilized. All cost centers are assigned to a company's legal entity. However, some cost centers may be assigned to business or operating units. The assignment of a cost center is distinguished by an area of responsibility, location, or accounting method.

Cost Management   Cost management is comprised of the fiscal processes, reporting, and analytics that support cost accounting, inventory accounting, and cost analysis.

Critical Application   A critical business application is one that a company must have to support major revenue activities, movement of goods to customers, a strategic manufacturing process, or to fulfill contractual or regulatory obligations. In addition, the application's availability is deemed by management to be vital to the continued functioning of company business. Examples of critical applications are: customer service support, order entry, inventory control, manufacturing resource planning, purchasing, warehouse control, quality assurance, and finance.

Critical Processes   A critical business processes is one that if disrupted or made unavailable for any length of time will have a significant negative impact on the success of the business.

Cycle Time   Cycle time is the total time from the beginning to the completion of a process. Cycle time includes process time, during which a unit is acted upon to bring it closer to an output, and delay time, during which a unit of work is spent waiting to take the next action.

[iv] Gartner, "IT Glossary," "Continuous Controls Monitoring (CCM)." Accessed March 2, 2019. https://www.gartner.com/it-glossary/continuous-controls-monitoring-ccm.
[v] Accounting Tools, "Contra Revenue." Last modified November 17, 2017. Accessed January 1, 2019. https://www.accountingtools.com/articles/what-is-contra-revenue.html.

Data Model A data model establishes data definitions and processes for reference, ensures data rules are utilized, and provides a schematic view of the underlying components comprising the data that drives the fiscal function.

Debt Covenant Debt covenants are agreements between a company and a creditor usually stating limits or thresholds for certain financial ratios that the company may not breach.

Disaster A disaster is defined as a loss of computing or telecommunication resources to the extent that routine recovery measures cannot restore normal service levels within 24 hours, which impacts the company's business significantly.

Enterprise Resource Planning (ERP) System An ERP is business process management software that allows an organization to use a system of integrated applications to manage the business and automate many back office functions related to technology, services, and human resources. Examples of ERP systems are the applicable ERP system, Oracle, SAP, Microsoft Dynamics, and Sage.

External Audit An external audit is a periodic audit conducted by an independent qualified auditor with the aim to determine whether the accounting records for a business are complete and accurate.

According to Wikipedia, "an external auditor performs an audit, in accordance with specific laws or rules, of the financial statements of a company, government entity, other legal entity, or organization, and is independent of the entity being audited. Users of these entities' fiscal information, such as investors, government agencies, and the general public, rely on the external auditor to present an unbiased and independent audit report. ...For public companies listed on stock exchanges in the United States, the Sarbanes Oxley Act (SOX) has imposed stringent requirements on external auditors in their evaluation of internal controls and financial reporting."[vi]

External Reporting Companies prepare external financial statements to report their business information to outside observers, including potential investors, stakeholders, shareholders, and the SEC.

Financial Accounting Standards Board (FASB) This is a private, nonprofit organization standard-setting body whose primary purpose is to establish and improve generally accepted accounting principles (GAAP) within the United States in the public's interest.

Financial Architecture Financial architecture is the structure in which components, processes, and systems for a finance function are organized and

---

[vi] Wikipedia, "External Audit." Accessed March 2, 2019. https://en.wikipedia.org/wiki/External_auditor.

integrated. This architecture is used to set the foundation for all finance and accounting processes and systems.

Financial Hierarchy   A company's financial hierarchy is usually structured with retained earnings at the top, followed by debt financing and then external equity financing at the bottom, and is supported by a structure of cost centers.

Fixed Assets   A fixed asset is a long-term tangible piece of property that a firm owns and uses in its operations to generate income. Fixed assets are not expected to be consumed or converted into cash within 1 to 2 years. Fixed assets are known as property, plant, and equipment (PP&E). They are also referred to as capital assets.

Financial Planning and Analysis (FP&A)   Financial planning and analysis (FP&A) is a group within a company's finance organization that provides senior management with a forecast of the company's profit and loss (income statement) and operating performance for the upcoming quarter and year.

Fiscal Close   The fiscal close process establishes a "cutoff" of fiscal activity so a company can generate monthly, quarterly, and annual financial reports for stakeholders and shareholders.

Forecast Process   A fiscal forecast is a financial management tool that presents estimated information based on past, current, and projected fiscal conditions. This will help identify future revenue and expenditure trends that may have an immediate or long-term influence on strategic goals.

General Data Protection Regulation (GDPR)   The GDPR was approved and adopted by the European Union (EU) Parliament in April 2016. The regulation took effect after a two-year transition period and, unlike a directive, did not require any legislation to be passed by government. GDPR came into force on May 25, 2018. The GDPR not only applies to organizations located within the EU but also applies to organizations located outside of the EU if they offer goods or services to, or monitor the behavior of, EU data subjects. It applies to all companies processing and holding the personal data of data subjects residing in the EU, regardless of the company's location.

The GDPR applies to "personal data," meaning any information relating to an identifiable person who can be directly or indirectly identified in particular by reference to an identifier. This definition provides for a wide range of personal identifiers to constitute personal data, including name, identification number, location data, or online identifier, reflecting changes in technology and the way organizations collect information about people.[vii]

General Accounting   Financial processes that support the close, general accounting, and intercompany processes.

[vii] European Union (EU), General Data Protection Regulation (GDPR), "GDPR FAQs." Accessed January 4, 2019. https://eugdpr.org/the-regulation/gdpr-faqs/.

Highly Significant Transaction A highly significant transaction is one that could reasonably result in a 10% or greater variance in revenues or would result in a 5% or greater variance in the net worth (assets minus liabilities).

Intercompany Accounting Intercompany accounting is the process of recording financial transactions between different legal entities within the same parent company.

Internal Audit The internal audit department is an independent, objective assurance and consulting activity designed to add value and improve an organization's operations and to identify and mitigate risk.

Internal Controls The integrated framework approach defines internal control as a process, effected by an entity's board of directors, management, and other personnel, designed to provide reasonable assurance regarding the achievement of objectives in the following categories: (A) reliability of financial reporting, (B) effectiveness and efficiency of operations, and (C) compliance with applicable laws and regulations.

Internal Reporting Internal financial reporting traditionally means compiling and distributing generic reports that show a company's past, short-term fiscal performance with budget results. Internal reporting can also be generated by divisions, profit centers, and regions.

International Accounting Standards (IAS) International Accounting Standards (IAS) are older accounting standards that were replaced in 2001 by International Financial Reporting Standards (IFRS), issued by the International Accounting Standards Board (IASB).

International Financial Reporting Standards (IFRS) These standards were issued by the IFRS Foundation and the International Accounting Standards Board (IASB) to provide a common global language for business affairs so that company accounts are understandable and comparable across international boundaries. IFRS is a set of accounting standards developed by an independent, not-for-profit organization called the International Accounting Standards Board (IASB).

What are International Financial Reporting Standards (IFRS)?

International Financial Reporting Standards (IFRS) are accounting standards and interpretations adopted by the International Accounting Standards Board (IASB). They include IFRS issued by the IASB since its formation on July 1, 2000, and International Accounting Standards (IAS) previously issued by the International Accounting Standards Committee (IASC) and adopted by the IASB upon its formation.

These standards focus on establishing general principles derived from the IASB conceptual framework reflecting the recognition, measurement, and reporting requirements for the transactions covered by the standards. IFRS tends to limit additional guidance for applying the general principles to typical transactions, thus encouraging management to use professional judgment in applying the general principles to specific transactions of an entity or industry.

What are the benefits of IFRS?

The global shift toward IFRS is intended to facilitate the movement of capital worldwide and provide more clarity and consistency to financial reporting in the global marketplace. IFRS is a more universally accepted, principles-based set of standards that should allow companies to better reflect the economic substance of transactions. It also provides for increased disclosure in footnotes, allowing analysts to "level set" companies in benchmark groups for improved comparability. Because IFRS enables companies to align their consolidated reporting frameworks with local and statutory reporting frameworks, it ultimately should be more efficient and cost-effective in the long term.

What are the drawbacks of IFRS?

In the short term, the significant costs related to the conversion and sustenance of IFRS reporting standards may make IFRS less efficient and cost-effective as compared to retaining local GAAP. In addition, the conversion process is a time-consuming project that requires the involvement of management at all levels of the organization. Because of the level of effort required, the conversion project itself may distract management's focus from the organization's primary goals and objectives.

Key Performance Indicator (KPI)   A KPI is a measurement or metric that demonstrates how effectively a process is working.

Merger and Acquisition (M&A)   In a merger, the boards of directors for two companies approve the combination and seek shareholders' approval. After the merger, the acquired company ceases to exist and becomes part of the acquiring company.

Net Income   Net income is equal to net earnings (profit) calculated as sales less cost of goods sold, selling, general and administrative expenses, operating expenses, depreciation, interest, taxes, and other expenses.

Organizational Controls   These controls should cover all aspects of a company's activity without overlap and be clearly assigned and communicated.

- Responsibility should be delegated down to the level at which the necessary expertise and time exist.
- No single employee should have exclusive knowledge, authority, or control over any significant transaction or group of transactions.
- Agreeing realistic qualitative and quantitative targets strengthens responsibility.
- The structure of accountability depends on continuing levels of competence of employees in different positions and the development of competence so that responsibility and reporting relationships can be regrouped in more efficient ways.

PEST Analysis　　PEST analysis is a simple and widely used tool that helps analyze the political, economic, sociocultural, and technological changes in your business environment. Looking at the impacts of these four quadrants provides an understanding of the big-picture changes and exposures that impact your company.

Peer Review Process　　The American Institute of Certified Public Accountants (AICPA) requires its member firms to undergo a peer review every three years. A peer review is a periodic external review of a firm's quality control system in accounting and auditing and is also known as the AICPA's practice monitoring program.[viii]

Policy Controls　　Policy controls are the general principles and guides for action that influence decisions. They indicate the limits to choices and the parameters or rules to be followed by a company and its employees. Major policies should be reviewed, approved, and communicated by senior management. Policies are derived by:

- Considering the business environment and process objectives
- Identifying the potential categories of risks that the environment poses toward achievement of the objectives

Procedure Controls　　Procedure controls prescribe how actions are to be performed consistent with policies. Procedures should be developed by those who understand the day-to-day actions.

Process　　A process is a systematic series of actions directed to some end, a continuous action or operation taking place in a definite manner.

[viii] American Institute of Certified Public Accountants (AICPA), "Peer Review Summary." Accessed March 19, 2019. https://www.aicpa.org/research/standards/peerreview/peer-review-summary .html.

Process Flow   A process flow communicates the actual process currently in place. It is a picture of the flow and sequence of work steps, tasks, or activities and will include the flow or sequence of steps throughout the process; the person responsible for each task; and the decision points and their impact on the flow of work.

Profit Center   A profit center is an area of responsibility for which an independent operating profit is calculated.

Project   According to the Project Management Institute (PMI), a project is temporary in that it has a defined beginning and end in time, and therefore defined scope and resources. And a project is unique in that it is not a routine operation but a specific set of operations designed to accomplish a singular goal.

Project Accounting   Project accounting is a specific form of accounting that corresponds to a defined project. This accounting process helps to adequately track, report, and analyze fiscal results and implications.

The Public Company Accounting Oversight Board (The PCAOB)   The PCAOB is a nonprofit corporation established by Congress to oversee the audits of public companies in order to protect investors and the public interest by promoting informative, accurate, and independent audit reports. The PCAOB also oversees the audits of brokers and dealers, including compliance reports filed pursuant to federal securities laws, to promote investor protection.

The Sarbanes Oxley Act of 2002, which created the PCAOB, required that auditors of U.S. public companies be subject to external and independent oversight for the first time in history. Previously, the profession was self-regulated.

The five members of the PCAOB, including the chairperson, are appointed to staggered five-year terms by the Securities and Exchange Commission after consultation with the chair of the Board of Governors of the Federal Reserve System and the secretary of the Treasury.[ix]

Related Parties   A related party is a person or an entity that is related to the reporting entity. A person or a close member of that person's family is related to a reporting entity if that person has control, joint control, or significant influence over the entity or is a member of its key management personnel. A related-party transaction is a business deal or arrangement between two parties who are joined by a preexisting special relationship.

Review Controls   These controls include an ongoing self-assessment process as required by the Sarbanes Oxley Act of 2002. A self-assessment is a series of questions that validate the effectiveness of the control environment.

[ix] PCAOB, "About the PCAOB." Accessed February 14, 2019. https://pcaobus.org/About.

A self-assessment must be conducted every fiscal quarter, in some situations; the manager of the operating unit may elect to conduct a self-assessment test more frequently. It is imperative that all weaknesses found in the testing process are remediated through a corrective action and follow-up process.

Revenue   Revenue is the amount of money that a company actually receives during a specific fiscal period, including discounts and deductions for returned merchandise. It is the top line or gross income figure from which costs are subtracted to determine net income.

Revenue Recognition   Revenue is one of the most important measures used by investors in assessing a company's performance and prospects. However, previous revenue recognition guidance differs in generally accepted accounting principles (GAAP) and International Financial Reporting Standards (IFRS)—and many believe both standards were in need of improvement. On May 28, 2014, the FASB and the International Accounting Standards Board (IASB) issued (press release) converged guidance on recognizing revenue in contracts with customers. The new guidance is a major achievement in the Boards' joint efforts to improve this important area of financial reporting.

Presently, GAAP has complex, detailed, and disparate revenue recognition requirements for specific transactions and industries, including, for example, software and real estate. As a result, different industries use different accounting for economically similar transactions.

The objective of the new guidance is to establish principles to report useful information to users of financial statements about the nature, amount, timing, and uncertainty of revenue from contracts with customers. The new guidance:

- Removes inconsistencies and weaknesses in existing revenue requirements
- Provides a more robust framework for addressing revenue issues
- Improves comparability of revenue recognition practices across entities, industries, jurisdictions, and capital markets
- Provides more useful information to users of financial statements through improved disclosure requirements
- Simplifies the preparation of financial statements by reducing the number of requirements to which an organization must refer[x]

Return on Investment (ROI)   ROI is a performance measure used to evaluate the efficiency of an investment. ROIs are also used in the decision-making

[x] Financial Accounting Standards Board (FASB), "Why Did the FASB Issue a New Standard on Revenue Recognition?" Accessed January 1, 2019. https://www.fasb.org/jsp/FASB/Page/ImageBridge Page&cid=1176169257359.

process when selecting an automated solution, new equipment, or other capital expenditures.

Roll Forward In accounting, this is the systematic establishment of new accounting period balances by using (rolling forward) prior accounting period data. There are two approaches: Roll forward both asset and liabilities on a consistent basis from a consistent earlier date (possibly the last annual review), or take the most up-to-date asset and liability figures as the starting point (which may be at different dates) to produce roll-forward estimates of assets and liabilities; in securities, it is when an investor replaces an old options position with a new one having a later expiration date (and same strike price).[xi]

Sarbanes Oxley (SOX) Act 2002 The act can be divided into three main points:

1. The scope of an external audit firm has been restricted in which CPAs no longer have the right to set standards for their practice.
2. There are new duties for boards of directors in general and for audit committees in particular. Corporate governance provisions include a required code of ethics or standards of business conduct.
3. There are new requirements for the CEO and CFO. Each SEC filing (10K and 10Q) states that:
   a. The report fairly represents in all material respects the company's operations and fiscal condition.
   b. The report does not contain any material misstatements or omit to state a material fact necessary in order to make the statements made, in light of the circumstances under which the statements were made, not misleading.
   c. The report containing financial statements complies with section 13(a) or 15(d) of the Securities and Exchange Act of 1934.
   d. The company's control system is in place and effective.

Securities and Exchange Commission (SEC) The U.S. Securities and Exchange Commission (SEC) is an independent federal government agency responsible for protecting investors, maintaining fair and orderly functioning of securities markets, and facilitating capital formation. The U.S. Securities and Exchange Commission (SEC) has a three-part mission: protect investors; maintain fair, orderly, and efficient markets; and facilitate capital formation.

[xi] Venture Line, "Definition of Roll-Forward." Accessed April 2, 2019. https://www.ventureline.com/accounting-glossary/R/roll-forward-definition/.

Segregation of Duties (SoD) An SoD control is one of the most important controls that your company can have. Adequate SoD reduces the likelihood that errors (intentional or unintentional) will remain undetected by providing for separate processing by different individuals at various stages of a transaction and for independent reviews of the work performed. The SoD control provides four primary benefits: (1) the risk of a deliberate fraud is mitigated as the collusion of two or more persons would be required in order to circumvent controls; (2) the risk of legitimate errors is mitigated as the likelihood of detection is increased; (3) the cost of corrective actions is mitigated as errors are generally detected relatively earlier in their lifecycle; and (4) the organization's reputation for integrity and quality is enhanced through a system of checks and balances.

Significant Deficiency This is a single control deficiency, or combination of control deficiencies, that adversely affects the company's ability to initiate, authorize, record, process, or report external fiscal data reliably. There is more than a remote likelihood that a misstatement of the company's annual or interim financial statements that is more than inconsequential will not be prevented or detected.

Standard Operating Procedures Standard operating procedures (SOPs) are formal written guidelines that denote daily operational procedures, assist in long-range planning, and provide instructions for incident responses.

While the exact layout and purpose of an SOP document varies somewhat from industry to industry, all SOPs share some traits in common. They have operational, system, and accounting standard components, and they are essential to a successful fiscal closing process. For the fiscal close process, SOPs should include roles and responsibilities, key stakeholders, procedures, flowcharts, templates, and checklists for every component of the fiscal close.

Standards of Internal Control The standards define a series of internal controls that address the risks associated with key business processes, sub-processes, and entity-level processes. The standards are the product of over 30 years of experience in the finance, accounting, and internal controls field. The standards are a body of work that leverages experience at large technology companies. They were developed when implementing internal control programs for approximately 80 business processes and sub-processes that include payroll, the fiscal closing process, logistics, procurement, accounts payable, and accounts receivable.

"Super User" A user of an ERP with special privileges needed to administer and maintain the system or a system administrator. The special privileges may include the ability to process a fiscal transaction and make changes in the general ledger to modify the transaction. "Super-user" privileges must be monitored to ensure that access rights are not used to incorrectly modify or falsify a transaction, resulting in risk to the company.

Supervisory Controls   Supervisory controls are situations in which managers ensure that all employees understand their responsibilities and authorities, and the assurance that procedures are being followed within the operating unit. They can also be considered as a compensating control in which a supervisory review is necessary to augment segregation-of-duties controls.

SWOT Analysis   According to Wikipedia, "SWOT analysis (or a SWOT matrix) is a strategic planning technique used to help a person or organization identify strengths, weaknesses, opportunities, and threats related to business competition or project planning. It is intended to specify the objectives of the business venture or project and identify the internal and external factors that are favorable and unfavorable to achieving those objectives."

"Strengths and weakness are frequently internally related while opportunities and threats commonly focus on the external environment. The name is an acronym for the four parameters the technique examines:

1. Strengths: characteristics of the business or project that give it an advantage over others
2. Weaknesses: characteristics of the business that place the business or project at a disadvantage relative to others
3. Opportunities: elements in the environment that the business or project could exploit to its advantage
4. Threats: elements in the environment that could cause trouble for the business or project"

Work Instruction   A work instruction is a step-by-step document that depicts the actions needed to complete an activity at the transaction level and is a detailed document that may include "keystroke" information. This is a very detailed "how-to" document.

Index